Women in the Church

ALSO BY LESLY F. MASSEY

*Women and the New Testament: An Analysis of
Scripture in Light of New Testament Era Culture*
(McFarland, 1989)

Women in the Church

Moving Toward Equality

LESLY F. MASSEY

foreword by THE REV. CHRISTINE TATA

McFarland & Company, Inc., Publishers
Jefferson, North Carolina, and London

ISBN 0-7864-1195-3 (softcover : 50# alkaline paper) ∞

Library of Congress cataloguing data are available

British Library cataloguing data are available

Manufactured in the United States of America

Cover photograph ©2001 Digital Vision

*McFarland & Company, Inc., Publishers
Box 611, Jefferson, North Carolina 28640
www.mcfarlandpub.com*

TABLE OF CONTENTS

113651

FOREWORD

This is a compassionate exploration of a complex and sensitive subject. Even in liberal or progressive churches, ordained women struggle with the chasm between the church's egalitarian vision and patriarchal past. As a woman ordained in 1993, when fully half of seminarians in my denomination were female, I recall that my colleagues and I were continually faced with the resistance and anxiety of well-meaning people of faith. Massey provides an accessible survey of how this resistance is figured in American Christianity, and offers sensible and sensitive strategies for hope and change.

Dr. Massey writes for the evangelical and conservative Christian, but he speaks to anyone concerned with how the church will live if it does not live for justice.

> The Rev. Christine Tata
> *United Church of Christ*
> *Dallas, Texas*

INTRODUCTION

On a Sunday morning in May 2001, services begin as usual at the First Christian Church (Disciples of Christ) in Rowlett, Texas. Music is led by a woman, and special music is presented by a male and female duet. At communion two elders preside, one male, the other female. Members of the diaconate, both male and female, serve communion. Associate minister Ann Dotson leads the Pastoral Prayer. The message is delivered by senior minister Dawn Weaks.

At the same time across Lake Ray Hubbard in Garland, services begin at the Saturn Road Church of Christ. All those who officiate are male—those who lead prayers, serve the Communion, make announcements, and lead singing. The message is delivered by a male minister. Women participate in singing, bow reverently during prayer, give an offering, and listen attentively during the sermon. Otherwise they remain silent and play no roles that involve leadership or public speaking.

The unmistakable difference between these two churches demonstrates divergent paths leading from the Stone-Campbell Movement of the early nineteenth century. It also illustrates one of the most critical theological and ecclesiastical issues of our time.

During the course of woman's elevation in the past two centuries, many Christian denominations have gradually acquiesced, either abandoning or radically modifying their interpretation of relevant biblical passages to accommodate inevitable social change. But for others, various biblical passages stand as divine authority for male domination and female subservience, and consequently the status of women remains cast in a mold from the first century synagogue.

The enormous volume of material published on the status of women during the past two decades is evidence of a desperate search for solutions. Relevant studies include the historical and cultural backgrounds to the New Testament, particularly as seen in ancient Greece and Rome and in the traditions of Judaism, and cover every phase of Christian church history to the present time. Also pertinent to the issue are sociological trends

3

and the psychology of male and female relationships. Some of the earliest writers in the feminist movement are not theologians, but sociologists. Of primary concern, however, are the exegetical studies in relevant biblical texts, principally Pauline. Scholars have dissected and analyzed these passages from every conceivable angle in a seemingly frantic effort to reconcile biblical doctrine with the growing acceptance of gender equality.

Certain conclusions are irrefutable. The simple gospel theme of social equity and justice, along with the clearly revolutionary attitude of Jesus Christ, provides ample justification for rejecting ecclesiastical tradition on the status of women. Gender equality is not only traceable to the attitude and teaching of Christ, in contrast to the male bias of all ancient cultures, but was expressed in a variety of ways in the early Christian community.

If that is the case, where did the church go wrong? Why did it take so long to find biblical justification for gender equity? And why is there still a dilemma today? The writings of the apostle Paul were the principal stumbling block, and for various reasons church tradition took a path reverting to patriarchal models which at once strengthened traditional female subjection. The tendency to codify Christian teachings arose largely in defense against Gnosticism and other "heresies" in the second century, and is apparent both in the rabbinism of certain Pauline doctrines and a reversion to a Jewish mode of hermeneutics. The result was the development of a complex Christian tradition which served to silence and subordinate women, both in the church and the home, but which as a theology of womanhood was radically opposed to the spirit of pristine Christianity.

Nineteenth century America provided the right environment for social advancement, including women's suffrage and the civil rights movement. In the process, many churches recognized women as the equals of men in terms of their right to serve and minister. Without the benefit of theological education and critical hermeneutics, plain people in the burgeoning American culture began to recognize as self-evident certain truths that had been obscured by church tradition and by an inordinate allegiance to biblical authority. Among those truths were principles of justice and human rights that stood in stark contrast to historical evils such as slavery, class discrimination, human exploitation, and the subordination of women.

However, the freedom of the early American culture also provided impetus for other areas of religious expression and exploration, including a renewal of biblical literalism and fundamentalism in distinctively American forms. This would include Pentecostal churches, the Church of Jesus

Christ of Latter Day Saints (the Mormons), the Seventh Day Adventists, and others. In this study attention is given to the work of Alexander Campbell, whose life and work gave rise to three denominations (the Disciples of Christ, the Conservative Christian Church, and the Churches of Christ) wherein today a polarity of views on the status of women is clearly evident. These are the author's roots. He writes from the perspective of a male clergyman having broken with the most conservative element of that tradition, and who rejects in its entirety the conservative posture on the status of women.

Today, advocates of feminine equality are clearly concerned about Roman Catholic and Orthodox traditions, as well as the doctrines of numerous Protestant denominations where no ground has been yielded on gender equality or the ordination of women. It is noteworthy that while rooted in the same biblical paradigm, the reasons offered by these churches for resisting change vary. Of equal significance is the fact that some churches have made superficial changes as a patronizing gesture to placate women without compromising traditional doctrines. This has prompted much criticism from feminists.

A resolution of the dilemma for these churches is complex and requires more than historical and exegetical studies. The psychological and sociological difficulty of change is in itself a significant factor at both corporate and individual levels. Also, as sociologists recognize, this sort of change has economic implications. But the fact remains that the conservative view of biblical inspiration and the authority of scripture, the foundation upon which church doctrine rests, is the true point of contention. Therefore, traditional arguments for female inferiority and subjection, and the entire paradigm upon which patriarchal traditions are based, quite simply must be challenged. Likewise, no conservative feminist model adequately resolves the dilemma because they are all predicated upon biblical authority.

From both theological and sociological points of view, the continuing debate on the status of women has monumental implications, and is clearly relevant to the credibility of the Christian message as a whole. The outcome will have a marked effect on future church doctrine and organization, as well as the role of churches in addressing genuine human needs in this rapidly changing and increasingly complex world. Therefore, apart from decisions at a denominational and organizational level, the most urgent and pressing need is an immediate and long-term strategy for change at the level of each local church.

ABBREVIATIONS

For multi-volume works and classical libraries, the following abbreviations are used in the notes at the ends of chapters:

ACW	Ancient Christian Writers
ANF	Ante-Nicene Fathers
BCL	Bohn's Classical Library
FOTC	The Fathers of the Church
ICC	International Critical Commentary
IDB	Interpreter's Dictionary of the Bible
ISBE	International Standard Bible Encyclopedia
LCL	Loeb Classical Library
LCC	Library of Christian Classics
LW	Luther's Works
MH	Millennial Harbinger
NBC	New Bible Commentary
NBD	New Bible Dictionary
NPNF	Nicene and Post-Nicene Fathers
NSHERK	New Schaff-Herzog Encyclopedia of Religious Knowledge
PG	Patrilogia Graeca
ST	Summa Theologica (Thomas Aquinas)
TDNT	Theological Dictionary of the New Testament

Chapter One

WOMEN IN THE LIFE AND MINISTRY OF JESUS

New Testament spokesmen claim Jesus Christ as their authority, whether by personal recollection of his teachings and deeds, by the witness of others, or by inspiration of the Holy Spirit. Moreover, the New Testament church claims Christ as its founder and author, and the source of its religious doctrines and way of life. Therefore, whatever status women may have occupied in the early church, and continue to occupy in the church today, should ideally have its roots in the attitude, example and teaching of Jesus in anticipation of a community of believers perpetuating the Gospel after his departure. The Christian church is without a doubt the direct outcome of the life and ministry of Jesus Christ.[1]

It is certain that Christ's ministry had numerous objectives directly relevant to his own social environment, but Jesus was neither a zealot, a political rebel nor a religious reformer.[2] There are elements in his manner which cause some to identify him with the Essenes, claiming that his doctrine and healing techniques were learned from that austere Jewish sect.[3] But there is far too much about the ministry of Christ which differs from Essene doctrine for this theory to have merit.[4] More appropriately, Jesus might be described as a religious and social revolutionary, with a revolutionary message and mission. Jesus' own ministerial thrust is expressed in the Lukan version of his synagogue message in Nazareth, based on Isaiah's vision of ministry to the outcast and oppressed of society.[5] His personal identity with this prophecy is suggested by the comment: "This day is the scripture fulfilled in your hearing." This, writes Vigeveno, was the revolutionary manner of Jesus.[6] He spoke out against social injustice and moral evil of every description, but avoided the cynicism and recalcitrant spirit of philosophers and rebels of his day. He despised exploitation of the poor in the name of justice, which had characterized nobility for centuries, and lashed out far more harshly at religious hypocrisy than at the sins of the common people.[7]

9

Jesus might well be described as a builder of a new society, founded on the principles of fellowship and social harmony.[8] As human life originates in love, so love becomes the greatest bonding force in all social systems. Contrary to the principles of the social gospel, Jesus did not seek to change the structure and nature of society in order to reach individuals, but conversely to change society by changing the hearts and lives of individuals. Shailer Mathews speaks of fraternity taught by Jesus as the functional principle of love towards mankind. He further asserts that the times and places where people "have come most under the influence of the words and life of Jesus have been those in which institutions at variance with fraternity—branding, polygamy, the exposure of children, slavery, drunkenness and licentiousness—have disappeared."[9]

These clearly were among Jesus' objectives. The undergirding of his redemptive sacrifice was the establishment of a potential lifestyle whereby the principles of sacrificial love might abolish social injustice. True greatness, Jesus taught, could not be obtained through military conquest, financial power, or social subjugation, but through individual humility and service to others. Cullmann sees this principle at work in the lives of early Christians, and the means whereby the example of Christ continued to influence the world after his departure.[10] For precisely these reasons women held a position of high esteem in the life and ministry of Jesus, and it becomes abundantly clear that Jesus held a view of women quite contrary to that of his contemporaries.[11] Most certainly in whatever sense Jesus hoped to minister to social needs and proclaim the principles of justice, mercy and love, so he sought to liberate women.[12]

Details of Jesus' life are available only in the Gospels. Yet scholars have noted the special kindness of Jesus toward women reflected in all four Gospels, and this must be carefully noted in the light of his mission.[13] From the very start women were responsive to his teachings and devoted to his person.[14] And Pratt comments that "women of all ranks in society found in him a benefactor and friend, before unknown in all the history of their sex."[15]

The Fourth Gospel gives special prominence to women as a class, and several women in particular. The record is problematic, however, in that many reputable scholars see it as the work of a second century Christian whose purpose was to represent Christian theology as it was interpreted by his community. Each character becomes a literary device to present to the readers a key message of the Gospel relevant to his day.[16] The discourses of Jesus contained therein might not, therefore, represent the actual historical Jesus, and what one might actually learn about the attitude of Jesus toward women from the Fourth Gospel is questioned by some scholars. However, it is certain that the writer sought to communicate a message that the spirit of Jesus in the Gospel was contrary to various traditions which held women in subjection. And scholars who have been most critical of the Fourth Gospel tend to see a tradition or source of factual events which pre-dates the Johannine author and his circle. In this regard Bultmann speaks of a "sign source"[17] and Schnackenburg discusses a "Cana tradition" from which the writer drew to present a preview of Jesus' signs and ultimate glory.[18] On this basis also Brown introduces his discussion of women in the Fourth Gospel, suggesting that the writer offers through discourses constructed from pre–Johannine traditions, "very perceptive corrective ... to some ecclesiastical attitudes of his (own) time."[19] Therefore all four Gospels are significant as witnesses to the attitude and teaching of Jesus concerning women, his interest in their welfare and his ultimate objectives, both on a spiritual and temporal plain.[20] Herein is to be found the genuine premise for a Christian theology of womanhood.

Concerning Mary, the mother of Jesus, an enormous body of tradition has developed over the centuries.[21] To some scholars the New Testament stories of Mary are genuine, offering brief glimpses into the humanity of Jesus and his attitude toward women as a class.[22] To others the mother of Jesus is, especially in the Fourth Gospel, a literary device and nothing in the traditions about her contributes to our understanding of Jesus' attitude toward women.[23] But Mary's ubiquitous presence in the Gospels from Jesus' birth until after his death makes a statement about the elevated role of women in and around Jesus' ministry, at least in the eyes of the four Gospel writers.[24] The Lukan account gives unusual attention to Mary, perhaps even suggesting her as a source of information on the early life of Jesus.[25] Twice Luke states that Mary kept all these events "in her heart."[26] The Fourth Gospel also gives special prominence to her, though not by name. The dialogue between Jesus and his mother at the wedding feast in Cana has suggested to many scholars the closeness between the two, perhaps even a prompting by Mary to demonstrate his identity by means of a miracle.[27] Jesus' reply, *ti emoi kai soi*, when she points out the lack of sufficient wine seems sharp, abrupt, and critical. But the expression was common in both Jewish and Hellenistic circles to mean "So what?" and displays no disrespect whatsoever.[28] Jesus calling her "woman" (*gune*) indicates no disrespect either, since he uses the same term in his dying hour when he consigns his mother to the care of "the beloved disciple."[29] So, while the person of Mary is of no great theological significance, Jesus' attitude toward her and her treatment by gospel writers contributes to a composite picture of womanhood that is above that recognized in Christian tradition.

Jesus' encounter with a Samaritan woman at the well of Sychar is significant.[30] The account is valuable in that it suggests that Jesus had little regard for the common pious avoidance of contact with Samaritans, nor was he concerned about suspicion of wrongdoing on the basis of public conversation with strange women.[31] The writer also points out this woman's knowledge of religious history and awareness of current affairs.[32] But more significant, perhaps, is the suggestion that Jesus would discuss with her the deepest implications of his ministry, identify himself as the Messiah, and declare to her that "God is spirit, and worshippers must worship Him in spirit and truth."[33] Jesus' statement "neither this mountain or at Jerusalem" further suggests a vision of service to God beyond the traditions and restrictions of the Jews and Samaritans. The role the Samaritan woman ultimately plays in evangelism, once she is convinced of Jesus' identity as the Messiah, is also significant.[34] The writer suggests that eventually many Samaritans came to believe in Jesus through her testimony. Therefore, neither Jesus nor the writer of the Fourth Gospel saw anything wrong with a woman preaching the Good News or informing men on spiritual matters. In fact, it would seem that this testimony endorses it.

Other accounts in the Fourth Gospel also illustrate a higher estimate of women on the part of Jesus than was common in his day. The story known as the Adulterous Woman, traditionally located at John 7:53–8:11, serves to demonstrate Jesus' rejection of typical bias against women in interpreting and enforcing religious laws.[35] While others were quick to condemn, Jesus called attention to the universality of sin and urged compassion and forgiveness. The account also demonstrates the common slant of rabbinic laws against women, with comparatively little condemnation of men guilty of the same sins.

The Johannine account of Jesus' relationship with Mary and Martha of Bethany emphasizes his capacity for personal friendship, and gives unusual attention to the personalities of these two women. In the account of the resurrection of Lazarus, Martha's confession of Christ as the Son of God is surprisingly similar to the better known confession by Peter and demonstrates a significant role of women in the Johannine Community.[36] The anointing of Jesus by Mary is attested to by two of the Synoptics, and therefore has greater credibility than perhaps some of the unique records in the Fourth Gospel in spite of confused details.[37] The significance lies, as Jesus points out, both in her sacrificial love and the symbolic act of anointing. Bultmann states that here she may have done more than she realized.[38]

Mary Magdalene has become famous in Christianity for her prominence and devotion during Jesus' ministry, his trial, crucifixion, burial and resurrection. Although she only appears twice in the Fourth Gospel, she is given prominence as a witness of the resurrection,[39] for which cause in the western church she became known as "the apostle to the apostles."[40]

The Synoptics offer various glimpses which are more readily accepted by scholars than those of the Fourth Gospel, and which reflect something of Jesus' opposition to traditional attitudes toward women. Bo Reike correctly notes that the Lukan writer emphasizes the attention given by Jesus to Samaritans, women and other despised classes,[41] and Swidler even suggests that a woman was responsible for the oral tradition and possibly a written proto–Luke.[42] The Lukan account of Jesus' visit to the home of Mary and Martha[43] demonstrates the right of women, at least in his eyes, to set aside domestic chores in favor of spiritual interests.[44] While Martha is busy with food preparation Mary chooses rather to sit talking with Jesus, which in her defense he suggests is more important.[45]

Luke's account of the sinful woman anointing Jesus might be a variation of an incident in the other three Gospels commonly identified with Mary of Bethany,[46] although some see it as a second anointing.[47] The unique details serve primarily as a didactic tool contrasting the self-righteous attitude of Simon the Pharisee with the spirit of forgiveness which Jesus embodied. However, the attention given to this incident by Luke also clearly demonstrates the concern Jesus felt for the plight of women, who as a class suffered humiliation and degradation not experienced by men. It is also noteworthy that tradition has identified Mary of Bethany with the sinful woman, clearly as an effort to discredit her and diminish any prominence she might otherwise attain as a witness to the resurrection.

Luke's unique account of the woman with a crooked spine[48] also has interest, first because Jesus noticed such an insignificant person and interrupted his teaching to address her needs. Some have speculated that her condition was *spondylitis deformans*, by which the bones of her spine were fused into a rigid mass.[49] Such was her state that she walked about bent over, unable to straighten her back. When Jesus healed the woman, the result was an immediate uproar among pious Jews because he had violated rabbinical law by healing on the Sabbath. Jesus responded by declaring that human needs take precedence over religious laws and traditions.[50] Oepke further points out that his calling her "a daughter of Abraham" would have been scandalous in his day, which clearly demonstrates his concern for the plight of women in Jewish tradition and his intention of effecting positive change.[51]

There are scholars who see the frequent references to women in Luke not as an attempt to elevate the status of women, but rather as Luke's attempt to appeal to the large number of women in his audience.[52] Luke being the only Greek among the gospel writers, his broader world view might be expected. However, there is no reason to expect more women in his audience than that of the other three Gospels.

Other significant incidents are recorded by either two or three of the Synoptists. Jesus' compassion for the woman with a hemorrhage demonstrates his unconcern for religious taboos and ceremonial impurities incumbent upon women,[53] and becomes a paramount example of salvatory faith.[54] This woman would have been considered perpetually unclean according to rabbinic law, and therefore was forbidden to touch a man. But Jesus appears more concerned for her needs than for either rabbinic law or religious and social taboos.

The woman who persistently begged healing for her demon-possessed daughter is also of great interest.[55] This encounter was in the region of Tyre and Sidon. But Matthew refers to the woman as a Canaanite, and Mark calls her a Greek, a Syrophoenician by race. In view of the Jewish orientation of Matthew, the writer's failure to state, as does Mark, that Jesus entered a house in this region is understandable.[56] While Mark records an immediate response to the woman grovelling at Jesus' feet in a house, Matthew leaves the impression that Jesus was outside, perhaps on the open road, and continued walking with the woman following behind. Matthew also adds that the disciples requested that Jesus dismiss her, perhaps annoyed by her persistence or fearing that she might create a commotion. Jesus' comment that it is not fit to cast the children's bread to the dogs is thought by some to represent the typical attitude of Jews toward Gentiles.[57] But the diminutive *kunaria* seems not to refer to mongrels of the street but to pet dogs who play in the house with children.[58] His initial refusal was simply to point out that the thrust of his preaching and healing ministry was for the Jews, and not for the Gentiles who live among the "children." The woman's retort adds another diminutive *psichia*, suggesting her willingness to accept even the smallest crumbs that fall from the master's table. Both writers imply Jesus' delight in her answer and faith, and record an immediate grant of her request.

In addition to these, several women in the Gospels are noteworthy because of giving money. The widow whom Jesus commended to the disciples for giving all she had into the temple treasury has become a well known illustration of sacrificial giving.[59] Perhaps of even greater significance are a group of women mentioned by name in Luke who "ministered unto him (Jesus) out of their substance."[60] It seems quite extraordinary that Jesus would reverse the usual order of financial dependency, accepting support from a group of women so that he could be devoted to public ministry. But this fact suggests a distinctly different view of women, of their worth and their rights, from that common in his day.

Lastly, the Synoptic divorce material is of great scholastic interest, partly because of the differences in detail between Matthew and Mark.[61] It is certain that the occasion for these statements is an attempt by Jewish leaders to draw Jesus into the current debate between the schools of Hillel and Shammai concerning the grounds for divorce suggested in Deuteronomy.[62] Yet all three Synoptics present Jesus as concerned with promoting marital fidelity, not with adjudicating grounds for divorce. He clearly attacks traditional divorce practices among the Jews, particularly their inclination to interpret Mosaic divorce laws for personal advantage. And while none of the accounts overtly extends to women the right to divorce an unfaithful husband, Jesus seems to be attacking the customary bias of laws and ethical traditions in favor of men.[63]

The teachings of Jesus appear to have brought together the more noble principles of all societies before his time, as well as pointing out the shortcomings of many social and religious traditions. However, Catchpole demonstrates effectively that Jesus' teachings were neither borrowed from contemporary society nor an accommodation of local religious sects, but rather were a refreshing, if not unique, response to the degenerate norms of the ancient world.[64] It is interesting also that in the long discourse on divorce in Matthew 19, Jesus appeals to the priestly Creation Story, rather than the Yahwist's story of Adam and Eve,[65] and then shifts to Genesis 2:24 to support the concept of marital devotion and oneness.[66] Jesus, or at least the writer, seems careful to avoid the implications of the Adam and Eve story which served as the basis for traditional rabbinic teachings on the subordination of women. Witherington also stresses that in discussing sexual sins Jesus seems to redirect attention from women, who generally bore the brunt of accusation and punishment in Jewish society, to men, who are duly responsible for controlling their aggressive passion.[67] Thus in Jesus' teaching traditional stereotypes are rejected.

Summary

It is quite significant that the attitude of Jesus toward women as represented in the Gospels is not that which is perpetuated in later Christian tradition. Instead, he appears to have suggested in various ways his rejection of the notion of female inferiority, often boldly challenging tradition. Holley words it succinctly:

> In Jesus' actions and attitudes, in his willingness to come up against the traditions of cultures, in his loving concern, he was revealing the will of God.... Jesus treated women of whatever sort as persons of value and worth, as genuine human beings, not just as inferior or despised females. There was never in his manner any condescending, sentimentalizing, jeering, patronizing or putting them in their place.[68]

Instead, it appears that Jesus attempted to elevate women in such a way as to demonstrate the remarkable change the kingdom of God would effect in a human life and in society. Both the Synoptic tradition and the Fourth Gospel offer strong evidence that within the broad framework of his ministry Jesus sought to elevate the status of women, in fact to teach principles by which all forms of discrimination against women might be abolished. However, Jesus does not reject the concepts of marriage and family. Witherington argues convincingly that Jesus not only upheld but in certain ways strengthend the concept of family, although his departure from the notion of paternal lordship and his rejection of various forms of injustice with regards to familial responsibility is quite remarkable.[69] Yet, Witherington concludes that Jesus sought to reform, but not reject, the patriarchal framework under which he operated.[70] Therefore the concepts of male dominance of the home and church in later Pauline tradition Witherington finds rooted in Jesus himself. This conclusion seems based more on silence than genuine evidence. To the contrary, the implications of evidence emerging from the Gospels is that Jesus was opposed to all forms of injustice, including those extensions of patriarchy evident in religion.

There is an increasing awareness of a disparity between various Christian traditions and those ideals which undergirded the early Gospel message. There is also a demonstrable difference between the thrust of Christ's teaching and the application of it by the early Christian community as demonstrated by Pauline and Petrine writings. Therefore, the attitude of Jesus toward women, as far as it can be established, is critical to a resolution of the dilemma faced by churches today. Because Christianity has its ultimate source in the mind and ministry of Jesus Christ, his own attitude toward women has critical significance in evaluating church doctrines and traditions today. As Scroggs points out, one cannot "explain the prevalence and equality of women in the earliest church if such attitudes were not initiated by Jesus himself."[71]

Chapter One Notes

1. Maurice Goguel, *Jesus and the Origins of Christianity*, Vol. I (New York: Harper Torchbooks, 1960), p. 18.

2. William Barclay, *The Mind of Jesus* (New York: Harper & Row, 1960), pp. 160, 230.

3. Marcello Craveri, *The Life of Jesus*, C.L. Markmann, trans. (New York: Grove Press, 1967, p. 72; J.W. Shepard, *The Christ of the Gospels* (Grand Rapids: Eerdmans, 1968), pp. xii–xiii.

4. W. Rauschenbush, "Jesus the Builder of the New Society," *Great Lives Observe Jesus*, Hugh Anderson, ed. (Englewood Cliffs: Prentice Hall, 1967), p. 126.

5. Luke 4:18–19; cf. Isaiah 61:1. "The Spirit of the Lord is upon me, because he anointed me to preach the gospel to the poor. He has sent me to proclaim release to the captives, and recovery of sight to the blind, to set free those who are downtrodden, to proclaim the favorable year of the Lord."

6. H.S. Vigeveno, *Jesus Was a Revolutionary* (Glendale: G/L Publications, rep. 1972), pp. 5–12.

7. Matthew 23:1ff; cf. Ezekiel 22:29; Ecclesiastes 5:8.

8. Rauschenbush, p. 126.

9. Shailer Mathews, "Jesus' Philosophy of Social Progress," *Great Lives Observed Jesus*, p. 122; cf. Mathews, *The Social Teaching of Jesus: An Essay in Christian Sociology* (New York: Macmillan, 1897), pp. 191–7.

10. Oscar Cullman, *The Early Church*, A.J.B. Higgens, ed. (London: SCM Press, 1956), p. 195.

11. Ben Witherington, *Women in the Ministry of Jesus* (Cambridge: University Press, 1984), pp. 125–131.

12. Albrecht Oepke, "*gune*," *TDNT*, Vol. I, G. Kittel, ed. (Grand Rapids: Eerdmans, rep. 1969), p. 784; Leonard Swidler, "Jesus Was a Feminist," *South East Asia Journal of Theology* XIII:1 (1971), pp. 102–4.

13. Henri Daniel-Rops, *Jesus in His Time*, R.W. Millar, trans. (London: Eyre and Spottiswoode, rev. 1956), p. 252.

14. Martin Debelius, *Jesus* (London: SCM, English edition, 1963), p. 54.

15. D.M. Pratt, "Women," *ISBE*, Vol. V. (Grand Rapids: Eerdmans, rep. 1955), p. 3102.

16. R. Bultmann, *The Gospel of John, A Commentary*, G.R. Beasley-Murray, trans. (Oxford: Basil Blackwell, 1971 edition).

17. Bultmann, *John*, pp. 113, 119.

18. Rudolf Schnackenburg, *The Gospel According to St. John*, Vol. I, K. Smith, trans. (New York: Herder and Herder, 1968), p. 326.

19. Raymond E. Brown, "Roles of Women in the Fourth Gospel," *Theological Studies* 36 (December, 1975), p. 689.

20. The difficulty of discovering the historical Jesus is acknowledged. R. Bultmann, *The History of the Synoptic Tradition*, John Marsh, trans. (Oxford: Basil Blackwell, 1963).

21. Craveri, pp. 9ff.; Otto Hophan, *Maria* (Turin: Marietti, 1953); Raymond E. Brown and K.P. Donfried, *et al.*, eds. *Mary in the New Testament* (Philadelphia: Fortress, 1978), p. 179ff.

22. Paul K. Jewett, "Mary and the Male/Female Relationship," *Christian Century* 90 (December, 1973), p. 1255.

23. Brown, "Roles of Women in the Fourth Gospel," p. 695; Eugene D. Stockton, "The Woman: A Biblical Theme," *Australian Journal of Biblical Archaeology* 1:6 (1973), p. 109.

24. Luke 1:27–38, the announcement of Mary's pregnancy. Bultmann regards this and the parallel in Matthew 1:18–25 an adaptation from Hellenistic sources, *Synoptic Tradition*, p. 296; C.M. Connick, *Jesus, The Man, The Mission, The Message* (Englewood Cliffs: Prentice-Hall, 1963), p. 104. A.R.C. Leaney, *A Commentary on the Gospel According to St. Luke* (London: Adam and Charles Black, 1958), pp. 20–27; W.C. Allen, "Matthew," *ICC* (Edinburgh: T & T Clark, third edition, 1965), pp. 18–22. Luke 2:1–18; the journey to Bethlehem and birth narrative. Matthew 2:1–16; the census, the shepherds, the magi and the slaughter of babies; cf. Bultmann, *History of the Synoptic Traditon*, pp. 297–8. Luke 2:41ff.; Jesus' dedication in Jerusalem at age 12. John 2:1–11; wedding feast at Cana. Cf. C.H. Dodd, *Historical Tradition in the Fourth Gospel* (Cambridge: University Press, 1965), pp. 297, 315–21; Bultmann, *John*, p. 118.

25. Norvel Geldenhuys, *Commentary on the Gospel of Luke* (Grand Rapids: Eerdmans, reprinted 1968), p. 114; Alfred Plummer, "Gospel According to Luke," *ICC* (Edinburgh: T & T Clark, fifth edition, 1964), p. 78; Jules Lebreton, *The Life and Teaching of Jesus Our Lord* (London: Burns, Oates and Washbourne, reprinted 1957), p. 27.

26. Luke 2:19, 51.

27. John 2:1–11.

28. Bultmann renders the expression, "What have I to do with you?" (p. 116); Barclay, "Let me handle this in my own way;" and Goodspeed, "Do not try to direct me." See Leon Morris, *The Gospel According to John* (Grand Rapids: Eerdmans, 1971), pp. 180–81. It seems rather to mean, "What does that have to do with you and me?"

29. John 19:26.

30. John 4:1–42. Martinus de Boer, "John 4:27– Women (and Men) in the Gospel and Community of John," *Women in Biblical Tradition*, G.J. Brooke, ed. (Lewiston: Edwin Miller, 1992), pp. 208–30.

31. D. Daube, "Jesus and the Samaritan Woman: The Meaning of *sugchraomai*," *Journal of Biblical Literature* LXIX (1950), pp. 137–47.

32. Rivalry concerning Mt. Zion and Mt. Gerizim, the history of Jacob's well, and prophecies concerning the Messiah.

33. John 4:24.

34. See verses 28, 39. Brown, p. 691; Barrett, p. 204; Swidler, p. 108.

35. Barrett, p. 492.

36. Brown, "The Roles of Women in the Fourth Gospel," p. 693. Sandra M. Schneiders, "Women in the Fourth Gospel and the Role of Women in Contemporary Church," *BTB* 12 (1982), p. 41.

37. John 12:1–9; Matthew 26:6–13; Mark 14:3–9.

38. Bultmann, *John*, p. 416. On the *semeion* of Jesus' burial see Dodd, *Fourth Gospel*, p. 370; Possible implications of Jesus' being anointed as prophet, priest and king, see Barrett, p. 341.

39. Also Mark 16:9.

40. Brown, "Role of Women…" pp. 692–3. From Hippolytus' Commentary

on the Canticle of Canticles. Elisabeth Schussler Fiorenza, *In Memory of Her* (London: SCM, 1983), p. 332.

41. Bo Reike, *The Gospel of Luke*, R. Mackenzie, trans. (Richmond: John Knox Press, 1962), p. 63.

42. Leonard Swidler, *Biblical Affirmations of Women* (Philadelphia: Westminster, 1979), pp. 261–2.

43. Luke 10:38–42.

44. Swidler, p. 104. The Tubingen proposition is that Martha represents Judaic Christianity trusting in works of the Law, while Mary represents Pauline Christianity, reposing simply on faith. See Plummer, p. 293.

45. Feminists like Fiorenza and Tetlow see in this the writer's intention of suppressing the activities of women. Fiorenza, "A Feminist Critical Interpretation for Liberation, Martha and Mary, Luke 10:38–42," *Religion and Intellectual Life* 3 (1986), pp. 21–36. Elisabeth Tetlow, *Women and Ministry* (New York: Paulist, 1980), pp. 101–108.

46. Luke 7:36–50.

47. Norvel Geldenhuys, *Commentary on the Gospel of Luke* (Grand Rapids, Eerdmans, rep. 1968), p. 234.

48. Luke 13:10–17.

49. Geldenhuys, p. 375, fn. 1.

50. Donald Guthrie, *Jesus the Messiah* (Grand Rapids: Zondervan, 1972), p. 207.

51. Albrecht Oepke, *"gune,"* *TDNT*, Vol. I, G. Kittel, ed. (Grand Rapids: Eerdmans, rep. 1969), p. 784.

52. Stevan Davies, "Women in the Third Gospel and New Testament Apocrypha," *Women Like This: New Perspectives on Jewish Women in the Greco-Roman World*, A.J. Levi, ed. (Atlanta: Scholars Press, 1991).

53. Leviticus 15:25–28; Cf. F Hauk, *"katharos,"* *TDNT*, Vol. III, G. Kittel, ed. (Grand Rapids: Eerdmans, rep. 1974), pp. 423–31; Bobby Lee Holley, "God's Design: Woman's Dignity," *Mission*, III:10 (April, 1975), p. 292; Letha Scanzoni and Nancy Hardesty, *All We're Meant To Be* (Waco: Word, 1974), p. 57.

54. Mark 5:25–34; Matthew 9:20–22; Luke 8:43–48.

55. Matthew 15:21–28; Mark 7:24–30.

56. R.C.H. Lenski, *The Interpretation of Matthew's Gospel* (Minneapolis: Augsburg, reprinted 1964), p. 595.

57. E.P. Gould, "The Gospel According to Mark," *ICC* (Edinburgh: T & T Clark, reprinted 1969), p. 136.

58. W.C. Allen, "The Gospel According to Matthew," *ICC* (Edinburgh: T & T Clark, reprinted 1965), p. 165.

59. Luke 21:1–4; Mark 12:41, 44.

60. Mary Magdalene, Joanna wife of Chuza, and Susanna; Luke 8:1–3. See Geldenhuys, pp. 238–9.

61. Charles C. Ryrie, *The Role of Women in the Church* (Chicago: Moody, 1978), pp. 40–49. The "except for fornication" clause in Matthew 5:32 and 19:9 has been the source of debate in church doctrine concerning grounds for divorce and remarriage. The clause does not appear in Mark 10:11 or Luke 16:18 and is generally considered to be the writer's insertion to accommodate a Jewish audience.

62. *Babylonian Talmud*, "Gittin" IX:10.

63. Matthew 19:4–9; Mark 10:3–12; Matthew 5:31–2; Luke 16:18; cf. Deuteronomy 24:1ff.

64. David Catchpole, "The Synoptic Divorce Material as a Traditio-Historical Problem," *Bulletin of the John Rylands University Library of Manchester*, 57:1 (Autumn, 1974), p. 93.

65. Genesis 1:27.

66. Matthew 19: 5–6.

67. Witherington, pp. 18–28.

68. Bobbey Lee Holley, "God's Design: Woman's Dignity," *Mission* VIII:10 (April, 1975), p. 294.

69. Witherington, pp. 11–18.

70. Witherington, p. 126.

71. Robin Scroggs, "Women in the New Testament," *The Interpreter's Dictionary of the Bible*, supp. vol. (Nashville: Abingdon Press, 1976), p. 967.

Chapter Two

WOMEN IN THE
EARLIEST CHRISTIAN
COMMUNITY

The status of women in the early Christian Church seems remarkably different from that of contemporary cultures, with the exception of certain Mystery Cults.[1] No doubt this phenomenon among the disciples of Christ represented the practical application of the revolutionary teachings of Jesus concerning social injustice and religious hypocrisy. The most obvious factor in this regard is that women were subject to the same personal response to the gospel message as men.[2] Beginning with the sermon of Peter on Pentecost, women were called to repentance, faith and confession of Christ without discrimination.[3] They were baptized, named among the believers, and encouraged to participate in various acts of godly service in the daily activities of the Christian community. The results of the Christian elevation of female status were far reaching and became especially evident in the writings of Paul and in the Lukan record of Paul's ministry. As churches were established in Palestine, Asia Minor, and Europe, women not only found meaningful roles but many also attained prominence and fame. This is the first picture of women in the church, and the first phase in their 2,000 year odyssey through church tradition until social and religious equality became a reality.

I. Prominent Women

During the early stages of the church the Apostles so dominate the historical picture that little treatment is given by the writer of Acts to the activities of converts individually, whether men or women. The narrative does, however, give sufficient detail so as to reveal the presence and significant role of women in the events surrounding the establishment of the church. Mention is made of certain women, including Mary the mother of Jesus, among approximately 120 disciples at Jerusalem.[4] Luke's mention of this group of women, which likely includes those who accompanied Jesus from Galilee and those present at the cross and grave, is perfectly in keeping with their prominence in the Gospels.[5] The 3,000 converts who made up the initial Jerusalem church doubtless also included many women.[6] In his quotation of the prophet Joel, Peter's mention of women prophesying has been understood by many as a strong hint of social and religious change which would mark the New Age.[7]

The first woman among the Jerusalem Christians to be discussed in detail is Sapphira, wife of Ananias. The story of this couple is one of two examples given by Luke to illustrate the practical results, both positive and negative, of the community of goods in the early Jerusalem church.[8] However, the most prominent woman in the Jerusalem church was Mary, mother of John Mark, identified by the writer as the sister of Barnabas.[9] The fact that Peter went to her house directly upon his escape from prison, and that a sizable group had assembled there, suggests that her home was well known by the Jerusalem Christians.[10]

Various other vignettes in Luke's Acts, in the view of numerous scholars, are clearly calculated efforts to demonstrate the elevation of women's roles in the Christian Community.[11] Dorcas, for example, a disciple in Joppa reputedly raised from the dead by Peter, is important in connection with benevolence among widows in her community.[12] Such is her significance in Acts that today "Dorcas Societies" perpetuate her memory, and in the modern city of Jaffa there is a memorial in the "Tabitha School" devoted to the care and education of underprivileged girls.[13]

The mother and grandmother of Timothy also receive prominence in Lukan and Pauline materials.[14] Presumably both Eunice and her son were converted during or subsequent to Paul's first visit to Lystra. Although married to a Greek, it appears that she and her mother Lois did all in their power to train Timothy in the fear of God and in the knowledge of holy scripture. Apparently Eunice had chosen Timothy's name, rather than his father, since its meaning is "one who honors God," further indicating a desire to rear her son according to Jewish, and then Christian, tradition.[15]

Among Paul's early converts in Philippi was a merchant woman of the Lydian city of Thyatira. The name Lydia by which she is identified is probably derived from her home country. Luke calls her as "a God-fearer," or "one who worshipped God," which was a common epithet for Gentiles who had some affiliation with the Jewish synagogue without actually proselytizing.[16] Euodia and Syntache were two women in the church at Philippi[17] whom Paul states had "labored" with him "in the gospel," strongly suggesting some practical role in evangelism or supportive ministry.[18] Chrysostom regarded the pair to be "the chief of the church which was there (at Philippi)."[19]

There is disagreement among scholars as to the meaning of "chief women" mentioned among the converts in Thessalonica.[20] The text reads *gunaikon te ton proton*, which might be understood as "wives of the leading men." The Western editors probably so understood it, for Codex Bezae omits the articles, leaving the text *gunaikon proton*.[21] But even this reduction could be construed as "leading women" or even "women of the best social standing," so the reason for the variation is unclear.[22] The precise meaning of Luke's adjective "chief" is also unclear. But there is significance in the fact that he drew special attention to these women, and their community influence due to both their status and number is unquestionable. Furthermore, the writer of Acts makes special mention of the honorable Greek women in the city of Berea,[23] whom some scholars believe to have been converted in greater numbers than the men and were of greater community influence and social status.[24] In Athens a woman named Damaris is listed among the converts, although nothing about her is known.[25]

Among Paul's closest companions in the Gospel were Aquila and Priscilla.[26] But of the two, there is reason to believe that Priscilla was the more capable and the more zealous in the faith.[27] Bruce, Harnack and others consider it possible that this couple had been converted elsewhere and were foundation members of the Roman Church.[28] Harnack was the first to suggest Priscilla as the author of Hebrews, a theory which might explain why early church tradition left the author anonymous. The history of textual transmission in the late first and early second centuries lends support to Harnack's theory, although the idea has not found much scholastic acceptance.[29]

Of critical importance is Paul's mention of Phoebe in his list of greetings at the close of Romans, where she is called a *diakonos*, translated "servant" in the Authorized Version.[30] This reference therefore becomes a key in establishing the office of deaconess in the first century church. Also in Romans 16 six of the twenty-seven people saluted by name are women, and two additional women mentioned are unnamed. These include Miriam, Tryphena and Tryphosa, and Persis, all of whom Paul says are to be noted because of their "labor (*kopian*) in the Lord."[31] Junias,[32] whom most scholars take to be a woman also, is said to have been a fellow prisoner of Paul, and along with Andronichus "of note among the apostles." Chrysostom understood this to mean that the couple were actually considered Apostles by the early church.[33] C.H. Dodd thought that the term

was used here in an unofficial sense, but he had no difficulty with the possibility that the early church sent out a woman on gospel missions.[34]

II. Women in Positions of Leadership and Service

There is also considerable evidence that in the earliest Christian
community women held offices and positions of leadership that eventually were eliminated from orthodox tradition or were modified so as to
diminish their significance and scope of influence.

Deaconesses

Probably the earliest office to develop in the church is that of deacon.[35] The origin of the diaconate is commonly sought in the selection of
the Seven at Jerusalem,[36] a view which has found favor with scholars in
general since the early church fathers.[37] These seven were selected from
among the Jerusalem Christians, and were appointed by the Apostles to
"serve tables," a work embraced by the term *diakonia*, so that the Twelve
could "continue steadfastly in prayer and in the ministry of the word."
The term "deacon" does not appear in this passage however, at least not
in reference to the Seven, and the qualifications mentioned do not parallel those prescribed later in the Pastoral Epistles.[38] Furthermore, Luke's
record has Stephen and Philip immediately appearing before the public
as miracle workers and evangelists, rather than carrying out any form of
benevolent ministry as deacons. The Seven can be called "deacons" only
in the sense that they were appointed to a benevolent ministry in the
church, and that they became the assistants or helpers of those holding a
superior office, in this case the Apostles.

The first use of the term *diakonos* as an official title is by Paul in his
letter to the Philippians, generally dated around A.D. 59–60, but the reference gives no details as to duties or qualifications. By this date there
appears to be a fixed order of officials in the church at Philippi including
both bishops (elders) and deacons.[39] The Pastoral Epistles of a later date
include certain guidelines for selecting both deacons and elders.[40] Com-
bining the root meaning of *diakonos* with the personal requirements to
hold such an office, it appears that deacons served as assistants to the
elders, ministering to the material needs of the church and working in all
areas of physical Christian service.[41]

It is difficult to state to what degree deacons should be thought of
as officers of the church, since the term means "servant" or "minister" and

is used by Paul to describe the work of apostles and evangelists.[42] But there is ample evidence that its primary use was in connection with official positions in social and religious life, even in numerous Mystery Cults which had attained great popularity throughout the Greco-Roman world.[43]

Although the offices discussed or implied by New Testament writers are almost totally occupied by men, there are hints that certain women in the early church held official positions, including that of deaconess. On this subject thoughts immediately return to Phoebe. Dodd states with confidence that whatever the deacons at Philippi were Phoebe was at Cenchraea.[44] Certainly the term must carry the same weight as when applied to Paul, Timothy or Titus, whether official or unofficial, and it must be admitted that even this description of a female Christian is unacceptable in many conservative Christian circles.[45] Significant also is Paul's term *prostatis* in describing Phoebe's relationship to the church at Cencharea, strongly suggesting some form of leadership and administrative status.[46] It is now known that in the Roman world many women were involved in finance, trade and commerce, and that by using their capital for patronage in worthy causes they often gained recognition and honor. Eumachia, for example, a priestess of Venus, donated a large building as a social club for business people in the city of Pompeii.[47] Like her, Phoebe was undoubtedly a highly influential and wealthy woman, and Paul recognizes her for using her status in various ways to promote the gospel.

Another possible reference to deaconesses in the early church is I Timothy 3:11. The context is that of the qualities desirable in candidates for elders and deacons. Verse 11 is immediately preceded by a list of characteristics desirable in deacons, which most naturally indicates that *gunaika* (women) must in some way parallel the above mentioned categories.[48] The Authorized Version renders this term "wives," implying that that certain qualities were expected also of the wives of candidates for either elder or deacon or both. But this translation clearly reflects the seventeenth century ecclesiastical attitude toward women, and appears to be intentionally misleading.

The absence of an article with the noun *gunaikas* in this case suggests that certain women, like elders and deacons in this context, were official servants in the church, the nature of their role demanding maturity and exemplary character in those so appointed. Had the passage been intended to describe wives of deacons and elders, one would expect to find such characteristics as subjection to their husbands, child rearing and hospitality as in Titus 2:4–5, and it would have been simple enough for the writer to use the possessive pronoun "their" to make himself clear. Instead, he used the term *hosautos* (likewise), which customarily introduces the second and third entities in a series and would seem to place these three groups in categories of similar nature. The same thing is suggested by the verb combination introducing each category, suggesting what qualities the candidates must have.[49] The qualities themselves further indicate the office or ministry of deaconess. Of the four adjectival expressions used here, two are found among the qualifications for elders and deacons, and the other two are paralleled roughly.[50] And, the fact that Paul inserts the women in the middle of his discussion of deacons suggests that their work is similar, and on a plane not quite the same as that of elders.[51]

Perhaps the strongest argument for the existence of deaconesses in the first century church is their mention in later patristic writings. Even if their roles changed during the development of the Catholic traditon, as clearly happened with other leadership roles, the fact of their existence cannot be denied.[52]

Widows

The Lukan reference to widows in Acts 6 gives rise to another possible office in the early church. Commentators commonly explain this reference as pertaining to poor widows needing special assistance out of church funds. Some scholars, however, see here a ministry performed by widows over which the Seven were selected as supervisors. The problem which came to the apostles' attention may have had to do with Palestinian widows being appointed to such a ministry while Hellenistic widows were being excluded. This would then be the beginnings of both the office of deacons, acting in a supervisory capacity, and the order of enrolled widows mentioned by Paul[53] who, in return for financial support, devoted their time to prayer, meditation and good works.[54]

A second reference to widows in Acts is in connection with Dorcas.[55] The writer is careful to point out that she was much loved and had abounded in deeds of charity and kindness, the widows showing Peter tunics and garments she had made. The concern is whether the phrase "while she was with them" suggests her ministry to them, or her affiliation with them as a member of an order of ministering widows. It is also noteworthy that after her recovery Peter called for "the saints and widows" to see her alive, which leaves the impression that the widows were a class or group in some way distinct from the rest of the community of believers. So it is quite plausible that early in the Palestinian church there was at least a rudimentary form of what later becomes an official "order of widows."[56]

The primary source of information concerning widows in the New Testament period is I Timothy 5:3–16. A substantial portion of this letter deals with church offices, perhaps more appropriately described as roles of service in the church, and Timothy's responsibility in selecting and working with each as a minister and evangelist. At times the specific subjects of the writer's discussion are unclear. For example, at the beginning of chapter five it is impossible to determine the status of the older and younger men and women, whether his terms refer to official roles or simply age groups. But in the thirteen verses which follow, the writer carefully identifies and discusses a class of women whose problems, needs and unique opportunity of service form a very special facet of the work of the early church. In fact, part of the complexity of this series of verses is to understand that widows were both the recipients of ministry and the instruments of ministry.[57] At least five categories of widows are distinguishable.

First, those who were legitimately destitute and therefore eligible for financial support from the church are called "real widows."[58] Second, a "widow with living relatives" or with other revenue needs no financial assistance from the Christian community and therefore should not be thought of as destitute.[59] Third, a widow who has guaranteed maintenance might well be listed among the idle rich, and is described as "self-indulgent" and "dead while she lives."[60] Fourth, concerning "the young widow," the writer recommends marriage, raising children and keeping a home. In this he sees a noble life style, quite in keeping with the principles and social standards of the day. He does not recommend any kind of celibate vow or dedication to an exclusive order which might prove too demanding or unfulfilling for a young woman full of life and passion, nor does he imply that being young necessarily excludes some widows from having a legitimate need for assistance.

Fifth, the primary group of widows discussed in this section are "enrolled widows." The term *katalegein* means "to place on a list," and implies an enrollment of widows for some special designation. As Lenski suggests, this group apparently constituted an honor roll among widows, or some type of widow's guild.[61] There can be no doubt that they were special in that stringent qualifications are set down comparable to those given for elders and deacons in the same letter.[62] Bruce is convinced that the enrolled widows of this era received support from the church, in return for which they cared for orphans, tended the sick, showed hospitality and gave themselves to spiritual meditation.[63] So, in spite of complexity of detail, there can be little doubt about the existence of some kind of order of widows in the apostolic church.

Women Elders

The primary office clearly functional in the first century church is that of the elder (or presbyter, *presbuteros*), also called bishop (or overseer, *episkopos*) or pastor (shepherd, *poimen*).[64] Although these and perhaps other terms are more descriptive than titles and may vary with locality, they represent a single leadership role which arose naturally from the Jewish concept of community and synagogue elders. Peter is careful to point out, perhaps in reflection of Jesus' own words to the disciples, that his role is one of gentle shepherding and example, rather than authoritative rule.[65] Nevertheless, the congregation is encouraged to submit to their guidance.

The Pastoral Epistles include certain noteworthy references to "the older women."[66] The identity of these women is obscure, but the qualities expected of them and the responsibility to teach could easily be associated with those who are elsewhere identified as "enrolled widows." But some suggest that the responsibility of teaching implies a status more appropriately described as "female elders."[67] Scanzoni and Hardesty point out that traditional translations seem to camouflage the possible administrative role of women here, avoiding terms that might imply women elders.[68] Therefore I Timothy 5:17–22 might conceivably include both men and women who deserve financial support because of their work in teaching, and who served the church as official shepherds.

Once the possibility of female elders is entertained, the common collective use of a masculine noun essentially includes women in any reference to "the elders" of a church, just as the masculine "prophets" would include "prophetesses," and "deacons" would include "deaconesses."[69] Therefore we have reason to at least entertain the possibility that in the earliest Christian community both men and women served in an official capacity as shepherds and overseers in some local churches.

Prophetesses

The participation of women in the formal assembly of the early church, along with their involvement in preaching, is probably a more controversial issue among churchmen today than is the possibility of female officers. It is relatively certain that women had a part in proclaiming the Gospel to non-believers. But evidence is strong that for a period of time during the first century, particularly where charismatic gifts were common, women participated in the formal church assembly both as speakers and engaging in open discussion with other speakers and teachers. Such noted women were called prophetesses.

Prophetism in early Christianity is essentially an extension of the same concept in Judaism.[70] In cultures antedating that of Israel and in some of its contemporary cultures, prophetism was marked by frenzy and ecstatic speech. It was believed that a seer, as many ethnic prophets were known, might be seized suddenly by a spirit causing him "to rave" as if possessed and in this state would utter messages from the spritual realm. Most of the prophetic practices in Egypt, Babylon, Assyria, Canaan and other ancient cultures are related primarily to magic and astrology, and the ecstatic experiences and dreams were often induced by artificial means.[71]

The Old Testament prophets were also involved, to a certain extent, with visions, dreams and forecasts, and were characterized by strange behavior. But as a whole they represent a more noble ministry than that of other ancient cultures. Essentially, the prophet of Yahweh was a proclaimer of religious truth and of the profound mysteries of the kingdom of God. He was the mouthpiece of God driven by his zeal and by the burden of a divinely inspired message to preach to God's people.[72] Merrill argues convincingly that the Old Testament prophet was neither ecstatic nor was he overwhelmed by his prophetic burden. His own personality was constantly evident, and he was in total control of his behavior even if such was somewhat unusual.[73] Neither was prediction of the future the principal element in Old Testament prophecy. Prediction was certainly employed by most prophets and the fulfilment of their prophecies served as evidence of divine calling. But the Old Testament "man of God" was primarily a man of the present. He related military defeats, grasshopper plagues and famines to the immediate spiritual needs of the people. He predicted the future and recalled the past for the purpose of present motivation to allegiance to God and to right living.[74] Their message was often directed at moral evils and social injustice.

Although men dominate the prophetic office in the Old Testament it would seem that women were not categorically excluded. The term "prophetess" is applied to Miriam, the sister of Moses;[75] to Deborah, one of the judges prior to the monarchy;[76] to Huldah, a contemporary of Jeremiah and apparently a functioning female prophet;[77] to Noadiah, a professional prophetess who opposed the work of Nehemiah;[78] and to the wife of Isaiah.[79] In the Gospel of Luke the term *prophetis* is applied to Anna, a prophetess somehow associated with the temple, who at the dedication of the child Jesus gave prophetic utterances concerning the expected Messiah.[80]

In the New Testament the concept of prophecy seems much the same as in the Hebrew Bible, except in the content of its message and context

of its utterance. The prophet in the early church was not so much a seer
of visions or a prophet of future events as an inspired preacher or teacher
and an organ of special revelation. In simpler terms, a prophet was a proclaimer of the word of God, moved by the Holy Spirit.[81] As suggested by
Lightfoot, the calling of the New Testament prophet was not so much to
"foretell" as to "forth tell."[82]

Some aspects of such prophetic preaching may have been apocalyp-
tic in nature, but for the most part it was straightforward and quite relevant to the lives of the audience. Therefore it can be said with reasonable
certainty that prophets in the apostolic church were essentially inspired
preachers of the will of God, whose primary service was the edification
of the Christian community.[83] They were not merely recognized as
prophets because of repeated utterances in assembly, but rather were
known in their own community as those having been endowed with the
gift of prophecy by the apostles.

During the Pentecost sermon Peter quoted the Old Testament
prophet Joel concerning signs of the New Age.[84] In view of the apoca-
lyptic nature of this prophecy, it is difficult to determine whether female
prophecy would be essential for it to find some degree of fulfilment. However, it does appear that some type of ministry by inspired women was
considered a sign of the presence of the Holy Spirit and the initiation of
the Kingdom of God. Also, reference to this particular prophecy would
suggest that the writer of Acts, if not Peter himself, thought so.

The majority of scholars, so it seems, hold that the 120 disciples of
the previous chapter were assembled on this occasion and that the entire
group, including a number of women, received the "outpouring" of the
Holy Spirit, evidenced by tongues of fire and the ability to speak in
tongues.[85] Whether that is so is challenged by certain details in Acts 2,
but it is likely that the facts are obscured by the writer's focus on Peter
and the Twelve.

The first clear mention of female prophetism in the history of the
early church is the the four daughters of Philip, described by the writer
as "virgins" (parthenoi).[86] They were present when the prophet Agabus
warned Paul of the dangers which awaited him in Jerusalem, but nothing is stated about their work or status in the church. By the time these
events transpired prophetic gifts had long been in use in Corinth, and Paul
had already written a letter dealing extensively with the misuse of charismatic gifts in that church. It could be argued that both they and Agabus
were remnants of Old Testament prophetism, as probably was Anna, or
that they were called to some special prophetic ministry such as that of
John the Baptist. But it would seem more logical to define their role

according to the implications of the clearest portion of evidence, that being I Corinthians 11–14.

However, concerning prophetesses in I Corinthians, commentators wrestle with what appears to be a blatant contradiction in policy, in that Paul in one chapter acknowledges such a ministry and in another chapter seems to deny them the right to speak.[87] The apparent injunction of silence in I Corinthians 14 will be discussed later, along with various contemporary exegetical efforts to reconcile the two passages. But at this point it is only necessary to assert that prophetesses did exist in the church at Corinth, and that they exercised their gift in the general assembly.[88]

Following John Calvin, Bachmann and a few others have argued that prophetesses were permitted to speak only in private home devotions, defined as assemblies of limited circles such as "house churches," or perhaps even at family devotionals.[89] But in I Corinthians 11 the clear relationship of the first section to the Lord's Supper discussion which follows cannot be ignored in favor of this theory.

Very similar to the above argument is the suggestion by Prohl that the agape (love feast) and the eucharist (Lord's Supper) were closed feasts, to which only "the initiated were invited."[90] He asserts that where no outsiders were present the wives were permitted to join the men in leading prayers and in prophesying. However, there is no suggestion in the New Testament that non-believers were prohibited from attending any of the assemblies, and I Corinthians 14 implies quite the opposite, that unbelievers were welcome.[91] It seems that secret or closed meetings only arose out of necessity during periods of extreme persecution, and as long as the Christians were in no physical danger their assemblies were open to any passerby.

Therefore, it is necessary to conclude that the proceedings implied by the term "prophesying" in I Corinthians 11:5 were involved with the assembly of the church, and that women who possessed prophetic gifts played an active role in inspired teaching and preaching, both in assemblies and in public evangelism.[92] One need not look for special references to prophetesses once it is established that they existed, for the masculine plural would doubtless include all females with the same prophetic gift.[93] And it should be noted that since most, if not all, male evangelists in the New Testament are generally considered by exegetes to be prophets, and in some way inspired, there is really no precedent for distinguishing their status from that of prophetesses. Nor is there reason to declare the role of prophetess irrelevant to female preaching and evangelism today, just because it is portrayed as charismatic.

Leaders in Prayer

The same statement by Paul which indicates that women engaged in prophecy in the assemblies of the Corinthian church also indicates female leadership in public prayer.[94] The term translated "praying" in this passage is used more than eighty times in the New Testament with the same meaning.[95]

A variety of prayer forms, such as petitions, supplications, praise, thanksgiving, and such, came into Christianity from Judaism. But the Gospels give the impression that Jesus initiated a shift to a more personal style of prayer, which no doubt motivated the disciples to say, "Lord teach us to pray."[96] Even in Judaism just prior to the life of Christ, prayer came to take the place of sacrifice in a shift of religious emphasis from the nation to the individual, and it would seem, as stated by Nash, that "The immense outflow of spiritual power and moral energy that founded the Christian church made prayer its spring and soul."[97]

New Testament examples and instruction concerning prayer reveal a surprising lack of liturgy, although psalms and devotional forms were incorporated into the wording of many prayers. Prayers appear to have been generally spontaneous and related to special needs and circumstances.[98] A common attitude of prayer was to hold the arms out with palms open and turned upward, either indicating a request for sustenance, symbolizing unconditional surrender to God, or even symbolizing moral purity.[99] But there is no indication that any special attitude was practiced ritually, for New Testament writers as a whole seem to regard virtually any position as acceptable. Many early Christians were accustomed to keeping hours of prayer, although this may have been true only among those converted from Judaism.[100]

Paul stresses the importance of congregational prayers, often soliciting prayers on behalf of himself and others whose circumstances were precarious.[101] As to whether prayers were recited in unison or worded by an individual, nothing concrete can be determined. The relationship between prayer and inspired prophecy is also obscure. Prayer is never listed among charismatic gifts, although some suggest that the prayer to which the Corinthian church would have responded "amen" was worded by a prophet.[102] Concerning the women who "pray and prophesy" in I Corinthians 11, it is difficult to know whether their prayers were charismatic or uttered by any prophetic authority. But it is likely that those who possessed prophetic abilities were devoted to extensive prayer and meditation, and were called upon most often to word prayers for edification when the whole church was together.[103]

A second text in the Pastoral Epistles which might indicate the participation of women as leaders in public prayer is I Timothy 2:8–10. The writer here seems to allude to public prayer, the expression "every place" referring to wherever Christians might assemble. But the overall tone of his statement has application in every sphere of Christian life, and not just to a formal assembly. Traditionally, Christian exegetes have argued that women in the assembly prayed only after the fashion of Hannah, who spoke in her heart; only her lips moved, but her voice was not heard.[104] There are other authorities, however, who contend that the use of "likewise" connects verse 9 with the subject of prayer in the previous eight verses. Ramsay, representing New Testament scholarship just after the turn of the century, wrote that "likewise" in this place is meaningless if it does not relate praying to women also, and later scholars have felt that the Greek conjunction might even carry on to women all that has been said concerning men in the previous verses.[105] If this is the case, the regulations concerning dress in verses 9 and 10 must be taken to represent the standards expected of those women who play a leading role in the assembly of the church, such as praying aloud. Much the same principle appears in I Corinthians 11 concerning the headcovering.

Women in the early church clearly participated in prayer when the church assembled and, at least in the context of prophesy, there is evidence that women led prayers. Arguments that such occasions were private gatherings rather than the general church assembly are unfounded, and fail to offer any sound basis for prohibiting women from praying publicly in churches today.

Consecrated Virgins

The subject of virginity is not a common topic in the New Testament, occurring only twice where some sort of special class might be implied. The first are the daughters of Philip, discussed also in connection with prophecy and about whom we know virtually nothing.[106]

The other occurs in a lengthy discussion of chastity by Paul in I Corinthians 7, although there is nothing therein which suggests an order of consecrated virgins in the early Christian community. The longest section of I Corinthians 7, verses 25–40, is a rather complicated discussion of those believers whom Paul identifies as *parthenoi*. The application of the term here is consistently a point of divergent opinion among scholars.

Ford, for example, argues that the equivalent term in Hebrew, Greek and Latin does not always refer to a man or woman who has never been married, but can be a term of status; that is, referring to one who has been married only once and who is pure by merit of faithfulness to one partner.[107] On this basis she approaches this section of I Corinthians, suggesting that Paul is referring to young widows and widowers and that the subject under discussion is some form of Levirate Marriage.[108] Her theory, however, makes too much of an obscure and questionable use of the term *parthenos* and wrongly presupposes the practice of Jewish Levirate marriage among Corinthian Christians, most of whom were of pagan background. Others, of whom Elliott is representative, understand *parthenos* to mean a "betrothed girl" and view the passage as dealing with engaged couples.[109] But the passage is quite understandable when *parthenos* is taken in its most common sense, "virgin." [110]

There can be no doubt that the Apostle Paul preferred a life of celibacy, which we must conclude pertained largely if not totally to his unreserved commitment to the Gospel.[111] In this vein Paul recommends such a life to others, since marriage has certain difficulties which might restrict one's spiritual service. Paul also recommends celibacy in view of the troublesome times and specific dangers encumbering believers in his day.[112] Persecution of some sort was virtually expected if one chose to become a Christian. And there is reason to think that an intense eschatological awareness on the part of Paul and many believers of his time contributed to their greater devotion to preaching and diminished interest in mundane matters.[113] But Paul does suggest that while a celibate life is noble, marriage is both natural, normal and acceptable as a Christian life style.[114] And he acknowledges that the ability to remain chaste is a "gift," perhaps possessed only by a few.[115] The alternative to celibacy, for those incapable of self-control, is marriage, "for it is better to marry than to burn."[116]

Verses 10–23 are essentially a discussion of marriage problems, primarily those relating to believers married to unbelievers and the tension and unhappiness which might result from their different life styles. Whether Paul made some concession for divorce and remarriage under these circumstances is difficult to determine.[117] But he clearly permitted remarriage of a widow, a doctrine he may have acquired from Gamaliel.[118]

With verse 25 Paul returns to his discussion of virgins, and he clearly distinguishes the unmarried woman (either a widow or divorced woman) from the virgin in verse 34. The section deals with the whole issue of marrying in view of difficult times, and on this subject no traditional teaching of Jesus had reached the Apostle.[119] Claiming no direct revelation on it, he offers his personal opinion.[120] Verse 36 must be understood in the light of the Roman *patria potestas*, a concept which had permeated most cultures of the West by Paul's day.[121] Paul gives advice concerning fathers who because of the critical times might have reservations about giving their daughters in marriage. Then concluding advice is given concerning widows, with a parallel axiom in Romans 7:1–6. The Apostle says a widow is at liberty to marry provided she marries a Christian,[122] which is quite harmonious with I Timothy 5:14 from a later Paulinist. But, as in all other cases, Paul is confident that a widow who is truly dedicated to the Lord will be happier if she imitates his choice to remain celebate.[123]

Considering the circumstance of the early Christian community, Paul's reasons for choosing and recommending celibacy are quite understandable. However, Fiorenza is right in suggesting that his advice was a frontal assault on the general cultural ethos, and the intentions of marriage laws instituted by Augustus was to increase the birthrate.[124] Paul's teaching created rather than resolved conflicts in the Christian community. It provided a basis for the later church rule of celibacy for the priesthood, and a mechanism for controlling the spiritual devotions of its women. Furthermore, considering that couples like Prisca and Aquila were serving effectively as married missionaries, Fiorenza finds Paul's theological error here quite remarkable.[125]

III. Pauline Vision of Equality

Galatians is possibly the earliest Pauline work, and therefore represents some of the apostolic concerns after the first two to three decades of evangelism.[126] In addition, Galatians 3:28 is a pivotal verse in the controversy over Pauline doctrine on women, both because of its implications in contrast to other Pauline texts and because of the way churchmen have interpreted it in order to harmonize Pauline teachings in defense of traditional subordination of women. Paul here draws upon three critical areas of social stratification to illustrate the objective of the Gospel and the nature of the kingdom of God: "There is neither Jew nor Greek, there is neither slave nor free man, there is neither male nor female; for you are all one in Christ Jesus."[127] And it is in this triad that practical theology with regard to the place of women in the church finds its critical moment. In whatever way the Gospel message applies to slavery and social discrimination, it applies to the status of women. But how this verse has been understood by the church through the centuries reflects the practical approach it would take to social ethics in general, and to the status of women today.

Spiritual Equality Only

Conservative scholars in general feel compelled to uphold the traditional position that male dominance, at least in the home and in church liturgy, is a divinely ordained pattern for all believers everywhere. Following a traditional approach to this and related passages, Paul's words are taken to refer only to the spiritual freedom and respect obtained in Christ. Quite obviously, freedom in Jesus Christ is, in the words of Caird, "one of the inseparable corollaries of his (Paul's) doctrine of justification by faith."[128] This in fact is the primary thrust of his letter to the Galatians in which the apostle compares legalistic Judaism to Hagar, a bondwoman rearing enslaved children, while Christianity, the heavenly Jerusalem and covenant of faith, corresponds to Sarah, the true wife whose children are free.[129]

But the liberty of which Paul speaks, so it is argued, is spiritual, not legal, political or social. Zerbst, for example, contends that Paul is concerned only with the spiritual value of people to God, declaring His accessibility to everyone regardless of social status. The immediate context of Paul's statement is the reconciliation of Jew and Gentile unto God through a spiritual body, and the mention of slaves and women is merely an extension of the same theme:

> The realm has nothing to do either with the body or external forms of human society, but is wholly of a spiritual nature. He (Paul) does not destroy the civil order or do away with the gradation of rank, without which human society cannot exist.[130]

Therefore, Paul's vision of the meaning of the Gospel is summarized in the good news that God is not exclusively the God of the Jews, of the rich, of citizens or of males only, but that all classes and both sexes have equal invitation to serve God and find spiritual harmony with Him.[131] As John Davis argues, the patriarchal structure of Jewish society remains "a providentially prepared social paradigm for the Christian Church."[132]

Naturally these principles of spiritual equality should have both personal and social implications, but only to the extent of expressions of love, compassion and fellowship in the church. They do not, according to this view, eradicate essential forms of social stratification. No New Testament writer overtly denounces slavery or any other form of social discrimination. Instead, the New Testament as a whole encourages all parties to carry out the obligations of their status in the spirit of Christ.[133] Likewise, the political hierarchy of the Roman Empire, with its technical distinction between slave and free classes and its opposition to the tenets of the Christian faith, was to be honored and supported by all believers.[134]

A further argument is based on the contention that God designed a hierarchy for marriage with the husband as the head and authority. Burton, advocating this line of interpretation, takes note of the "ineradicable distinction of sex," concluding that the passage has nothing to do directly with the practical merging of nationalities, annulling class distinctions or abolition of slavery, and therefore cannot abolish the practical subordination of the wife to her husband and all its implications.[135] Chadwick also sees Paul's words as the offer of moral choice and the responsibility of spiritual behavior, but not a program of emancipation. The role of the husband and wife, he says, stays the same by God's authoritative design.[136]

Witherington sees Paul's statement as a response to the common emphasis in his day on marriage and procreation. Paul had to affirm that in Christ there was a place and a meaningful role for a single person. In this, the text has clear social implications for the woman in Christ. But to Witherington, this "does not lead to an agenda of obliterating or ignoring such (social) distinctions or their advantages."[137]

As a whole, advocates of this interpretation of Galatians 3:28 acknowledge that there are certain social distinctions which are inevitable in any culture. There will always be leaders and followers, teachers and pupils, rich and poor, employer and employee, governor and citizen; there will always be male and female. The New Testament does not instruct that such social distinctions are to be disregarded by Christians, or even that such should not persist within the body of believers, but that these standards have nothing to do with salvation or quality of service in the kingdom of God. Therefore, Paul is only stating that in God's eyes there are no social distinctions, and everyone can enjoy a station of dignity in the body of Christ, even a Gentile, a slave and a woman. As Hailey sees it, the principles taught on both theological and sociological levels are redemption in Christ, value of the individual, and unity among believers.[138]

Complete Social Liberation

In contrast with the traditional line of reasoning, many scholars are inclined to see Galatians 3:28 as a statement of the ideal attainable if and when Christian principles lead to spiritual maturity in people and attain their objectives in socially meaningful ways. In the words of Roger Haight, this verse is "a rather direct expression of the substance of Jesus' revelation of a God of boundless love," and a concise statement of the essence of Christianity.[139] Most exegetes today reject an interpretation of this passage which obviates the practical issue of social relationships.[140] Paul must

be understood to declare, at least as a potential for a mature church and
for a Christ-oriented society, dignity and equality for all.[141] As Barbara
Hall words it, Paul has opened a door of social and civil equality that "no
man can shut without severely hurting the church's life and witness to
the world."[142]

The first objection to the traditional view limiting this passage to
spiritual relationships is that it renders Galatians 3:28 meaningless, even
in spiritual terms. In almost every religion of the ancient world, including Judaism, women enjoyed the same status as men when considered from
the standpoint of blessings received from and relationship to their deities.
As was the case with Israel, many cults were nationalistic and no individual could be thought of as having a greater or lesser degree of spiritual importance than anyone else, with the exception of priests and
prophets. But the outward form of spiritual expression clearly discri-
minated against women—the exclusion from certain cultic rituals, along
with the ceremonial encumbrances and traditional taboos that made the
lot of women unduly harsh. And, according to Paul, it was this useless
body of tradition from which Jews could be freed through the sacrifice of
Jesus Christ.[143] Therefore, if her only benefit was acknowledgment by God
as the spiritual equal of male Jews, without equitable treatment in the
assembly or at home, then converting to Christianity would offer a Jew-
ess no tangible benefits or advantages.

A further objection to the traditional line of reasoning is that it tends
to create a monstrous contradiction between what is commonly recognized
as Christian ideology and actual New Testament doctrine. While New
Testament writers, and more significantly Jesus himself, encourage the
support of government officials, even if they happen to be evil and their
form of rule tyrannical, the underlying principles of New Testament theology clearly oppose tyranny.[144] However, Paul himself instructs slaves to
submit to their masters and masters are encouraged to treat slaves fairly,
which when considered according to the hermeneutic of some fundamentalists, should be taken as supportive of slavery. In direct contrast, the
underlying principles of love, mercy, equity, and justice clearly oppose
slavery.[145] One must assume, therefore, that the fulfillment of the Christian message and the development of a mature church requires time, so
that as the principles of the Gospel are encouraged and slowly permeate
social structure, they will supplant tyranny and injustice. This implicit
phenomenon is essential to the fulfillment of evangelism in any community, even the maturation of a single congregation of believers.

Some scholars are not convinced that Paul was that farsighted.[146] As
stated by Terrien:

> Paul may not have intended or foreseen the momentous consequences
> of his statements in terms of social ethics, even though he stated its
> consequences in terms of ritual and racial exclusion.[147]

But other visions and aspirations Paul had for the Church, as well as fears
and warnings, suggest his awareness of what the Gospel seed could produce should it find a suitable place to grow.[148] Therefore, it is quite reasonable to conclude that Galatians 3:28 represents perhaps the clearest
New Testament declaration of the egalitarian nature of the kingdom of
God and Paul's vision for a mature and perhaps ideal church, even if he
was not able later to resolve all the tensions that arose in churches due to
this transition and could not totally rid himself of his patriarchal roots.

Further evidence that Paul had more in mind than mere spiritual status are the practical and social implications of Christianity to Jews and
Gentiles.[149] The three pairs mentioned in Galatians 3:28 denote the three
deepest divisions which split society in the first century, and were the
three specific classes mentioned in the Jewish morning prayer. In his ministry and writings Paul openly sought to abolish the social walls between
Jew and Gentile.[150] He was often involved in mediating between Jewish
and Gentile factions, especially where Jewish Christians attempted to
impose upon Gentile converts at least certain aspects of Mosaic law to
satisfy their traditional prejudice.[151] Paul claims to have opposed Peter
face to face over a similar issue.[152] As Paul saw it, such resistance to change
was contrary to the true meaning of the Good News and served to quench
the spirit of Christ. No doubt similar tension developed between members of different socio-economic strata. There was some consolation in
knowing that God did not measure their spiritual worth in terms of material possessions.[153] Various New Testament writers draw attention to the
practical implications of the Gospel in response to social inequity. From
the outset wealthy Christians were encouraged to share their abundance
with the poor, and to avoid discrimination against them in the affairs of
the church.[154] Likewise, the poor were encouraged to maintain faith, and
the lazy were admonished to work in order to have possessions with which
to support their own relatives and to share with others who might have
nothing.[155]

This leads to the conclusion that same vision existed concerning the
status of women. In Galatians 3:28 the apostle Paul reveals the ultimate,
the ideal, in Christian objectives, setting aside in theory all practical rules
of subordination and declaring the freedom of all subjected classes, slaves,
Gentiles and women, from social discrimination. The implications of such
a teaching are summarized by Glen:

Both Jew and Gentile were to be reconciled in their actual outward
relationships as well as in spirit and mind. The Gospel is the power
that shattered and continues to shatter slavery, not only as a spiritual
and mental form of bondage, but as an institution; no less that form
of slavery, the formal institution of subordination of women to men.[156]

If, therefore Paul's words do not suggest the practical emancipation
of women, to be evidenced first in the role of women in the church and
second in the sphere of social relationships, then they have no meaning
at all. And as Paulsen suggests, Paul would here have provided the church
with a model which stands starkly opposed to reality.[157]

Summary

The status of women in the earliest Christian community appears
that of remarkable elevation. Women responded to the gospel and were
baptized, and spiritual gifts such as prophecy and tongue speaking were
evident among them with no form of discrimination. Women appear to
have rendered a variety of forms of service in the church, and there is substantial evidence also that women were appointed to certain positions of
responsible leadership. They preached, taught and prayed, both publicly
and privately, and in some places may have served as overseers and coun-
sellors. This evidence does not represent any sort of fully developed doctrine, but simply the elemental and natural response of early Christians
to the principles of the Gospel of Christ in their own time and locality.
In this sense, in the words of Paul, they did not conform to the world but
were transformed by new thinking (Romans 12:2).

While there continue to be tensions within the early church, including significant problems concerning the status of women, Galatians 3:28
represents a long range projection of the application of the Gospel in
socially meaningful ways and in favor of female equality. It is a vision of
a New Age, not framed by the standards of the Old World.[158] It therefore becomes a concise canon for measuring social and religious traditions
concerning the status of women, and against which patriarchal paradigms
are exposed as inferior and unacceptable in Christian doctrine.

Chapter Two Notes

1. Greek women, a century later Roman women also, had opportunities for
spiritual leadership in the Eleusian and Dionysian cults, among others. Frederick

C. Grant, *Hellensitic Religions* (New York: The Liberal Arts Press, 1953), pp. 24, 117–22; C.K. Barrett, *The New Testament Backgrounds* (New York: Harper and Row, 1961), pp. 91–100.

2. Oepke, p. 785.

3. Acts 2:37ff., 5:12–14.

4. Acts 1:14–15.

5. Matthew 27:55ff.; Mark 15:20, 16:1; Luke 24:10; John 19:25.

6. Acts 2:37ff.

7. Acts 2:17–18; Joel 2:28.

8. Acts 5:1–11; 2:45; cf. 4:32–37; F.F. Bruce, *The Acts of the Apostles* (Grand Rapids: Eerdmans, rep. 1970), pp. 131–6.

9. Acts 12:12; Colossians 4:10.

10. Louis Matthew Sweet, "Mary," *ISBE*, Vol. III (Grand Rapids: Eerdmans, 1955), p. 2006; cf. William Ramsay, *St. Paul the Traveller*, p. 385.

11. Witherington, *Women in the Ministry of Jesus*, p. 129.

12. Acts 9:36; her name is given as Tabitha in Aramaic, translated into Greek as *dorcas*, meaning "a gazelle." She is called a disciple (*mathetria*), the only place in the N.T. where the feminine form occurs.

13. S.F. Hunter, "Dorcas," *ISBE*, Vol. II, p. 870.

14. Acts 16:1ff.; II Timothy 1:5, 3:15.

15. John Rutherford, "Eunice," *ISBE*, Vol. II, p. 1037.

16. Acts 16:12ff.; Cf. Bruce, p. 314.

17. Philippians 4:2–3.

18. Carrington, p. 181.

19. Chrysostom, *Homilies on Philippians*, XIII (*NPNF*, XIII, p. 244).

20. Acts 17:4.

21. B.M. Metzger, *A Textual Commentary on the Greek New Testament* (London: United Bible Society, 1971), p. 453; Rackham, p. 295.

22. A.T. Robertson, *Word Pictures in the New Testament*, Vol. III (London: Harper, 1930), p. 243. This illustrates the tendency in Bezae to remove ambiguities but is not necessarily part of an anti-feminist effort.

23. Acts 17:12.

24. R.C.H. Lenski, *The Interpretation of the Acts of the Apostles* (Minneapolis: Augsburg, 1961), p. 703.

25. Some have insisted that she was an aristocrat and of considerable influence. Cf. D.M. Beck, "Damaris," *IDB*, Vol. I (New York: Abingdon, 1962), p. 757; Lenski, p. 741. Her mention is omitted by Codex Bezae.

26. Acts 18:19–23; a shorter form, Prisca, appears in I Corinthians 16:19.

27. Her name is mentioned first in Romans 16:3 and II Timothy 4:19; Early church tradition held her in high esteem, considering her to have been the more productive in the faith; Chrysostom, *Homilies on II Timothy*, X, (*NPNF*, XIII, p. 515). Bruce also contends that she was of Roman nobility, bearing the title *gens Prisca*; F.F. Bruce, *The Spreading Flame*, (Paternoster, 1970), p. 15.

28. Bruce, *The Spreading Flame*, p. 137.

29. Donald Guthrie, *New Testament Introduction* (Downer's Grove: Inter-Varsity Press, 1973), pp. 696f.

30. Romans 16:1–2. The masculine noun cannot correctly be rendered "deaconess," but in view of the male domination of society in that day a masculine noun in connection with a woman strongly argues in favor of its official and titular use.

31. Romans 16:6, 12. Hauck states that in the New Testament the term *kopian* has a distinctive use for Christians toiling in and for the community; Friedrich Hauck, *"kopos, kopian" TDNT*, G. Kittel, ed., Vol. III (Grand Rapids: Eerdmans, 1974), pp. 828–9.

32. Romans 16:7.

33. Chrysostom, *Homilies on the Acts of the Apostles and the Epistle to the Romans*, XXXI (*NPNF*, Vol. XI, p. 555).

34. C.H. Dodd, "The Epistle of Paul to the Romans," James Moffatt, ed., *The Moffatt New Testament Commentary* (New York: Harper and Brothers, 1932), p. 239.

35. *diakonoi*, "servants," or "ministers." The primary meaning is "a waiter at a meal" or "a servant of a master." H.W. Beyer, *"diakonia," TDNT*, Vol. II, G. Kittel, ed. (Grand Rapids: Eerdmans, 1964), pp. 88, 91–2.

36. Acts 6:1–8.

37. W.A. Heidel, "Deacon," *ISBE*, Vol. II, p. 800.

38. I Timothy 3:8–12.

39. Philippians 1:1.

40. I Timothy 3:1–13; Titus 1:5–12.

41. Walter Lock, "The Pastoral Epistles," *ICC* (Edinburgh: T & T Clark, rep. 1966), p. 40.

42. Paul: Ephesians 3:7; Colossians 1:23, 25; Timothy: I Timothy 4:6; Titus: Colossians 4:7.

43. James H. Moulton and George Milligan, *The Vocabulary of the Greek New Testament* (London: Hodder and Stoughton, 1949), p. 149.

44. Dodd, p. 235.

45. Ephesians 3:7, 6:21; Colossians 1:7, 23, 25; 4:7; I Timothy 4:6.

46. *prostatis*, translated "helper," often denotes a technical or official status of "patron" as does the Latin *patronus*, a title given to certain wealthy and influential individuals appointed by a city as guardian of the poor. Cf. W. Sanday and A.C. Headlam, "The Epistle to the Romans," *ICC* (Edinburgh: T & T Clark, rep. 1968), p. 418–20. The verb form of the word is used elsewhere in reference to the role of elders and deacons; I Timothy 3:4–5, 5:17; Romans 12:8.

47. E. Lyding Will, "Women's Roles in Antiquity: New Archaeological Views," *Science Digest* (March, 1980), pp. 35–39. R. MacMullen, "Women in Public in the Roman Empire," *Historia* 29 (1980), pp. 208–18.

48. R.C.H. Lenski, *The Interpretation of St. Paul's Epistles to the Colossians, to the Thessalonians, to Timothy, to Titus, and to Philemon* (Minneapolis: Augsburg, 1961), p. 598.

49. *dei einai*, "must be" in verse 10, 11 and 12.

50. *nephalious*, "sober minded" (cf. I Timothy 3:2); *semnas*, "grave" (cf. verse 8); *me diabolous*, "not devilish"; *pistas en pasin*, "faithful in all things."

51. James B. Hurley, "Women in Ministry," Shirley Lees, ed. *The Role of Women* (Leicester: Inter-Varsity Press, 1984), pp. 138–9. It is interesting that Hurley, a conservative, sees the deaconess as a non-authoritative role under the direction of men, therefore harmonizing with his interpretation of I Timothy 2.

52. J. Stephen Sandifer, *Deacons: Male and Female?* (Houston: Keystone, 1989).

53. I Timothy 5:1–12.

54. Rackham, p. 82; Bruce, p. 151. MacKenzie represents the traditional

view that the widows here were totally recipients of charity, with no service required on their part; Donald MacKenzie, "Widows," *Dictionary of the Apostolic Church*, Vol. II, James Hastings, ed. (New York: Charles Scribner's Sons, 1919), p. 676.

55. Acts 9:46ff.

56. Bruce, p. 212.

57. Roger Gryson, *The Ministry of Women in the Early Church*, J. Laporte and M.L. Hall, trans. (Collegeville: Liturgical Press, 1976), p. 9.

58. Concerning the plight of destitute widows in ancient Palestine, see Chayim Cohen and Ben-Zion Schereschewsky, "Widow," *Encyclopedia Judaica*, Vol. XVI (Jerusalem: Macmillan, 1971), pp. 487–95.

59. Family members are strongly urged to care for their own, verse 4.

60. Verses 5–6.

61. Lenski, p. 670.

62. The age of sixty is that set by Plato for men and women who join the priesthood in his ideal state; *Laws* (*LCL*, p. 579). *enos andros gune* ("wife of one man") Lenski renders "true and faithful to one man," p. 669; cf. I Timothy 3:2, 12.

63. Bruce, *The Spreading Flame*, p. 189. Bonnie B. Thurston, *The Widow: A Woman's Ministry in the Early Church* (Minneapolis: Fortress, 1989).

64. I Timothy 3:1ff; Titus 1:5–9; Acts 14:23.

65. I Peter 5:3; Mark 10:42.

66. I Timothy 5:1–2; Titus 2:1–5.

67. "apt to teach," cf. I Timothy 3:2.

68. Scanzoni and Hardesty, p. 63.

69. Examples include prophets of I Corinthians 11–14 and the use of collective terms like "disciples," "saints," and "believers."

70. The Hebrew term *nabi'* occurs more than 300 times in the masculine in the O.T. and six times in the feminine. The root meaning is "to utter a sound," or "to announce, speak, or proclaim;" Francis Brown, S.R. Driver and C.A. Briggs, eds., *A Hebrew and English Lexicon* (Oxford: Clarendon Press, rep. 1968), s.v. A synonymous term is *roeh*, "a seer," one who sees and hears beyond natural perception; C. Von Orelli, "Prophecy," *ISBE*, Vol. IV, James Orr, ed. (Grand Rapids: Eerdmans, 1955), p. 2459.

71. Karl Burger, "Prophecy and the Prophetic Office," *The New Schaff–Herzog Encyclopedia of Religious Knowledge*, Vol. IX, S.M. Jackson, ed. (Grand Rapids: Baker, rep. 1964), p. 271; Helmut Kramer, "*prophetes*," *TDNT*, Vol. V, Gerhard Friedrich, ed. (Grand Rapids: Eerdmans, 1971), pp. 786–7.

72. A.B. Davidson, *Old Testament Prophecy* (Edinburgh: T & T Clark, 1903), p. 89.

73. Eugene H. Merrill, "Prophecy," *Christianity Today* (March 12, 1971), p. 541.

74. Von Orelli, p. 2461.

75. Exodus 15:20; Numbers 12:2.

76. Judges 4:4, although this is likely a late inscription.

77. II Kings 22:14; II Chronicles 34:22.

78. Nehemiah 6:14.

79. Isaiah 8:3.

80. Luke 2:36.

81. Gerhard Friedrich, "*prophetes*," *TDNT*, Vol. VI, Gerhard Friedrich, ed. (Grand Rapids: Eerdmans, rep. 1971), p. 829. Ben Witherington III, *Women in the Earliest Churches*, Society for New Testament Studies, Monograph Series 59 (Cambridge: University Press, 1988), pp. 92–4.

82. J.B. Lightfoot, *Notes of the Epistles of St. Paul, From Unpublished Commentaries* (London: Macmillan and Co., 1895), p. 83. Cf. H.B.Swete, "The Prophets in the Christian Church," *The Biblical World*, XXVI (September, 1905), p. 208.

83. I Corinthians 14:6, 24ff.

84. Joel 2:28; Acts 2:17.

85. Bruce, p. 88; Rackham, p. 17. Others believe the Pentecost event centered upon the Apostles only, which seem more harmonious with other references in Acts and does no harm to the prophecy; cf. Acts 2:43; 4:33; 5:12; G.H.C. Macgregor, "The Acts of the Apostles," *The Interpreter's Bible*, Vol. IX (New York: Abingdon, 1954), p. 34.

86. Acts 21:7–14. This record, however, would have been written after Paul's mention on prophetesses in I Corinthians, dated around A.D. 55. See also Witherington, pp. 151–2.

87. I Corinthians 11:4–5; 14:1–26.

88. The entire section 11:2–14:34 seems to deal with matters concerning the church assembly: cf. 11:18, 20; 14:5; etc. Carroll Osburn, "The Interpretation of I Cor. 14:34–35," *Essays On Women In Earliest Christianity*, Vol. 1, Carroll Osburn, ed. (Joplin: College Press, 1993), pp. 224ff.

89. John Calvin, *I Corinthians*, I, 356; H.A.W. Meyer, *Critical and Exegetical Handbook to the Epistles to the Corinthians* (New York: Funk and Wagnalls, 1884), p. 247; Abel Isaksson, *Marriage and Ministry in the New Temple: A Study with Special Reference to Matthew 19:3–12 and I Corinthians 11:3–16* (Lund: Gleerup, 1965), p. 155.

90. Russell G. Prohl, *Women in the Church: A Restudy of Woman's Place in Building the Kingdom* (Grand Rapids: Eerdmans, 1957), p. 30.

91. I Corinthians 14:23ff.

92. One further reference, Revelation 2:20, suggests the possibility of prophetesses in the early church, although this one is entirely negative. Concerning whether the prophetess Jezebel was a real figure in the church in Thyatira, see R.H. Charles, "A Critical and Exegetical Commentary on the Revelation of St. John," Vol. I, *ICC* (Edinburgh: T & T Clark, rep. 1963), p. 70; G.B. Caird, *A Commentary on the Revelation of St. John the Divine* (New York: Harper & Row, 1966), p. 43. Harnack was probably correct in seeing Jezebel in *Revelation* as a figure for emperor worship, Gnosticism or any other heresy; Adolf Harnack, *The Mission and Expansion of Christianity in the First Three Centuries*, Vol. II (London: Williams and Norgate, 1908), p. 69.

93. E.g. Romans 12:6.

94. I Corinthians 11:4–5.

95. *proseuchesthai*, cf. Liddell, Scott, Jones, and McKenzie, s.v.

96. Luke 11:1.

97. H.S. Nash, "Prayer," *NSHERK*, Vol. IX (Grand Rapids: Baker, 1964), p. 154.

98. Philip Schaff, *History of the Christian Church*, Vol. I, p. 463; cf. Matthew 6:5–15; Philippians 4:6.

99. Cf. I Timothy 2:8, Lock, p. 30.

100. E.g. Peter in Acts 10:9.

101. Romans 12:12; 15:30–32; II Corinthians 1:11; 9:12ff.

102. Friedrich, p. 853.

103. Luke 2:36–38; Acts 13:1–3; I Thessalonians 5:17ff.

104. Cf. I Samuel 1:13; William Hendriksen, *A Commentary on 1 and 2 Timothy and Titus* (London: Banner of Truth, 1964), p. 102–3.

105. W.M. Ramsay, "Historical Commentary on the First Epistle to Timothy," *The Expositor*, VIII (September, 1909); Walter Lock, "A Critical and Exegetical Commentary on the Pastoral Epistles," *ICC* (Edinburgh: T & T Clark, rep. 1966), p. 31.

106. Acts 21:9.

107. J. Massyngberde Ford, "The Meaning of Virgin," *New Testament Studies* 12:3 (April, 1966), pp. 293–8.

108. Ford, "Levirate Marriage in St. Paul (I Cor. 7)," *New Testament Studies* 10:3 (April, 1964), p. 361.

109. J.K. Elliott, "Paul's Teaching on Marriage in I Corinthians: Some Problems Considered," *New Testament Studies* 19:2 (January, 1973), pp. 219–25.

110. Meaning a woman never having been married, and therefore assumed to be a virgin. It refers to women only in verses 28, 34, 36, 37 and 38; cf. Revelation 14:4.

111. This fact sets Paul at odds with his rabbinic background; cf. Witherington, p. 27.

112. Suggested by "the present crisis" (v. 26).

113. Verse 31; cf. I Thessalonians 4:13–18. Ruth Tiffany Barnhouse and Urban T. Holmes III, *Male and Female* (New York: Seabury Press, 1976), p. 24.

114. Witherington, pp. 28–9; Witherington also points out that Paul sees marital intercourse as an obligation for both partners, not an option, which discounts the possibility that he is advocating "spiritual marriage."

115. Verse 7; Paul is careful not to give ascetics grounds for using his words to command others to abstain from marriage, which in later years happens anyway.

116. Verse 9; The use here of *purousthai* is also debatable. Traditionally it has been taken to refer to the fire of passion. Barre has argued that it refers to the fires of judgment for wrong doing. M.L. Barre, "To Marry or To Burn: *purousthai* in I Cor. 7:9," *Catholic Biblical Quarterly*, 36:193–202 (1974).

117. "Not under bondage" has been a controversial expression known as "the Pauline privilege," the issue being whether he is allowing divorce (and therefore remarriage) when an unbelieving partner departs. Witherington, among others, understands *aphiemi* (verses 10 and 15), to mean "divorce;" p. 32. Others see it as meaning "separate" while actually maintaining the legal marriage. See also Elliott, who argues that the circumstances do not include the implications of adultery should the believer remarry. J.K. Elliott, "Paul's teaching on Marriage in I Corinthians: Some Problems Considered," *New Testament Studies* 19:2 (1973), pp. 219–25.

118. Vss. 8, 39. Cf. I Timothy 5:14, Romans 7:2–3; Gamaliel, "M. Yebamoth," 16:7 (*DM*, pp. 244–5).

119. Verse 25.

120. Suggested both by *gnome* "judgment" and by the verb *nomidzein* in verse 26.

.

121. Otto Kiefer, *Sexual Life in Ancient Rome*, Gilbert and Helen Highet, trans. (London: George Routeledge and Sons, Ltd., 1941), p. 43; see above, p. 27 concerning the father's rights.

122. This interpretation has been disputed by Harnack and others; see A. Robertson and A. Plummer, "A Critical and Exegetical Commentary on the First Epistle of Paul to the Corinthians," *ICC* (Edinburgh: T & T Clark, second edition, rep. 1967), p. 135.

123. Witherington's discussion of I Corinthians 7 is thorough and his observations sensible. He is correct in concluding that Paul does not think sexual relations or marriage are either evil or questionable, and approaches this discussion out of concern for the Christian's attitude toward relationships in view of troubled times. Paul's advice to the unmarried to remain as they are is part of his general advice to remain in whatever status or situation one is found upon conversion. But he further stresses that the Christ event has called the believer to live unattached to things of this world, therefore offering each one a choice about how best to serve God. Witherington correctly concludes, however, that Paul was not an ascetic; pp. 26–42.

124. Elisabeth Schussler Fiorenza, *In Memory of Her: A Feminist Theological Reconstruction of Christian Origins* (London: SCM, 1983), pp. 225–6; P.E. Corbett, *The Roman Law of Marriage* (Oxford: Oxford University Press, 1930), pp. 106–46.

125. Fiorenza, p. 226.

126. Considering the two mentioned visits to Jerusalem (Galatians 1:18 and 2:1) the latter being fourteen years after his conversion, most scholars settle on a date around A.D. 48 or 49.

127. The format of antithetical pairs is also found in I Corinthians 12:13 and Colossians 3:11, which suggests to Witherington that Paul may here be working with a set piece; p. 77.

128. G.B. Caird, *Paul and Women's Liberty* (The Manson Memorial Lecture, University of Manchester, 1971), p. 271.

129. Galatians 4:22.

130. Fritz Zerbst, *The Office of Women in the Church: A Study in Practical Theology* (St. Louis: Concordia, 1955), p. 35.

131. Romans 10:12; Colossians 3:11; I Corinthians 12:13.

132. John Davis, "Some Reflections on Galatians 3:28, Sexual Roles, and Biblical Hermeneutics," *Journal of the Evangelical Theological Society*, 19:207, 1976.

133. Philemon; I Peter 2:19; Colossians 3:22.

134. Romans 13:1ff.; I Peter 2:13ff.

135. E. de W. Burton, "The Epistle to the Galatians," *ICC* (Edinburgh: T & T Clark, rep. 1968), p. 206; H.N. Ridderbos, *The Epistle of Paul to the Churches of Galatia* (Grand Rapids: Eerdmans, rep. 1970), p. 149.

136. Henry Chadwick, *The Early Church* (Grand Rapids: Eerdmans, 1967), p. 58–9.

137. Witherington, pp. 76–8. See also Ben Witherington, "Rite and Rights for Women—Galatians 3:28," *New Testament Studies* 27:5 (1981), pp. 593–604.

138. Jan Favor Hailey, "Neither Male Nor Female" (Gal. 3:28), *Essays on Women in Earliest Christianity*, Vol. 1, pp. 164–6.

139. Roger Haight, "Women in the Church: A Theological Reflection," *Toronto Journal of Theology*, 2:113, 1986.

140. E.S. Gerstenberger and W. Schrage, *Woman and Man*, Douglas Stott, trans. (Nashville: Abingdon, 1981), p. 150.

141. Norman Parks, "Set Our Women Free," *Integrity* (January, 1973); J. B. Lightfoot, *The Epistle of St. Paul to the Galatians* (Grand Rapids: Zondervan, rep. 1972), p. 150; F.F. Bruce, *The Epistle to the Galatians* (Paternoster, 1982), pp. 188–90.

142. Barbara Hall, "Church in the World: Paul and Women," *Theology Today* 31 (1974), p. 52.

143. Galatians 3:13; Colossians 2:14.

144. Romans 13:1–14; Mark 12:16–17.

145. Ephesians 6:5–9; Colossians 3:22–4:1, Philemon 1–25.

146. A comparison of Acts 2:39, 10:1ff. and Galatians 2:7–13 suggests that Peter did not envision Gentiles becoming part of the New Age, and had trouble adjusting to it when it occurred. I Corinthians 13:12 might be taken to mean that Paul also recognized his inability to grasp the total implications of the Gospel.

147. Samuel Terrien, "Toward a Biblical Theology of Womanhood," quoted by Ruth Tiffany Barnhouse and Urban T. Holmes III, *Male and Female* (New York: Seabury Press, 1976), p. 24.

148. Ephesians 4:13–16 concerning growth of the Church to maturity; Acts 20:28–9 concerning later apostasy; also I Timothy 4:1ff if accepted as Pauline.

149. Daniel P. Fuller, "Paul and Galatians 3:28," *TSF Bulletin* 9:9–13, 1985.

150. Ephesians 2:14–22.

151. The Jerusalem Council, Acts 15.

152. Galatians 2:11–21.

153. James 1:9–10.

154. James 1:9–10; 2:1ff.; I John 3:13–18.

155. A particular problem at Thessalonica; II Thessalonians 3:10–12. Cf. Ephesians 4:28.

156. J.S. Glen, *Pastoral Problems in First Corinthians* (Philadelphia: Westminster Press, 1964), pp. 137–8.

157. H. Paulsen, "Einheit und Freiheit der Sohne Gottes-Gal. 3:26–29," *Zeitschrift fur die Neutestamentliche Wissenschaft*, 71:95, 1980. Cf. Maahs, p. 21.

158. Robin Scroggs, "Paul and the Eschatological Woman," *Journal of the American Academy of Religion* 40 (1972), p. 287.

Chapter Three

SOLUTIONS TO TRANSITIONAL PROBLEMS

Most of the teachings on the status of women in the early Christian community are traditionally ascribed to Paul, with various allusions to or quotations from the Genesis Creation Narrative. And this corpus of passages comes to serve as the ultimate proof texts for the subordination of women in Christian tradition. Galatians 3:28, discussed in the previous chapter, has been understood by many as an emancipation proclamation for women with Paul as the great New Testament champion of female liberation.[1] But this passage, representing what is now being viewed as a principal element of the Christian message, clearly stands in juxtaposition to Pauline doctrine as a whole and to mainstream Christian tradition. Therefore, developments in both theology and sociology in the modern world demand a careful and critical reexamination of relevant passages, challenging both social myth and religious dogma on this issue.

Maahs argues convincingly that Paul is neither a chauvinist nor a liberationist, but is ambivalent on the issue of women.[2] In his thinking, Pauline passages are self-consistent, although in apparent tension because of disparate foci. Gaden, on the other hand, contends that scripture, and Paul in particular, simply presents two opposite positions which cannot be reconciled.[3] He is in favor of a pluralist stance allowing churches, parishes and dioceses to take either position without enforcing one upon all. Most conservative exegetes, however, are set on harmonizing Pauline doctrines, while at the same time explaining away any teaching on the status of women which may be strained by current social trends and defending those they consider to be universal and divinely authoritative.[4] This position is the most problematic of all.

It is likely that some Pauline texts have been misunderstood, and certainly misapplied, all through the history of Christianity. But it is undeniable that, as a whole, relevant Pauline texts support traditional male dominance, and Galatians 3:28 does indeed stand in disharmony with that entire religio-sociological tradition. Paul is therefore, in the words of Elaine Pagels, "a man in conflict."[5] The tension between Galatians 3:28 and the rest of Pauline teachings is quite understandable in light of the unique dialectic of the first century, and represents an attempt on the part of the Apostle to construct a harmonious atmosphere within the Christian community to allow development and maturation of the principles of the Gospel. But the traditional elements of his teaching must be regarded as a concession to inferior social norms, much like Moses' concession to divorce, and not to be taken as divine mandate for all generations.[6] In fact, Paul seems to have found himself in a strait between the ideals implied in the Gospel and the practical realities of life in a complex culture.[7] The same must be said of other writers who contributed to materials in the Pauline tradition, particularly the Pastoral Epistles, which clearly represent an attempt to define and standardize rigid patriarchal norms.[8] Perhaps Paul's earliest conflict on the issue of women arose in the Corinthian church, in specific connection with the work of prophetesses. In dealing with those problems his teaching left a number of hermeneutical difficulties for future generations.

I. Husband as the Head of the Wife

The traditional Christian family structure is rooted in I Corinthians 11:3, which has been taken as divine authority for the husband's role as head of the wife and the household, and which, coupled with later Pauline statements, consign the wife to a role of submission.[9] This hierarchy of authority has been a paradigm for social relationships throughout the Judeo-Christian tradition.[10] Larry Christenson sees the structure of headship as vital to a functional family, each member living under the authority of some other individual filling a role designated by God:

> The husband lives under the authority of Christ and is responsible to Christ for the leadership and care of the family. The wife lives under the authority of her husband, and is responsible to him for the way she orders the household and cares for the children. The children live under the authority of both parents ... the authority of the mother is a derived authority. She exercises authority over the children on behalf of and in the place of her husband.[11]

Others, like David Field,[12] find support for the authority paradigm in the concept of governments and political officials serving as God's agents to keep peace,[13] the authority of parents over their children,[14] and even the authority of God the Father over the Son.[15] An exhaustive discussion of this subject from the traditional point of view has been published by Stephen Clark, director of a large Christian community in Ann Arbor, Michigan. He states that God is a God of order and that the New Testament presents a pattern which if followed will produce the most stable and harmonious marriages possible.[16] Proponents of this order for family structure see no danger or wrong in the husband being in the power position purely by reason of gender, for he in turn is in a subordinate position to God and Christ and is instructed to love his wife and sacrifice himself for her welfare.[17]

Since this interpretation is typically rooted in the belief that such biblical teachings are fully inspired of God and are divinely authoritative for all believers, the logical conclusion is that if this is God's plan it must be the best.[18] Therefore exegesis easily becomes an exercise in apologetics, to defend and prove by additional argumentation what has already been decided to be the correct interpretation.

The topic of discussion at the thirty-eighth meeting of the Evangelical Theological Society, held in Atlanta late in 1986, was "Male and Female in Biblical and Theological Perspective." A major area of concern was the meaning of the classical Greek term *kephale*, used by Paul in I Corinthians 11:3 to describe the relationship of the husband to wife, and that of God to Christ.[19] Wayne Grudem, of Trinity Evangelical Divinity School, represented the traditional position arguing that *kephale* in the New Testament carries the connotation of authority, as do its Hebrew and Latin equivalents, and essentially means "boss" or "chief." [20] Catherine Kroeger, Gilbert Bilezikian, and other participants suggested that the term refers to "source," as in the English concept of the headwaters of a river, reflecting the Genesis account of woman being taken out of man and having her origin in him.[21] This is the meaning of the term understood by Bartchy, Fiddes, Scanzoni and Hardesty, and numerous other conservative scholars who also advocate feminine equality.[22]

Mickelsen demonstrates that where the Hebrew *ro'sh* is used metaphorically in the Old Testament to mean leader or an authority figure, the Septuagint prefers the term *archon* in most cases.[23] And based on this and comparable studies Maahs concludes that there is no reason to assume that a Hellenized Jew would understand *kephale* to mean "one having authority over someone."[24] The motif in this passage, he argues, is one of propriety and respect for one's source.[25] If this is correct the term cannot be taken as supportive of the traditional subordination of the wife to the husband, and refers to a deeper implication of social and personal relationships. Since the true basis of marital unity is love, this concept naturally leads to the conclusion that the husband should be viewed as the source and initiator of love. A later work edited by Piper and Grudem reinforces their rejection of this interpretation, concluding that the traditional understanding of *kephale* is the more natural and accurate.[26]

Karl Barth represents those older scholars who have advocated "submission in equality," drawing from the concept of mutual love and submission in Ephesians 5:21. Barth observed that the untidy order in which Paul mentions man, Christ, woman and God in I Corinthians 11 makes it clear that they are not being arranged by scale, although he concluded that female subordination is proper.[27] This role, he believed, is one like Christ's in that through submission and suffering there is great honor and dignity.

Following this approach, Witherington is convinced that Paul tried to reform, while still supporting, traditional patriarchy by redefining the cultural concept of headship in terms of love and mutual submission, a view which is becoming more common among Christian family counselors today.[28] Fiddes stresses, however, that an exact correspondence of origins cannot be found since even Paul points out in I Corinthians 11 a reciprocity in the male-female relationship that is not true of God and Christ. While the rabbinic tradition viewed woman as having been taken out of man, Paul states that it is also by being born of woman that man comes to be. Therefore male and female depend on each other. Nor, as Fiddes stresses, is there any basis for the idea that woman is only related to Christ through her husband for both are "in Christ." Also, while woman may reflect the glory of man in some sense, Paul does not deny that both man and woman were created in the image of God.[29]

Michael and Valerie Griffiths, also evangelical feminists, further argue that the thrust of New Testament teaching on marriage relationships is that of reciprocal love, dependency and care, and not one of authority.[30] In fact, modern feminists feel strongly that the submission and domination ethos was of Greek origin and was introduced into Christianity principally through the "household tables."[31] Aristotle's ethics of submission and rule clearly defined the household hierarchy of husband-wife, father-child and master-slave as the foundation of stable society.[32] Thus alleged apostolic teachings became the means whereby Greco-Roman patriarchy was codified and imposed upon Christians as holy scripture.[33] Fiorenza seems correct in asserting that this was no accident, but a calculated effort on the part of some Christian writers to defend their community against charges of anti-social and destructive practices, disrupting the Greco-Roman order of patriarchal house and state.[34] No doubt such charges came from traditional Jews as well.

A Balanced Alternative

Today a growing number of conservative scholars are recognizing that while the authority paradigm is to be rejected, the "submission in equality" argument is weak and patronizing if it is applied only to the female.[35] The ideal marital relationship must be sought in love without a power or authority of either one over the other.

This more acceptable alternative is presented by S. Scott Bartchy based on papers presented in 1987 at the "Consultation on a Theology of the Family" at Fuller Theological Seminary.[36] Bartchy contends that the ideal approach to decision making and problem resolution in marriage is that a couple share responsibility in an attitude of love and mutual submission. This, rather than the concept of male dominance, he suggests is the true theology of the family in Pauline writings and represents the spirit of the New Testament as a whole. Such a Partnership Paradigm is becoming the predominant approach among evangelical scholars where a devotion to the authority of scripture is preserved while also addressing the issue of social equity.[37]

Bartchy focuses on a number of points and problem areas he sees as the core of the family power issue today. First, a law which assigns the husband the role of authority simply because he is male invites and provokes the wife to manipulative attitudes and actions. This is the natural response in all social "power down" positions. Second, there is no sound basis for the notion that one person has to be in charge. Paradigms often set forth from military and government life as models for such reasoning are invalid.[38] Third, there is no evidence that God grants any blessing to families on the basis of the traditional structure. The large number of battered women and abused children in so called "Christian homes" suggests that such a structure is open to abuse by men who feel compelled to verify their masculinity through domination. Bartchy writes:

> Many women, including more Christian women than generally acknowledged, rightly perceive their marriage as situations in which their psychological health if not also their physical well-being is at risk. Yet for many women who are not in such immediate danger, fear of being rejected if they become "too assertive," frustration with always being in the "power-down" position, and resentment against "being told" rather than being consulted, all encourage them to become manipulators of their husbands in a culture that gives so much permission to men to dominate others simply because they are males.[39]

Fourth, religious language and pious feelings are commonly appealed to for the purpose of reinforcing male domination in relationships, while in reality the power paradigm is incompatible with the Spirit of Christ. Fifth, this system demands the stifling of natural talents in wives for the sake of maintaining their proper place in the "Christian marriage." Sixth, an excessive degree of importance has been attached to the term "Christian marriage," suggesting that the mere acknowledgment of male dominance and female subordination will produce the happiness desired in marriage. And seventh, there is a general absence of recognition in the Christian world for the mutual subordination model for marriage, which is silently proving to be the accepted and superior structure.[40]

Jesus seems to have totally rejected the ethos of power and control of others, according to Mark's Gospel.[41] The spirit of his ministry was that of servitude, not domination. And this more than anything else he attempted to communicate to his followers. This is without a doubt the message behind the washing of the disciples' feet in the Fourth Gospel.[42] The apostle Paul seems to have recognized this and plays upon it in the famous Christological Hymn of Philippians 2:2–8. In this vein he frequently sets forth an ideal for human relationships based on self-subordination and service. This dominates the portion of his letter to the Christians at Ephesus which is so often quoted in support of male domination in the home,[43] and also appears strongly in the Epistle to the Romans.[44]

Therefore, there is quite sufficient reason to reject the traditional interpretation of Paul's teaching as an essential pattern for male authority in marriage in favor of a partnership paradigm, which seems more sensible, noble and just—in fact, a self-evident truth. However, it cannot be ignored that among conservatives this is generally accomplished by diluting the inegalitarian nature of Pauline views of husband-wife relationships and focusing on mutual love and consideration in other passages. The primary motive for this approach is to maintain allegiance to the Bible as divine authority and at the same time to find a feasible application of its doctrines. This approach does not effectively explain the clearly traditional hierarchy of male authority in I Corinthians 11 and other passages. Therefore, in reality even the best exegetical efforts of conservative feminists leave an inexplicable conflict within Pauline doctrine, and appear to be a halfway house between old ideologies and real solutions to the current dilemma.[45]

It must be noted, however, that in both Ephesians and Colossians, Paul addressed the subordinate status of women and slaves in the same context. And if all exegetical methods fail to find a sensible solution to the enigma of Pauline doctrines, perhaps logic will. If Paul's teaching on women makes them subordinate for all times, then so does his teaching on slavery. But if it is evident that Paul's exhortation to slaves to be subordinate to their masters was not an endorsement of slavery, but rather an accommodation of a gross social injustice amidst overwhelming odds, then so is his teaching on the status of women. If slavery is a social injustice to be rejected by Christians, though Paul instructed slaves to be subservient, then it is at least conceivable that the same might be true of the subordination of women.

II. Headcovering in Worship

The issue of authority does arise in I Corinthians 11:10 where Paul states that in order for a prophetess to speak she should have "authority on her head because of the angels."[46] Traditionally the point of discussion here has been understood to be a veil, an artificial headcovering, as a "sign" or "symbol" of authority, an interpretation traceable at least as far back as the gnostic Valentinus.[47] There can be no doubt that the prime concern was somehow related to husband-wife relationships and traditional subordination of wives, which had become a problem because of prophetesses speaking out in the church assembly.[48] But the whole passage is troublesome, reflecting a number of customs and social ideologies perhaps lost to the modern exegete.

The first exegetical problem concerns veiling customs in the ancient world and the meaning of *katakalupto*.[49] In spite of prolific research into historical backgrounds, it remains difficult to disclose Paul's full intent concerning head-coverings.[50] It is commonly argued that in Jewish circles of the first century there was a strong aversion to women praying without a veil, but that lacks supportive evidence.[51] However, it is more likely that the issue involved Greek customs, perhaps even specific to Corinth. And while there is evidence for headcoverings among Greek women, customs are not consistent over the centuries surrounding the birth of Christianity. Paul's suggestions here neither harmonize with Jewish customs nor are they clearly relevant to a Corinthian setting.[52] Witherington finds evidence that this teaching came from Tarsus, and that Paul's upbringing influenced his opinion here.[53] Many exegetes, including Witherington, have relied on the work of C.M. Galt in the 1930s, concluding that headcoverings were customarily required for women in all rituals, funerals, weddings and religious gatherings.[54] But more recent studies suggest quite the opposite.[55] Witherington himself is convinced that the Corinthians would have met in private homes, and if so the primary motive of hiding a wife from view in public disappears.[56]

Paul's reference to hair in this passage is also troublesome. Hurley has argued effectively that the whole point of concern was actually hairstyle, the idiom "covered" meaning "having the hair tied up in a chiton" as becoming a married woman.[57] This is suggested particularly by verse 15 where Paul states that woman's hair is given to her "for a covering,"[58] supported by the illustration of "shaving and shearing" and the alleged shame of long hair for men.[59] All this leads to the conclusion that Paul was referring to a particular hairstyle which symbolized submission to one's husband. While Hurley's argument is plausible, it has gained little scholastic acceptance. Most conclude that the subject is a traditional veil or head covering.

Scholars agree that very little can be said about what "nature" teaches concerning hair length, either for men or women, and here Paul might have been referring rather to "custom" and to social propriety in that specific locality.[60] Paul's allusion to "shaving and shearing" suggests that such would be shameful for a woman,[61] and serves simply as support for his argument that the woman's head should be covered. It has been commonly argued that prostitutes were made to wear shorn hair, but there is no substantial evidence that this was so.[62]

Paul's reference to angels adds to the confusion. It is ludicrous to suggest that an angel would be offended or inflamed with passion upon seeing a bareheaded woman praying, although this has been the interpretation of many for centuries.[63] Some have suggested that the term "angel" here refers to the ministers of the church, in danger of temptation if women did not properly cover themselves.[64] But it is more likely that Paul drew on common beliefs that angels were present in and concerned with human service to God,[65] and therefore would delight in a Christian assembly conducted with propriety, decency and order.[66]

Many commentators assume the term *egzousian* to refer to the authority of the husband over the wife, and the unmentioned veil a sign or symbol of such authority.[67] Robertson represents the traditional application of this passage in a modern context, warning that "the freedom of women to minister in church must not overthrow or disregard the leadership role of men in families and church."[68] This exegesis has been challenged by others who see Paul alluding to the woman's own authority to speak and share in the assembly proceedings under the new Christian order.[69]

In spite of all the difficulties, the most reasonable conclusion is that Paul here refers to some form of veiling in compliance with social expediency, and that he uses hairstyles, common beliefs concerning angels, and other customs as arguments to support his case. Whether the authority in question is that of the husband over the wife, or that of the wife to speak on her own merit, there can be no question that Paul's advice in the end defers to traditional male domination and customs that required wives to be in subjection. Even prophetesses had to conform.[70]

Paul's conclusion in verse 16 is as difficult as the rest of the passage, but appears to be an appeal to unity and peace.[71] But there is nothing about the passage which should cause a believer to think that God has ordained that women should cover their heads in a religious assembly, either to pray or to speak, or that the customs and doctrines contained in this section of scripture constitute a universal mandate for church assembly. The fact that few modern churches require a veil for women, or long hair, or any particular hairstyle, indicates the ability even in conservative tradition to recognize the cultural nature of some New Testament teachings, and therefore disregard them as modern church dogma.[72]

III. Silence in the Assembly

I Corinthians 14:34–36 is a conundrum by contrast to chapter 11, in that it appears to abolish what was clearly taking place under the auspices of prophetic gifts. For this reason some have concluded it to be a post–Pauline interpolation.[73] An appeal to the Law seems quite out of the ordinary for Paul, although the reference may be to rabbinic law rather than the Law of Moses.[74] However, evidence for interpolation is lacking from the standpoint of textual criticism,[75] and there are various internal reasons for accepting it as Pauline.[76]

It appears that most scholars have felt compelled to harmonize chapters 11 and 14, and to harmonize Paul with contemporary tradition and general church dogma even if this is accomplished by means of fantastic conjectures. A variety of theories have been offered. Moffatt suggested that women were so susceptible to the mysterious and ecstatic that a potentially beneficial practice soon got out of hand.[77] Von Dobschutz suggested that chapter 11 came from fragments of an earlier letter, and sometime after writing it Paul simply changed his mind on this issue. The two portions came to be copied as one letter very early.[78]

Various other exegetes have suggested that the problem addressed here is not that of prophetesses at all, as was the case in chapter 11, but women who were interrupting and confusing the assembly with questions, or even idle chattering by women of the church.[79] This theory allows for women speaking as prophetesses, but not in circumstances that created an unacceptable disruption. Witherington concurs, seeing no contradiction between the implications of chapter 11 and the injunction of silence in chapter 14, since he feels the latter deals with a specific problem of propriety and order.[80]

However, in verse 28 there appears a command of silence on the part of those who were addressing the congregation in charismatic tongues without an interpreter. Under these circumstances, Paul says, a speaker should "keep silence in the church, and speak to himself and to God."[81] This does not suggest total silence, but refraining from speech so as to maintain order.[82] And it appears that the problem addressed is indeed related to those who possessed charismatic gifts, and therefore would include prophetesses.

Hurley suggests that the answer lies in verse 35, which pertains to judging the validity of prophecy. The prophetesses were continually firing questions at the speakers, perhaps with the motive of learning, but assuming the anomalous role of judging men and creating a general atmosphere of disorder. Paul instructs that they be quiet, and ask such questions at home.[83] Witherington's exhaustive exegesis yields much the same conclusion.[84] Peterson makes a distinction between prophecy, which he feels was an acceptable practice for women in the early church, and teaching, which was not. The latter, he says, was "an authoritative function concerned with the faithful transmission of apostolic doctrine or tradition," and was committed to men only.[85] Therefore, Paul states that those women who were attempting to teach should stop.

Kaiser, Odell-Scott and others find a radically different way of explaining the injunction of silence. They see Paul here referring to some earlier communication from Corinth, which he completely rejects. The strong particle *he* in verse 36, usually translated "What?" introduces a sentence contrary to the one preceding it. Paul therefore is saying: "What? Did the Word of God originate with you (men), or are you the only ones it has reached?" With this interpretation, the injunction of silence becomes a heretical doctrine which Paul rejects and denounces, and the traditional proof text for the silence of women is removed altogether.[86]

Although attempting to choose from a number of such interpretations is frustrating, it is probable that Paul meant essentially what he has been understood to mean for centuries and that his teaching reflects the rabbinic models of his heritage. However, it is also plausible that his intention was merely to solve a problem at Corinth only, and that he did not intend to set down a mandate for all churches. In either case, we are forced to view the entire passage as written from a transient cultural perspective, and influenced both by Greek and Jewish tradition.

Summary

There can be no doubt that Paul was concerned with order and propriety in the assembly, as well as general unity in the whole church. In view of various social traditions, a doctrine of female subordination was essential to those objectives. It must be recognized also that prophetic gifts were a transient element of the early church destined to disappear with time, and that female prophetism represented an element in the church that contradicted the norm.[87] While many exegetes seem to be obsessed with harmonizing and justifying Paul, a more rational alternative is to accept that in view of the circumstances his doctrine on women was simply less than ideal, and that dedication to Christianity in a modern world does not require a fundamental application of all he taught or recommended on this issue. As Dwight Pratt suggests, regardless of the immediate problems Paul addressed, his prohibition was applicable only to the peculiar circumstances at the time and are irrelevant to church life today.[88]

Chapter Three Notes

1. Scroggs, p. 283.

2. Kenneth H. Maahs, "Male & Female in Pauline Perspective: A Study in Biblical Ambivalence," *Dialogue & Alliance* 2, No. 3 (Fall, 1988), pp. 17ff. Similarly, Witherington concludes that Paul is neither a chauvinist overly influenced by his Jewish past, or an early feminist. Ben Witherington III, *Women in the Earliest Churches*, Society for New Testament Studies, Monogram Series 59 (Cambridge: University Press, 1988), pp. 24–5.

3. J.R. Gaden, "For the Ordination of Women," *MOW* (Melbourne, 1985); also in *St. Mark's Review* (March, 1986).

4. David Peterson, "The Ordination of Women—Balancing the Scriptural Evidence," *St. Mark's Review* (March, 1986), p. 20.

5. Elaine Pagels, "Paul and Women: A Response to Recent Discussion," *Journal of the American Academy of Religion* 42:544, 1974.

6. Jesus considered the Mosaic toleration of divorce a concession to human weakness; Matthew 19:8.

7. Conservatives like David Field denounce this idea in the strongest terms. "It is difficult to take such a suggestion very seriously. Apart from the grave implications it has for the authority and inspiration of scripture it effectively makes Paul seem either an idiot or a muddle-headed communicator." Field, "Headship in Marriage: the Husband's View," Shirley Lees, ed. *The Role of Women* (Leicester: Inter-Varsity Press, 1984), p. 50.

8. This takes into consideration the general tendency among scholars to reject the Pastorals as Pauline, written instead in the early second century by an anonymous Paulinist.

9. Generally the verb *upotassein*, a common term meaning "to rank, to place under, to subordinate;" Ephesians 5:21–24; Colossians 3:18; I Timothy 2:11; I Peter 3:1–5; cf. Genesis 3:16.

10. Roberta Hestenes, "Women in Leadership: Finding Ways to Serve the Church," *Christianity Today* (September 3, 1986), pp.7–1f. Noteworthy also is the instruction by Paul that a wife should "reverence" her husband (Eph. 5:33), and the mention in I Peter 3:6 of Sarah calling Abraham "lord." Both are clear reflections of the social expectations in the first Christian century.

11. Larry Christenson, *The Christian Family* (Minneapolis: Bethany Fellowship, 1970), p. 17–18.

12. Field, p. 58.

13. Romans 13:1–7.

14. Ephesians 6:1–3.

15. I Corinthians 11:3; 15:28.

16. Stephen B. Clark, *Man and Woman in Christ: An Examination of the Roles of Men and Women in Light of Scripture and the Social Sciences* (Ann Arbor: Servant Books, 1980), p. 285.

17. Ephesians 5:25.

18. Some advocates of the traditional position note the use of *aner kai gunaikos* by Paul for "husband and wife" in all related passages. Therefore the authority relationship is only applicable in marriage, not of men in relationship to women. But the intimate relationship between families and church demands male headship also in the church. This has become more or less the official position among Churches of Christ. James O. Baird, "The Role of Women in the Church," *Introducing the Church of Christ*, John Waddey, ed. (Ft. Worth: Star, 1981), pp. 121ff.

19. David Neff, "The Battle of the Lexicons," *Christianity Today* 31:44 (Jan. 16, 1987), p. 44.

20. See also Peterson, p. 16.

21. Also the meaning of Christ's relationship to the church, Colossians 1:15–18, Ephesians 1:22.

22. Paul S. Fiddes, "Woman's Head is the Man," *The Baptist Quarterly*, Vol. 31, No. 8 (1986), pp. 370–83; Letha Scanzoni and Nancy Hardesty, *All We're Meant To Be* (Waco: Word, 1974), pp. 30–31; Witherington, *Women in The Earliest Churches*, pp. 84–5.

23. Berkely and Alvera Mickelsen, "The 'Head' of the Epistles," *Christianity Today*, 20:264, 1981.

24. Maahs, p. 23; Jerome Murphy-O'Connor, "Sex and Logic in I Corinthians 11:2–16," *Catholic Biblical Quaterly*, 42:196–215, 1980. Aristotle's reference to to the husband as "head of the household" seems to mean this, although it could be seen as the source of sustenance for all in household; i.e., the chief provider. *Politics*, 1254–55 (*LCL*, 21).

25. Figurative references to Christ as "head" of the church can also be understood as "source of life" rather than "authority over," especially Colossians 2:9–10. However, the natural sense of Ephesians 1:22 is authority, strengthened by the preposition *huper*, "head over all things to the church."

26. John Piper and Wayne Grudem, eds. *Recovering Biblical Manhood and Womanhood: A Response to Evangelical Feminism* (Wheaton: Crossway, 1991), pp. 425–468.

27. Karl Barth, *Church Dogmatics*, Vol. III, Part 2; *Humanity in the Thought of Karl Barth*, S.D. McClean, ed. and trans. (Edinburgh: T & T Clark, 1981), p. 181.

28. Witherington, *Women in the Ministry of Jesus*, p. 129. Witherington also attempts to demonstrate, unsatisfactorily, that apparent contraditions in Paul's teachings on female leadership are not caused by tension between his rabbinic background and his Christian theology, but but were inherent in the teachings of Jesus which Paul echoes.

29. Fiddes, p. 371; cf. Genesis 1:28.

30. Valerie Griffiths, "Mankind: Male and Female," and Michael Griffiths, "Husband/Wife relationships: a practical Christian viewpoint," Shirley Lees, ed. *The Role of Women* (Leicester: Inter-Varsity Press, 1984). Specific reference to I Corinthians 7:3–4, concerning conjugal rights of both husband and wife.

31. Ephesians 5:21–6:9; Colossians 3:18–4:1; I Peter 2:11–3:12. Elisabeth Schussler Fiorenza, *In Memory of Her: A Feminist Theological Reconstruction of Christian Origins* (London: SCM, 1983), pp. 251–79.

32. *Politics* I: 125b.

33. Elisabeth Schussler Fiorenza, "Breaking the Silence—Becoming Visible" in "Women: Invisible in Church and Theology," Elisabeth Schussler Fiorenza and Mary Collins, eds., *Concilium: Religion in the Eighties* (Edinburgh: T & T Clark, 1985), pp. 5ff.

34. Elisabeth Schussler Fiorenza, *In Memory of Her* (London: SCM, 1983), p. 266.

35. Witherington discusses at length the implications of *hupotasso* in Pauline Haustafel (Ephesians 5:21–22 and Colossians 3:18). Since the concept of submission is predicated of all believers in their relationships to each other, as well as to children, wives and slaves, the verb appears to be used by Paul to describe the nature of Christian humility and service appropriate to any social role; pp. 50ff.

36. S. Scott Bartchy, "Issues of Power and a Theology of the Family," *Mission* 21, No. 1 (July–August, 1987), pp. 3–15.

37. Hestenes, p. 8–1f.

38. The argument has been made against monarchial bishops in churches for the very reason that where one person is in charge there is the potential for "lording over the flock" and leading the church into heresy. If this argument is valid, the same principle would apply to one leader over a family.

39. Bartchy, p. 10.

40. Rooted in Ephesians 5:21. Paul Tournier writes extensively on in-depth relationships in marriage, stressing that sharing is a mutual need. In his opinion the ideal relationship is one of balance where neither dominates the other. *The Gift of Feeling* (SCM: 1981), p. 102ff. Cf. Valerie Griffiths, "Mankind: male and female," *The Role of Women*, Shirley Lees, ed. (Leicester: Inter-Varsity Press, 1984), pp. 80–1.

41. Mark 10: 32–45.

42. John 13:1–20.

43. Ephesians 5:19–21.

44. Romans 12:3–21.

45. R.K. Johnston, *Evangelicals at an Impasse* (Atlanta: John Knox Press, n.d.), p. 69; Griffiths, p. 81.

46. M.D. Hooker, "Authority on Her Head: an Examination of I Cor. XI: 10," *New Testament Studies*, 10:415f., 1963–4.

47. Valentinus, circa. A.D.160. On the veiling of virgins, see Tertullian.

48. Paul's use of *aner kai gunaikos* in several passages pertains to "husband and wife," not "man and woman" as generic categories. Abel Isakssen, *Marriage and Ministry in the New Temple; a Study With Special Reference to Matt. 19:3–12 and I Cor. 11:3–16* (Lund: Gleerup, 1965), p. 165.

49. Used in verses 5, 6, 7, 13 and 15. *kata kephales echon* ("having the head covered") appears in verse 4, and *peribolaiou*, "a mantle" (literally, "a throw-around") occurs in verse 15. The common terms for "veil" (*kalumma, kredemnon*, and *kaluptra*) do not appear here.

50. Background studies in recent years have contributed immensely to our understanding of the problems suffered in the Corinthian church. Jack Finegan, "Corinth," *Interpreter's Dictionary of the Bible*, I (New York: Abingdon, 1962), p. 682; W.R. Halliday, *The Pagan Background of Early Christianity* (New York: Cooper Square Publishers, rep. 1970).

51. Johannes Weis, *The History of Primitive Christianity*, Frederick C. Grant, trans. (New York: Wilson-Erickson, 1937), p. 584; Clarence Tucker Craig, "The First Epistle to the Corinthians," *The Interpreter's Bible*, Vol. 10 (New York: Abingdon, 1955), p. 126; C.K. Barrett, *A Commentary on the First Epistle to the Corinthians* (New York: Harper and Row, 1968), p. 251.

52. Goudge stated that both men and women prayed with the *tallith*; H.L. Goudge, *The First Epistle to the Corinthians* (London: Methuen, 1911), p. 94. But there is a dispute as the whether this head covering existed in Jewish tradition before the fourth century A.D. See A. Robertson, "First Corinthians," *ICC* (New York: Charles Scribner's Sons, 1925), p. 229; Paul Billerbeck and H.L. Strack, *Kommentar zum Neue Testament ans Talmud und Midrash*, Vol. III (Munchen: Beck, rep. 1956), pp. 423–6.

53. Witherington, p. 82.

54. Fritz Zerbst, *The Office of Women in the Church; a Study in Practical Theology* (St. Louis: Concordia, 1955), p. 37; Hurley, p. 196; Roland de Vaux, "Sur le voile des femmes dans l'orient ancien," *Revue Biblique* 44 (1935), p. 408; Hooker, pp. 410ff.; Witherington's conclusions are based on alleged evidence collected by Galt that in Greece during the Hellenistic period women wore headcoverings during religious rites and dances. She describes them as "facial veils" which "covered the face up to the eyes, and fell over the neck and back in folds." C.M. Galt, "Veiled Ladies," *American Journal of Archaeology*, 35:373–93 (1931). See also Witherington, pp. 82ff.

55. Albrecht Oepke, "*katakalupto*," *Theological Dictionary of the New Testament*, Vol. III, ed. G. Kittel (Grand Rapids: Eerdmans, 1965), pp. 560ff.

56. Witherington, p. 80.

57. James B. Hurley, "Did Paul Require Veils or the Silence of Women? A Consideration of I Corinthians 11:2–16 and I Corinthians 14:33b–36," *The Westminster Theological Journal*, XXXV, 2 (Winter, 1973), pp. 190–220. Hurley's understanding of Paul's terminology is derived in part from the LXX wording of key phrases in Leviticus 13:45 and Numbers 5:18 where *akatakaluptos* suggests "loose hair." But Hurley also notices that Paul's teaching is contrary to the Old Testament regulations, which required a headcovering for the priests and implied long hair.

58. *peribolaion*. Witherington sees a clear distinction between a veil and a mantle, the former of which he believes covered the face. He is convinced Paul uses the *peribolaion* as an illustration of woman's need for a covering, and not that the hair is sufficient for a covering.

59. Verses 6 and 14.

60. The term *phusis* describes the natural form or constitution of a thing, the way things happen to be according to physical laws. Practically speaking, the term refers to the way things are done in a society by reason of custom, habit, or doing whatever comes naturally. Many scholars feel that universally long hair on men is disgraceful and in discord with the nature of men; F.W. Grosheide, *Commentary on the First Epistle to the Corinthians* (Grand Rapids: Eerdmans, 1953), p. 260. Marcus Dods, *The First Epistle to the Corinthians* (London: Hodder and Stoughton, 1900), p. 253. However, such conclusions appear to represent the same kind of unfounded traditional prejudice which Paul addressed at Corinth.

61. Lucian, *The Runaways* 27 (*LCL*, V, p.85). This classical writer was critical of Spartan women who looked masculine due to short hair.

62. F.W. Grosheide, *Commentary on the First Epistle to the Corinthians* (Grand Rapids: Eerdmans, 1953), p. 254; H.A.W. Meyer, *Critical and Exegetical Handbook to the Epistles to the Corinthians* (New York: Funk and Wagnalls, 1884), p. 248.

63. Tertullian, "On the Apparel of Women," II (*ANF*, IV, p. 15, 32); John R, Rice, *Bobbed Hair, Bossy Wives and Women Preachers* (Wheaton: Sword of the Lord Publishers, 1941), p. 73; Leslie Greer Thomas, *Women and Their Veils* (Knoxville). Of course, the nonsensical character of such a belief does not preclude it from Paul's thinking.

64. As suggested by Ambrose and Primarius; see Robertson, pp. 233ff.

65. J.A. Fitzmyer, "Features of Qumran Angelology and the Angels of I Cor. XI 10," *New Testament Studies*, IV (1957–8), pp. 48–58. Chrysostom said: "Do you not know that you stand in the midst of angels? With them you sing, with them you chant, and do stand laughing?" quoted by Robertson, p. 233; cf. Hebrews 12:1.

66. Henry Alford, *The Greek New Testament*, Vol. III (London: Gilbert and Rivington, 1861), p. 566.

67. *exousian ... epi tes kephales*. Maahs, p. 24. The conventional understanding is supported by the Arabic word for veil, *shultana*, which means "authority."

68. Robertson, p. 17.

69. Hooker, pp. 410–16; C.K. Barrett, *A Commentary on the First Epistle to the Corinthians* (London: A & C Black, 1968), pp. 253–5; F.F. Bruce, *I and II Corinthians* (London: Oliphants, 1971), p. 106.

70. Sir William Ramsay believed, based on Dio Chrysostom, that veiling of women was prescribed more strictly in Tarsus than any other place. Therefore Paul was greatly influenced by his upbringing. *The Teaching of St. Paul in Terms of the Present Day* (Grand Rapids: Baker, 1979), p. 214. He wrote in conclusion: "In this matter we must, I think, recognize an instance of the Apostle's occasional inability to rise above the ideas of his own time. Old prepossessions, dominant in his mind from infancy, made him see a moral duty where in our modern estimation only a social custom was really in question."

71. Scholars disagree as to whether *toiauten* means "no such" or "no other,"

and whether the "custom" he refers to is that of headcoverings, throwing off head-coverings, or being contentious about it, one way or the other. I Cor. 14:40 suggests that Paul is concerned with order in the assembly. With this Lenski agrees, quoting the Augsburg Confession: "It is proper that the churches should keep such ordinances for the sake of love and tranquility, so far that one does not offend the other, that all things be done in the churches in order, without confusion." R.C.H. Lenski, *The Interpretation of St. Paul's First and Second Epistle to the Corinthians* (Columbus: Lutheran Book Concern, 1946), p. 452.

72. Generally true also of wearing gold, braided hair, expensive garments, etc.; I Timothy 2:9–10, I Peter 3:3.

73. Elaine Pagels, p. 544, 1974; James Moffatt, *The First Epistle of Paul to the Corinthians* (New York: Harper, n.d.), pp. 231f. C.B. Caird, *Paul and Woman's Liberty* (The Manson Memorial Lecture, University of Manchester, 1971), p. 371. Susanne Heine, *Women and early Christianity: Are the Feminist Scholars Right?* (London: SCM, 1987), p. 135.

74. Tertullian noticed this also, "Against Marcion," V, 8 (*ANF*, III, p. 446). No such law exists in the Old Testament, unless it is a loose allusion to Genesis 3:16. Dick and Joyce Boldrey suggest that here *ho nomos* refers to "propriety;" "Women in Paul's Life, *Trinity Studies* 2:13 (1972). But such a use is not common to Paul. Witherington (p. 103) believes it refers to silence when a word of counsel is spoken, from Job 29:21.

75. B.M. Metzger, *A Textual Commentary on the Greek New Testament* (London: United Bible Societies, 1971), p. 565.

76. Various exegetes have defended verses 33–6 because of the link of terms such as *laleo*, *sigao*, and *hupotasso* in verses before and after, as well as the pattern of instructing submission in close proximity to an exhortation involving inspired speech (Col. 3:18ff.; Eph. 5:19ff); Witherington, p. 91.

77. Moffatt, pp. 207–18. Witherington also stresses the likelihood that the Corinthian Christians were highly prone to practices originating with Mystery Cults; p. 92.

78. Ernst Von Dobschutz, *Christian Life in the Primitive Church*, p. 38; quoted by J. Weis, *The History of Primitive Christianity*, Vol. I (New York: Wilson-Erickson, 1937), p. 332.

79. Heinrich Schlier, "*kephale*," *Kittel*, Vol. III, p. 680. There is evidence that the verb *lalein* was commonly used for "chattering" as might occur at a party or social gathering; Moutlon and Milligan, *The Vocabulary of the Greek New Testament*, p. 386. The verb *sigao* means "to hush," "be quiet," "refrain from talking;" See Liddell, Scott, Jones, s.v. However, the same term appears some eighteen times in I Corinthians 14, in each place apparently meaning "speaking to communicate a message," and in most referring to public speaking (I Cor. 14:3, 19, 21, 29). See R.C. Trench, *Synonyms of the New Testament* (Grand Rapids: Eerdmans, 1963), p. 286; W.E. Vine, *I Corinthians* (London: Oliphants, 1965), p. 199.

80. Witherington, p. 104.

81. Verses 28–9; also suggests the general church assembly.

82. G. Friedrich, "*prophetes*," *TDNT*, Vol. VI, G. Kittel, ed. (Grand Rapids: Eerdmans, 1956), p. 829. Total silence has not meant for the women either, for they partook in singing and said "amen" in response to prayers.

83. Hurley, p. 217.

84. Witherington, *Women in the Earliest Churches*, pp. 101–2. More specific-ally, that wives were becoming insubordinate to their husbands through judging prophecy.

85. Peterson, p. 19.

86. Kaiser, p. 12–I; D.W. Odell-Scott, "Let the women speak in church, and egalitarian interpretation of I Cor. 14:33b–36," *Biblical Theology Bulletin*, 13:3 (1983), pp. 90–3.

87. Schlier argues that the use of prophetic gifts by women was an excep-tion to the general rule of propriety. Henry Schlier, "*kephale*," *TDNT*, Vol. III, G. Kittel, ed. (Grand Rapids: Eerdmans, 1965), p. 680.

88. D. Pratt, "Women," *ISBE*, V, p. 3103.

Chapter Four

REVERSION TO PATRIARCHAL MODELS

As time went by problems similar to those at Corinth arose in other places, and it became clear that shifts in gender roles in the church created an intolerable strain on the peace and harmony sought by each congregation of believers. It appears also that the stability of marriages were being threatened because of a general reluctance, primarily on the part of men, to abandon the traditional paradigm of patriarchy. Some wives flaunted their freedom, compounding the growing tension in their marriages. Church leaders attempted to follow the spirit of early apostolic doctrine as they groped for solutions.

Comments concerning women are numerous in the Pastoral Epistles, particularly in I Timothy, and scholarship in general has come to view these works as representative of a later stage of doctrinal and organizational development in the church than reflected in Paul's epistles.[1] On this subject in particular the writer of I Timothy seems to revert to a very conservative rabbinic exegesis of the Old Testament to defend what was evolving into a general church doctrine.[2]

I. Ontological Inferiority of Women

Perhaps the greatest myth concerning women, the one from which all others arise, is their alleged natural and ontological inferiority to men. In the Judeo-Christian tradition this notion is derived from the Creation narrative, but in the New Testament it is taught in I Timothy 2:13–15. Here traditional rabbinism is evident in the writer's appeal to the Genesis to strengthen his argument for the subordination of wives to their husbands.[3] Each of the three distinct elements in his argument hinges upon the Jewish concept of woman's secondary creation and essentially inferior nature, following a literal interpretation of Genesis 2. Paul implies

65

much the same thing in I Corinthians 11:2–16 by stating that man was created first, that woman was taken out of man, and man is the glory of God.[4]

The point is raised by Maahs that the use of the J creation account becomes a major problem for modern exegetes. Since scholarship is becoming less inclined to defend the historicity of Adam and Eve, much less the literal details of the Second Creation story, doctrine based on those details becomes highly dubious.[5] Maahs correctly suggests that rather than using Paul or any other writer as an inspired entree to Genesis, one has to view this use of Genesis critically. Assuming Pauline authorship of I Timothy, Maahs writes:

> This would mean that Paul is not attempting to establish a permanently valid exegesis of Genesis, but rather is willing to use traditional interpretation as a means of keeping a lid on an explosive issue to which ideological pursuits were willing to link the very life of the church.[6]

Fiddes points this out in connection with I Corinthians 11 where Paul seems to hold with the rabbinic view of androgyny in the original creation,[7] which would also fit his belief in "one flesh" in marriage and his view of reciprocal submission and devotion.[8] But it is also clear that Paul rejected the kind of literal asexuality fostered by various Gnostic groups, who taught that all sexual distinctions were abolished in the new creation so that marriage and procreation were to be disdained. The writer of I Timothy does not suggest this at all.

A major problem lies in the fact that the argument in I Timothy 2 is not really valid. The Second Creation account indeed suggests that woman was taken out of, or made from man, but this does not make her subordinate or inferior to men any more than man's being made out of dust makes him subordinate to the earth, or males' being born of women makes them inferior to and perpetually subordinate to their mothers or to women as a class.[9] In Genesis this notion is implied in the fashioning of Eve when Adam discovers that there is no suitable mate ("help meet") for him among all the animals. Therefore she becomes an afterthought, necessary only because of the male's "needs." The writer of I Timothy, following rabbinic doctrine, ventures to say much more than can be found in Genesis but clearly what was believed by his contemporaries.

I Timothy also seems to appeal to the Adam and Eve story to support the notion of woman's intellectual inferiority, which it does not do.[10] It should be noted that Eve leaps to God's defense when the Serpent discredits Him, and she engages in a discourse with her tempter concerning the consequences of the prohibition. Churchmen as far back as Ambrose have pointed out that Adam was tempted by his own partner, a mere human, while the woman fell to the trickery of a fallen angel, a creature superior to a human.[11] If this implies anything at all, it implies male inferiority.

Maahs, who assumes Pauline authorship of I Timothy, also stresses the growth in Paul's perspective concerning the Gospel and theoretical social equality. As the church grew Paul came to be more an accommodative missionary than a philosophical theologian, willing to delay full implementation of various ideals in order to ensure survival and growth of his missionary efforts.[12] Therefore, some of his teaching was very much beneath his own view of ideal Christianity, and calculated to keep a lid on potentially explosive situations *till* the church developed enough to survive. This indeed is possible. But Maahs might be giving Paul too much credit. One cannot set aside the fact of his Jewish background and traditional views which could have influenced his judgment in difficult didactic circumstances. It is probable that he accepted the Genesis creation story as literally true, and constructed the major part of his doctrine on it. This becomes especially evident when considering that female prophetism in the church caused problems because of its contrast with the Jewish understanding of the Old Testament, and preserving both traditional marriage and social order became a major priority for church leaders.

Nevertheless, it is evident that the writer of I Timothy appealed to the Creation in a careful and calculated manner as a literary device in controlling unpleasant developments. Whether this was done by Paul or by a Paulinist of a later date, and whether or not he believed the Genesis Creation to be literally true, the doctrine constructed upon it offers nothing which should today be construed as evidence of woman's ontological inferiority. If the writer meant this by his comments, or if he believed it to be so, he was in error.

II. *The Cause of Sin and the Fall*

Hays finds virtual universal evidence for the myth of feminine evil in primitive societies. While woman is viewed with desire by the male, she is at the same time considered to be the source of uncleanness, a debilitating influence and a threat to male virility.[13] The male psyche appears to perceive the female as a castrated male, bleeding and deprived of masculine aggression and strength, yet at the same time graceful and alluring. Therefore, in some bizarre sense, woman becomes both the object of his lust and the scapegoat for his guilt. Holding her in subjection both gratifies his ego and satisfies his need to punish her for being naturally appealing to him.

The story of the temptation and fall in the Garden of Eden contributes heavily to the perpetuation of blame placed on women for all human struggles. I Timothy 2:14, in addition to its contribution to the myth of female inferiority, finds in woman the cause of sin. The writer clearly states that it was Eve, not Adam, who was deceived by the Serpent, and for this she was in transgression.

Most scholars, even conservative ones, acknowledge that the "forbidden fruit" represents something more serious than the stated act of disobedience, but there is no way of determining the nature of it.[14] A very old tradition says that it was sexual intercourse, although this cannot be harmonized with the divine commission "be fruitful and multiply" of the earlier account, nor with the logical purpose of the sexes. Some also have suggested Eve's tendency toward liberation as the initial sin, or perhaps her presuming to encroach upon man's exclusive role in theology. There does appear in various traditions a fear of the female ability to lure and deceive, as if she has inherited a special penchant for evil from her mother Eve.[15] Early feminist Judith Murray suggested that the story represents an effort on the part of woman to intellectual pursuits. The Hebrew account, she believed, has *Isha* as being tempted because she represented in that time the sacred, the intellect, the one desiring knowledge and man's link with the divine, not because she was thought to be weaker.[16]

For the writer of I Timothy the story of Eve's temptation becomes the premise upon which hangs his advice that wives should allow their husbands to play the role of leadership, both in the social aspects of marriage and in the spiritual guidance of the home. But he refrains from mentioning that Adam accepted Eve's offer of the "forbidden fruit" without question and in total disregard of the instructions of God.[17] The account offers no explanation of the failure on the part of Adam to exercise his authority over her in the light of her apparent imperception. Nor can it be overlooked that the account has God pointing a finger of guilt at Adam, and on this basis in Pauline doctrine Adam becomes the type of fallen man and the source of death.[18]

However, it is not the husband's role or guilt in the Fall that is stressed here. It is the role of the woman in the fall. This implies that among the recipients of this epistle there existed an unwillingness of some women to accept a subordinate role in marriage, and also that husbands were having some difficulty in coping with the changes Christianity brought about in relationships and the liberty afforded their wives in Christ. Witherington argues that Paul was not accusing women of being weak and susceptible to deception, but was using Eve as an illustration of the evil that can result from being led astray. Therefore, those women who were inclined to overstep the bounds of propriety should be reminded to exercise caution and restraint.[19]

The consequences of the Fall in Genesis are also noteworthy. They are not set forth as divine rules but tendencies, clearly an attempt to explain social customs from the standpoint of the writer. "He shall rule over you" is not a divine command or pronouncement, but a description of the disorder and perversion which would result from sin.[20] Even scholars like Prohl, who believes in a created order of subordination of the wife to the husband, rejects this as a proof text for male domination:

> God is not here issuing a special commandment, "Be thou ruled by him!" or, "Thou shalt not rule!" But here in Genesis 3:16 we have a statement, a prediction, a prophecy of how man, degenerated by sin, would take advantage of his headship as a husband to dominate, lord it over, his wife. Nowhere in the Bible is Genesis 3:16 quoted or referred to as establishing a general subordination of woman to man.[21]

Therefore, it would seem that reflections on this account in I Timothy serve simply to remind women of their weaknesses and tendencies to err, for which reason all men and women have suffered since the sin of Eve. But sadly, in Christian tradition these highly symbolic myths from Genesis through Pauline tradition become not only a divine seal upon male domination of women, but the source of many related doctrines degrading and shaming women.[22] Yet in reality, the Genesis record cannot be taken as a historical account of the first act of sin, or of woman's role in bringing sin into the world. Instead, it is a reflection of the social and religious degradation of women in the time of the writer of that portion of Genesis, and its use in I Timothy is a reflection of similar norms in the cultural environment of the early church. Therefore, in drawing upon that Old Testament story the writer of I Timothy, whether Paul or a later Paulinist, clearly aligns himself with a traditional belief which is unacceptable as an ideal model.

III. Unsuitable to Teach or to Have Authority Over the Man

It is generally agreed that I Timothy 2 pertains largely to the formal assembly of the church,[23] although the writer's concern for appropriate attire is paralleled elsewhere clearly with reference to general lifestyle.[24] But of critical concern is the traditional allegation that I Timothy 2, supported by the writer's appeal to Genesis 2, declares a theological paradigm of male authority.[25] His advice that women "learn in silence" is then taken to mean refraining from speech during a church assembly,[26] and the remainder of the charge prohibits women to play any role where they might appear to have authority over a man, such as holding a church office or in public ministry or teaching.[27] Eenigenburg summarizes the traditional understanding of this passage: "A woman who by divine ordinance is subject to her husband in the home can hardly bear rule over him in the house of God."[28]

The writer does seem very concerned here with a violation of social propriety on the part of some wives, perhaps in a context identical with that of I Corinthians 11–14. The term *hesuchia* refers to a quiet and peaceful manner, suggesting an attitude of life which is orderly and submissive.[29] The term *authentein* here is an *hapax legomenon* in the New Testament which Hommes understands to be a "good, pithy colloquial expression" very nearly equivalent to the modern expression "wearing the pants."[30] Rather than "playing the boss" over their husbands, the writer advises that wives should be quiet and remain within the scope of social expediency.[31] The verb *epitrepo* should be translated "I am not permitting," and suggests that this is the writer's timely and expedient prohibitive judgment, but not one based on the Law nor suggesting a timeless divine ordinance.[32]

Although these exegetical points are clear, there is still uncertainty as to the problem which gave rise to such advice. Kaiser contends that traditional exegetes have overlooked the point of verse 11, that women need to be taught. Considering that in the first century women generally lacked the education to impart knowledge and expound scripture, women in the church were unsuitable as teachers and the writer recommends that they refrain from trying to play that role. The appeal to Eve serves to stress her lack of instruction and understanding of God's commands.[33] Therefore, Kaiser argues, if and when women receive the essential education to equip them to be teachers, the entire situation changes.[34]

Witherington states emphatically that there is no universal and unqualified prohibition of women preaching and teaching in this text regardless of the immediate point of concern, nor does it speak to the issue of female ordination.[35] And, as Barclay points out, the real problem for the church today lies in thinking that the advice in I Timothy 2, regardless of its specific nature, constitutes a divine prescription for our practice today. It is simply wrong to make this teaching a universal rule for the church.[36]

IV. Created for Pleasure and Procreation

Christian tradition also has seen woman as created specifically for man's benefit, essentially following the Jewish interpretation of the Genesis account of creation. Woman is man's "help meet," which entails a combination of subordinate roles including sex for the pleasure of the male and for procreation.[37] This position appears in early Pauline doctrine (I Corinthians 11:9) where he states that woman was made "for (*dia*) the man," and was further developed by Paulinists who viewed woman as a creation secondary to man and for the purpose of meeting man's needs. As stressed earlier, a literal interpretation of Genesis 2 is to be rejected, but one is forced to assume that Paul and the writer(s) of later Pauline literature held the same view as their rabbinical contemporaries as to the implications of the Creation story.[38]

In connection with this view, a complex assertion is made in I Timothy 2:15 that woman will be saved in childbearing. Two main streams of thought have arisen concerning this meaning of this statement. The first is that despite Eve's foolish deception, which brought sin, pain and death into the world, woman became the essential instrument for producing the Savior, specifically the motherhood of Mary. This view was suggested by various church fathers, revived by Ellicott, von Soden and Wohlenberg, and upheld by a few modern scholars.[39] The second view is that childbearing, including the rearing and instruction of children and keeping of the home, is the highest ideal in Christian womanhood and is the lifestyle by which a Christian wife attains eternal life.[40] The fact that the New Testament frequently discusses womanhood in terms of marital responsibilities, and the fact that in the immediate context the writer deals with the subordinate demeanor of wives, favors this interpretation. But this in no way implies that salvation is dependent upon fertility, nor that marriage and childbearing are a requirement for every woman.[41] Rather, the writer employs an expression that embraces the entire role of a woman who submits to the duties of marriage. By playing that role well, she has a far greater potential for influencing mankind toward Christianity, and for obtaining her own salvation, than by attempting to dominate her husband and playing the role of a teacher. These words certainly must be taken as an expression of the dignity of motherhood. Hendriksen probably summarizes the original meaning well:

> The path that leads to salvation is ever that of obedience to God's ordinances. It is His will that woman should influence mankind "from the bottom up" (that is by way of the child), not "from the top down" (that is, not by way of the man).[42]

However, from the modern perspective such a view of womanhood fails to address reality. As a paradigm for life styles it reduces woman to her sexual parts, and defines her value and purpose totally in terms of her sexual relationship to a man. Furthermore, it hopelessly minimizes the numerous contributions women can and do make to the social economy outside the scope of homemaking, and it fails to address the roles to be played by millions of childless and single women who do not fit the pattern of motherhood and subordination to a husband.[43] Having grown beyond the *patria potestas* and the rigid rabbinism of Paul's day, exact scholarship today rejects any interpretation of this passage which seeks to bind on Christian women the stereotype of motherhood and confinement to domestic chores. Consequently, one is forced to see a tension between what Paul and his school might have believed, and what is ideal and right in various contexts. Playing the role of submissive wife was, in the eyes of these early Christian spokesmen, the right behavior for a woman in order to please God and find salvation. But it fails as a universal model for the spiritual woman.

V. *The Weaker Vessel*

I Peter 3:7, traditionally ascribed to Peter, is generally quoted in support of the idea that women are weaker than men. Although it is not paralleled in Pauline literature, we shall consider it here as part of the basis of later tradition:

> Likewise ye husbands, dwell with them according to knowledge, giving honour unto the wife as unto the weaker vessel, and as being heirs together of the grace of life; that your prayers be not hindered.[44]

This work also represents a reversion to rabbinic thinking, perhaps not so much because of a later date as because of its closer association with the Jewish community. The verses which precede this one call for behavior in women modeled after the reverential submission of Sarah to Abraham, who honored him as her "lord."[45] Admittedly, this one verse exhorts husbands to exercise a higher degree of kindness toward their wives than might have been common among Jews. But it does not teach mutual submission, as do Paul's epistles, and this one exhortation hardly compares with the six verses describing what is to expected of submissive wives.

However, the major issue here is the suggestion that women are weaker than men, and what this might imply for later church tradition. The term "weak" is a relative. It is true and undeniable that universally human females are characteristically shorter and physically weaker than males. But this idea has lent itself to support various mythical notions in the polarity of the sexes, and has been exploited in defense of traditional female subordination. Even in modern times, particularly in education, there have been claims that women were innately inferior to men in certain academic fields—mathematics, physics, chemistry and such like—and that emotionally they are unstable and therefore unsuited for certain forms of leadership.

As Scanzoni and Hardesty point out, traditionally women are thought to be Narcissistic, subjective, dependent, passive, intuitive, fragile, irrational, frivolous and weak. This is the "feminine mystique."[46] But adages and observations in early cultures eventually became prescriptions rather than descriptions, and with time came to be viewed as divine institutions.

Today in Western society it might be observed that little boys use toys and blocks to construct outdoor scenes of action, with animals, cars and trucks. Little girls, in contrast, build interiors and play housekeeping, serve tea, dress dolls and pretend to be mothers. This childhood play is seen by traditionalists as an enactment of man's world and woman's place it, complete with a whole set of traits, attitudes, roles and obligations proper for a woman, and all so designed by God.[47]

Most of the pioneers in the field of psychology were also inclined to view the polarity of the sexes as a result of innate characteristics. Erik Erickson represents traditional typology in stating that men are active, interested in things and ideas, whereas women are passive and intuitive, interested in people and feelings:

> Stand in the sun and experience light, hot active, positive male yang.... Move under cover and feel the dark, moist, cold, passive force of female yin.[48]

In the middle twentieth century behavioral scientists challenged this belief, contending that gender traits are not determined by genetics or even by hormonal balance, but by conditioning and role modeling in each given society.[49] Likewise the male image, dominated globally by machismo, power, dominance, acquisition and achievement, is also a learned behavior.[50]

Sociological studies of various cultures offered ample support for this theory, demonstrating that the characteristics assigned to each sex by the Judeo-Christian tradition are neither global nor innate. In Iranian culture, women are expected to be practical and cool while men are emotional, sensitive and intuitive. The Tutsi of Africa consider women to be naturally stronger, and for this reason many African peoples associate their women with hard labor. Among the American Indian tribes, the Navaho and Hopi specifically, weaving has been traditionally regarded as men's work while pottery making was only for women.[51] Margaret Mead found illustrations of this in various tribes of New Guinea.[52] Among the Arapesh both males and females are mild tempered, gentle and submissive, while the Mundugumor men and women are equally ruthless and aggressive. Tchambuli women, on the other hand, are energetic, impersonal, unconcerned with personal beauty and the dominant social managers, while the men are less responsible, emotionally dependent, and are described as spending their time in gossip, dancing and adorning their hair.[53]

However, in the late twentieth century the explanations of gender differences became less polarized, and there is now a general recognition that gender traits are more highly complex than before thought, influenced by genetics, hormones, parental role models, and a variety of sociological factors.[54]

There is a strange paradox in myths about women. The apparent weakness and universal subordination of women in a way has been a mask for power. For example, the male's acute desire for sex has been perceived by women as a weakness, and therefore has proved to be a means by which women are able to manipulate males. There are also a variety of ancient beliefs about the mystery of feminine power, many undergirding fertility cults and magic. In some African tribes women are considered the owners of grain and vegetable crops because of their principal role in cultivation and harvest, and thereby they have a considerable degree of community power. Studies in Japanese marital relationships have discovered an interesting paradox. In public a woman appears to honor her husband as lord and master, but in private she becomes the mother of another child in desperate need of love and maternal care.[55] Hence femininity has a subtle power greater than the masculine pretense. It may be that through centuries women in general have been willing to acquiesce in the myth of subordination in favor of a more subtle power.[56] It is possible also that there exists within males a deep psychological fear of women, and systems of subordination are mechanisms of defense. In the future, studies in human psychology are certain to discover within us, and perhaps in our past, the keys to unlock these mysteries.

Summary

The stress of shifting gender roles in the earliest apostolic churches resulted in a reversion to rabbinic models rooted in Genesis. The difference between Paul's restrictive teachings on women and those of later Paulinists is simply this: the earlier teachings dealt with transient conflict, conceivably with no intention of establishing a global church doctrine; the latter teachings were a clear and intentional reversion to ancient patriarchal paradigms. The motive might have been either malicious or misogynous, but represented a conviction that this is how things always have been, and should be, because it is God's design. By the early second century the doctrinal foundation of Christian tradition had taken shape.

Chapter Four Notes

1. The authorship of I Timothy has been disputed by Schleiermacher, Baur, Holtzmann, Dibelius and others, primarily because of its omission from Marcion's Canon of a.d. 140. The Pastorals were likely written in the second century by a Paulinist, developing and applying Pauline doctrine in a more advanced ecclesiastical context. Whether the Pastorals were written by Paul or by a later Paulinist, they still represent a development of Pauline thought. But a question must be asked as to whether that development is an enhancement of earlier teaching, or against and beyond it. There are clear linguistic parallels between I Timothy 2 and I Corinthians 14 , and some have even suggested that if I Corinthians 14 is an interpolation it came from I Timothy 2. See Witherington, pp. 117ff.

2. Heine suggests that by this time Charismatic elements had disappeared, structures of order had replaced the prophetic word, and there were vigorous campaigns against Gnostic teaching. "The Pastoral Epistles are evidence of the last stage of the development indicated in the New Testament." Heine, p. 139. See also Constance F. Parvey, "The Theology and Leadership of Women in the New Testament," R.R. Ruether, ed. *Religion and Sexism* (New York: Simon and Schuster, 1974), p. 137.

3. Kevin Giles, *Created Woman* (Canberra: Acorn Press, 1985).

4. Peterson, p. 17.

5. E.F. Kevan, "Genesis," *NBC*, F. Davidson, ed. (London: Inter-Varsity Fellowship, rep. 1967), pp. 78–9. See also Louis Praamsma, *The Church in the Twentieth Century*, Vol. IV (St. Catharines, Paideia, 1981); on the approach to scripture and myth in Genesis by Barth, pp. 53–7; Brunner, pp. 58–60; Bultmann, pp. 61–4; Niebuhr, pp. 64–9.

6. Richard Longenecker sees in Gal. 3:19f., 4:29f., and II Cor. 3:13–18 Paul using *argumentum ad hominum*, interpreting OT passages in typically rabbinic fashion to his own advantage. *Biblical Exegesis in the Apostolic Period* (Grand Rapids: Eerdmans, 1975), p. 120f.

7. Genesis 1:28.

8. Ephesians 5:31–33; "Androgyny" meaning that the original Adam carried within himself (itself) the potential for both sexes. Keil and Delitzsch discount this possibility in light of Genesis 1; C.F. Keil and F. Delitzsch, "The Pentateuch," Vol. I, *Commentary on the Old Testament* (Grand Rapids: Eerdmans, 1959), pp. 65, 90.

9. Scanzoni and Hardesty, p. 28.

10. E.g., Bengel, *Gnomon*; cf. N.J. Hommes, "Let Women be Silent in the Church: a Message Concerning the Worship Service and the Decorum to be Observed by Women," *Calvin Theological Journal*, April, 1969, p. 21.

11. Andre Dumas, "Biblical Anthropology and the Participation of Women in the Ministry of the Church," in *Concerning the Ordination of Women* (Geneva: World Council of Churches, 1964), p. 32.

12. Maahs, p. 27.

13. Hays, p. 96–8.

14. Reinhold Neibuhr, *The Nature and Destiny of Man*, Vol. I (New York: Charles Scribner's Sons, 1964), pp. 178ff. Neibuhr sees the Genesis Fall as representing human pride, i.e., his presumption to know truth without and apart from a relationship with God.

15. Walter Wagner, "The Demonization of Woman," *Religion in Life* XLII (Spring, 1972).

16. Tavard, p. 14.

17. Genesis 3:3, 11.

18. Romans 5:14–19; I Corinthians 15:21–45. Tavard totally rejects I Timothy 2:13–15 as Pauline, because it is out of step with these other passages where Adam bears the stigma of Original Sin, pp. 27f. See George Tavard, *Women in Christian Tradition* (Notre Dame University Press, 1973), pp. 27ff.

19. Witherington, p. 122.

20. Maahs, p. 19.

21. Russell C. Prohl, *Woman in the Church* (Grand Rapids: Eerdmans, 1957), p. 39.

22. Walter Wagner, "The Demonization of Woman," *Religion in Life*, XLII (Spring, 1973); H.R. Hays, *The Dangerous Sex: The Myth of Feminine Evil* (New York: G.P. Putnam's Sons, 1964).

23. Richard Longenecker sees in Gal. 3:19f., 4:29f., and II Cor. 3:13–18 Paul using *argumentum ad hominum*, interpreting OT passages in typically rabbinic fashion to his own advantage. *Biblical Exegesis in the Apostolic Period* (Grand Rapids: Eerdmans, 1975), p. 120f.

24. Titus 2:7–8; I Peter 2:12ff.

25. Peterson, p. 17.

26. As was the case in I Corinthians 14:33ff.

27. Roger E. Dickson, *International New Testament Study Commentary* (Church of Christ: 1987), p. 593; James O. Baird, "Role for Women in the Church," *Introducing the Church of Christ*, John Waddey, ed. (Ft. Worth: Star, 1981), pp. 123–4. In fact, some conservatives understand I Timothy 2:9 to imply that only males could lead public prayers. I. Howard Marshall, "The role of women in the church," *The Role of Women*, Shirley Lees, ed. (Leicester: Inter-Varsity Press, 1984), pp. 191–2.

28. Elton M. Eenigenburg, "The Ordination of Women," *Christianity Today* 3:15–16 (April 27, 1959).

29. A.T. Robertson, *Word Pictures in the New Testament*, Vol. IV (New York: Harper and Brothers, 1931), p. 570; J.H. Moulton and G. Milligan, *The Vocabulary of the Greek New Testament* (London: Hodder and Stoughton, rep. 1963), p. 281. Cf. I Peter 3:4.

30. N.J. Hommes, "Let Women Be Silent in the Church: A Message

Concerning the Worship Service and the Decorum to Be Observed By Women," *Calvin Theological Journal*, April, 1969, p. 6.

31. For a variety of possible causes of the upset, see Scanzoni and Hardesty, p. 71. It should be noted that the spirit of Christ would not approve of anyone "playing the boss" over another, not even a church elder; Mark 10:42, I Peter 5:3–4. If this denies women the right to fill roles of leadership, teaching, or authority, then it does so for everyone.

32. Witherington, p. 120. Not like the rabbinic formula of I Corinthians 14:38 "it is not permitted."

33. This is also stressed by Witherington who sees the problem as the susceptibility of women to false teaching and their being easily led into apsotacy. The Pastorals are likely dealing with proto–Gnosticism. Pp. 117–127.

34. Walter C. Kaiser, "Shared Leadership," *Christianity Today*, Vol. 30, No. 14 (October 3, 1986), p. 121ff.

35. Witherington, p. 122.

36. William Barclay, *The Letters To The Corinthians* (Edinburgh: The Saint Andrews Press, rep. 1965), p. 152.

37. Cf. I Corinthians 7:34. See also Scanzoni and Hardesty, pp. 119ff.

38. A question is raised concerning the credibility of a writer who knowingly appeals to mythology as if it were factual. But it is probable that Paul believed Adam and Eve to be genuine historical figures and the details of Genesis 2–3 to be factual. The mythical nature of the Adam and Eve story is perhaps one reason Jesus made no reference to it. An example of a totally mythical legend incorporated into scripture is the lame man at the pool of Bethesda (John 5:4). The writer of the Fourth Gospel offers as a setting for the story the legendary troubling of the waters, to which a later copyist added the explanatory verse 4. But nowhere in the account is there any hint of its fallacy. Another example is the dispute over the body of Moses (Jude 9) taken from the apocryphal work *The Assumption of Moses*.

39. E.g., Ignatius, Justin, Tertullian and Theophylact; See P.B. Payne, "Libertarian Women in Ephesus; A Response to Douglas Moo," *Trinity Journal*, 2 (1981), pp. 169–97; Walter Lock, "The Pastorals" *ICC* (Edinburgh: T & T Clark, rep. 1966), pp. 32–33.

40. Titus 2:5. R.C.H. Lenski, *Interpretation of Colossians, Thessalonians, Timothy, Titus and Philemon* (Minneapolis: Augsburg, rep. 1968), pp. 572–3; F.D. Gealy, "I Timothy," *The Interpreter's Bible*, Vol. XI, G.A. Buttrick, ed. (New York: Abingdon, 1955), pp. 406–7.

41. Attention has already been given to Paul's recommendation of celibacy for both men and women.

42. William Hendriksen, *I and II Timothy and Titus* (London: The Banner of Truth Trust, rep. 1964), p. 111.

43. Scanzoni and Hardesty, pp. 133f.

44. Although some have placed this work in the early second century, a Petrine source is strongly attested. A likely date is around A.D. 63–4, just before Nero's persecution.

45. See verses 1–6.

46. Scanzoni and Hardesty, p. 73.

47. Janeway, pp. 13–15.

48. Erik Erickson, *Childhood and Society*, 2nd edition (New York: W.W.

Norton, 1963), pp. 97–108. Sigmund Freud believed that all women considered themselves to be castrated males, incapable of any great cultural achievement. Most of his assertions are answered by feminist Kate Millet in *Sexual Politics* (Garden City: Doubleday, 1970), pp. 176–203. For a thorough treatment of the religious implications of Erikson's views, see Patricia Martin Doyle, "Women and Religion: Psychological and Cultural Implications," *Religion and Sexism*, Rosemary Radford Ruether, ed. (New York: Simon and Schuster, 1974), pp. 15–40.

49. Erik Erickson, *Identity, Youth and Crisis* (New York: W.W. Norton, 1968), pp. 268–74.

50. Scanzoni and Hardesty, pp. 73–82.

51. Scanzoni and Hardesty, p. 77.

52. It is noteworthy that the works of Margaret Mead and Ruth Benedict still carry considerable scholastic weight, though dating from the 1930s. See Adriana Valerio, "Women in Church History," Elisabeth Schussler Fiorenza and Mary Collins, eds. *Concilium* (Edinburgh: T & T Clark, 1985), p. 66.

53. Margaret Mead, *Sex and Temperament in Three Primitive Cultures* (New York: William Morrow, 1935), p. 280.

54. Jack O. Balswick and Judith K. Balswick, *Family: A Christian Perspective on the Contemporary Home* (Grand Rapids: Baker, 1989), pp. 189–94.

55. Robert Jay Lifton, "Woman as Knower," *The Woman in America*, R.J. Lifton, ed. (Boston: Houghton Mifflin Co., 1965), p. 44.

56. Janeway, 54–5.

Chapter Five

THE COURSE OF CHURCH TRADITION

An ocean of time lies between the events of the New Testament and the modern church. Although there are some exceptional women in the era immediately following the apostolic period, and clear evidence of an elevated station for women in the pristine church, there occurred an immediate reversion to patriarchal models. During the post-apostolic and medieval periods of church history Pauline texts and the Genesis Creation narrative became the foundation for a solid church tradition that, in the name of God, would hold women in subjection for nearly 2,000 years.

I. Notable Women in the Post-Apostolic and Medieval Church

During the early centuries of Christianity there were many women of renown in the church whose lives and deeds represent the spirit of freedom and equality evident in the Gospel. Thecla of Thamyris was not mentioned earlier since she does not appear in the New Testament. But she does feature prominently in the apocryphal work *The Acts of Paul and Thecla*, ascribed by Tertullian to a presbyter in Asia who allegedly compiled the work out of adoration for Paul.[1] Thecla was converted at Iconium and is credited with teaching, preaching and baptizing. And until recently scholarship in general has concluded that these claims are exaggerated, if not totally fabricated.[2] But today a growing number of scholars are coming to believe that Thecla is only one of many who featured prominently in evangelism during the early history of the Christian church.[3] Drusiana, heroine of the Apocryphal *Acts of the Apostles*, is another example.

Among famous martyrs, Eusebius tells of the ordeal of a great woman, Blandina, who died in the persecution of Vienna and Lyon under Marcus Aurelius (A.D. 177).[4] Under the persecution of Severus of Carthage in A.D. 203 two other female martyrs are noteworthy. Vibia Perpetua died for the faith in North Africa, and Felicitas was put to death in Rome with her seven sons. Both were considered to be prophetesses.[5] Perpetua left a diary of her ordeal up to the day of her death, and therefore provides us one of the earliest documents of the early Latin Church.[6] Paula (A.D. 347–404) was a wealthy Roman noblewoman who assisted Jerome in translating the Vulgate, in addition to founding a monastery, convent and hospice in Bethlehem.[7] Melania (A.D. 383–439) is also an exceptional figure. She was from a wealthy and aristocratic Roman family and was praised by the Imperial family, Serena in particular, for her life of piety.[8] She allegedly founded two monasteries, one for women and one for men. *Life of Saint Melany* was written by her disciple and devoted friend, the priest Gerontios.

The religious pilgrimages of Etheria throughout the Mediterranean world are also noteworthy. She visited many sites of interest, tracing Old Testament history and making notes of all she found. Tavard cites her as a "very attractive type of Christian woman who meets bishops and monks on terms of equality and manifests freedom even from social conventions."[9]

Other great women of medieval Europe include Marcelina, famous sister of Ambrose, Marcella the wealthy ascetic whose home in Rome was a center for Christian influence, Gertrude of Nivelles, abbess during the period A.D. 626–653, and Radegunda, former queen of the Franks and wife of Chlothar I, who studied at the monastery of the Holy Cross at Portiers (d. A.D. 587).[10] Much later in France the eighteen-year-old Jeanne d'Arc led her army against the English during the Hundred Years' War (A.D. 1412–31). The church condemned her as a witch and burned her at the stake in 1431, but twenty-five years later retried her case and found her innocent. In 1909 she was beatified and then canonized in 1920.

One contributing factor to the exceptional power of some women during this period was the ability to inherit land and wealth, a provision of the old Germanic law codes that prevailed in parts of Spain and France. This often led to matrilineal dynasties in which women were able to endow monasteries, build churches, appoint abbots and abbesses, and in some cases serve in the capacity of priests.[11] Dale Pauls stresses the fact that the Gregorian reform of the papacy beginning in A.D. 1073 brought an end to lay control of church patronage, and had a generally negative impact on the influence of women over the Medieval church.[12]

It is difficult to know whether such women were rare exceptions, or if there were many others whose significance is simply lost in historical oblivion. Adriana Valerio suggests that history is not and could never be an aesthetic and objective exercise, since each historian chooses to record what he deems worthy of recorded memory. Since history has traditionally been read from a masculine and elitist standpoint, it therefore gives attention to great figures, institutions and political events, leaving out accomplishments by radicals and nonconformists, and the experiences of common people, obscure people and women.[13] It also portrays movements and events largely from the standpoint of mainstream thinkers. Therefore since the involvement of women in otherwise male dominated systems was not welcome, it was carefully edited out of history, or portrayed in a bad light. Since there are at least a few outstanding women in this period, in spite of the prejudicial forces, one might conclude that there had to have been others and that their invisibility in church and theology was a matter of intense manipulation of historical memory. But more important, the evidence is strong that in the earliest stages of Christianity women enjoyed a degree of freedom and leadership status which was denied them in later Christian tradition.

II. Female Officers in the Post Apostolic Church

The presence of certain offices for females in the early church is a further indication of the spirit of the Gospel in its pristine form. But such offices very quickly became a subject of confusion and debate, and in time disappeared altogether.

Deaconesses

As far as can be determined none of the Ante-Nicene fathers makes reference to Phoebe as a deaconess. But Pliny, a Roman noble in the service of the Emperor Trajan, wrote a letter in A.D. 112 reporting on an investigation he had conducted among Bithynian churches. Admittedly, Pliny does not appear to be well informed concerning Christian beliefs, for he speaks of torturing two women in an attempt to extract information from them concerning their religion. Whether hoping to find evidence of cannibalism, incest or some other lurid crime we do not know, but what we learn is that they were recognized by the church in some way as deaconesses. Pliny writes:

> I judged it so much the more necessary to extract the real truth, with
> the assistance of fortune, from two female slaves, who were styled

deaconesses; but I could discover nothing more than depraved and
excessive superstition.[14]

Again, the Latin term Pliny used was *ministrae*, which could have been
rendered "servants" or "ministers." In either case the typical New Testament use of the term suggests some kind of official status.

Further evidence appears in various works of Clement of Alexandria,
written in the late second century. In his treatment of I Corinthians 9:5
where Paul discusses the right of apostles to "lead about a wife who is a
sister," Clement makes reference to the role of deaconesses. Although his
interpretation of this particular passage seems incorrect, he does express
an awareness of deaconesses in the early church, whose role he defines as
assisting the apostles to bring the doctrine of the Lord into women's apart-
ments, eliminating suspicion of blame if men were to do so. Clement also
discusses the role of deaconesses in his *Stromata*, stating that the service
they render has to do with showing hospitality, menial service to the
needy, and various supportive roles in teaching and evangelism.[15]

Other than the references of Pliny and Clement, there is silence concerning deaconesses until the middle of the third century. The silence is
broken by a very lengthy treatment of the subject in the *Apostolic Constitutions*, a compilation of Syrian material from various sources and written to regulate various church orders and liturgy. The first six books are
the oldest dating from as early as A.D. 250. Passages in these works show
deacons and deaconesses to hold stations of honor functioning as medi-
ators between the presbyters and the congregation.[16] Of this collection
the eighth book, known as the *Didascalia Apostolorum*, is the most recent,
united with the rest around A.D. 325. Here the office of deaconess is more
defined and appears to be a prominent feature of church organization.[17]

Few authorities attempt to explain the long literary silence on the
subject between the New Testament and the *Apostolic Constitutions*, but
the office either existed continuously from the apostolic era with little
occasion for mention, or was suddenly revived in the third century due
to changing needs in the church. Either explanation presupposes an order
of deaconesses in the first century church.

This is not to suggest that it did not change or become more technically defined. It is certain that all church offices went through considerable evolution after the apostolic era, in some cases drifting away from
the original concept. Schaff recognizes that in post-apostolic times the
bishop came to be elevated above the presbyter, the presbyter developed
into the priest, and the deacon "became the first of three orders in the
ministry and a stepping-stone to the priesthood."[18] Observing these and

other significant changes in church dogma, it becomes difficult to accept that the third century order of deaconesses was maintained unaltered from the start.

According to the *Apostolic Constitutions*, deaconesses were ordained by the laying on of hands, as were deacons. The same is suggested in the *Apostolic Tradition* of Hippolytus (A.D. 170–235). In the case of a deacon, however, a prayer was made that he might achieve a higher standing, no doubt referring to the eldership.[19] At that time it seems that deaconess was the highest office in the church obtainable by a woman. This ministry involved numerous practical duties in the daily life of the community and in certain religious ceremonies, but appears to be confined almost totally to caring for the needs of other women, benevolence, keeping orphans, and teaching. Deaconesses assisted women with baptism by keeping the doors, anointing and receiving after immersion, but not performing the baptism itself.[20] They also stood by the doors of the worship assembly to keep order among the women, serving as intermediaries between lay women and other church officers. It seems also that widows were expected to hold them in high esteem as they would male officials.[21]

It is strange, however, that the *Teaching*, which is the oldest portion of the *Constitutions*, makes no mention of deaconesses or any female officers in its section concerning the ordination of church officials.[22] This might indicate that deaconesses only came to be a recognized office in the Eastern church in the early fourth century, after the *Teaching* was completed. In support of this suggestion is the fact that the first appearance of the word *diakonissa* in Christian literature is in the canons of the Council of Nicea, A.D. 325, and even there cautions are issued to the effect that deaconesses should not be considered as among the clergy. In the *Apostolic Constitutions* this rather advanced and technical term appears only in Book VIII, the Didascalia Apostolorum which supports a completion date around the time of the Council of Nicea.[23]

After this era references to deaconesses are more plentiful, and most writers assume the order to have originated in the New Testament continuing up to their own day. The first patristic reference to alleged deaconesses in I Timothy 3:11 is made by John Chrysostom:

> Some have thought that this is said of women generally, but it is not so, for why should he introduce anything about women to interfere with the subject? He is speaking of those who hold the rank of deaconess.[24]

It is impossible to trace accurately the changes in definition of the role of deaconesses as well as the changes in attitude toward them. By the fourth century restrictions were being placed on the appointment of deaconesses, especially with regard to their ordination. The sacramental concepts associated with ordination in the minds of church officials set it above the worthiness of women. *The Apostolic Constitutions* insist that women should obey their husbands since it was official church doctrine that "the man is head of the woman."[25] Women are advised not go to the public baths and generally to avoid the mores of pagan women.[26] Women were forbidden to teach in the church or usurp any priestly function, for women were not allowed to have any authority over a man. Nor were women allowed to baptize, Christ having not granted them that power.[27]

In Syria deaconesses were ordained by the bishop in the same way as deacons, but later sections of the *Constitutions* outlawed women from sacred functions, and this view became the universal norm. The Council of Laodicea in A.D. 381 prohibited women from approaching the altar, implying some liturgical function to that date. The Synod of Orange in A.D. 441 forbade the ordination of women, although deaconesses still existed as a church order by A.D. 533 at the second Council of Orleans.[28]

At about this time also special orders of nuns were developing, and their austerity and separation from association with ordinary people made them more acceptable to current theology. Therefore nuns gradually took over the role of deaconesses, and the latter disappeared from the Western church by the eighth century and from the Eastern church by the eleventh century.[29]

Widows

As one might expect, the "order of widows" mentioned in I Timothy 5 becomes much more elaborate in definition and function in postapostolic history. They are discussed as a special group long before lengthy treatments of deaconesses appear, and their role is essentially that of ministers to special needs.[30] The first mention of widows by the apostolic fathers is in a much disputed passage by Ignatius, writing around A.D. 110–117: "I salute the households of my brethren, with their wives and children, and those that are ever virgins, and the widows."[31] Both virgins and widows came to be significant classes of women in the church at a later stage, and at the time of Ignatius it can be accepted that an "order of widows" existed in perhaps every congregation. But no mention is made by Ignatius of their functions nor the requirements for enrollment. Early in the second century Polycarp wrote to the Philippians:

> Teach the widows to be discreet as respects the faith of the Lord, praying continually for all, being far from all slandering, evil speaking, false

witnessing, love of money, and every kind of evil; knowing that they are the altar of God...[32]

Justin in his *First Apology*, dated around the middle of the second century, mentioned widows briefly in connection with the Sunday assembly of Christians, stating only that they and orphans were among those assisted out of the funds given each week.[33] No mention is made of an order of widows or a special enrollment. Lucian, also of the middle second century, satirizes Christian practice in his account of the imprisonment of Proteus Peregrinus. Lucian says that Christians:

> ...left no stone unturned in their endeavor to procure his release. When this proved impossible they looked after his wants in all other matters with untiring solicitude and devotion. From earliest dawn old women (widows) and orphan children might be seen waiting about the prison doors, while the officers of the church, by bribing the jailors, were able to spend the night inside with him. Meals were brought in and they went through their sacred formulas.[34]

From this testimony one might conclude that widows at this stage took responsibility for orphans and that they visited prisoners routinely, perhaps lingering outside in prayer. Although Lucian's work is fiction, it is based on his own observations of Christian behavior and must be regarded as a valid witness.

Tertullian, representing the church in North Africa around A.D. 220, indicates that enrolled widows had to be at least sixty years of age, single-husbanded, mothers, educators of children and counselors to women with problems. He complains that in a certain place a virgin of less than twenty years was placed in the order of widows, much to the detriment of its purpose.[35]

The most comprehensive treatment of widows in post-apostolic history appears in the *Apostolic Constitutions*. In these documents a careful distinction is made between "enrolled widows" and those widows who were merely the recipients of charity. Enrolled widows were expected to spend much time in prayer for the church, and were instructed not to run about from house to house. They also were employed to tend to the sick, instruct the younger women, and to teach Christianity to heathen women.[36]

The requirements for enrollment, the nature of duties, and the distinction between "enrolled widows" and "widows indeed" appear to have remained fairly constant from New Testament times down to the fifth century, which was not the case with deaconesses. It also appears that eventually the two became blended in the East and deaconesses replaced widows altogether in the West till both were abolished.

At the time of the *Apostolic Constitutions* confusion was being felt about the two orders. Deaconesses were in some sense considered church officers, being appointed by the imposition of hands, but this was not so of widows. They were clearly distinct groups, with widows subject to the authority of deaconesses. However, the Council of Nicea speaks of deaconesses as the only recognized female order in the church, while the Council of Orleans, around A.D. 533, speaks of "widows who are called deaconesses."[37] Concerning the two orders, Lightfoot says: "Whatever confusion may have been in later times, in the apostolic age and for some generations after Ignatius they were distinct."[38]

Prophetesses

An intense desire to maintain the spirit of the early church contributed to the rise of various prophetic movements, of which Montanism is of note, representing varying degrees of spiritual fervor. Since charismatic gifts had all but disappeared by the middle of the second century, female prophetism in this movement contributed heavily to its opposition by the church as a whole. Two prophetesses, Priscilla and Maximilla, were very close to Montanus himself and were considered to be very special instruments of the Holy Spirit. Both Hippolytus and Epiphanius considered the movement to be heretical because of its female bishops and openly named Maximilla a false prophet.[39]

Irenaeus of Lyon (A.D. 130–202), however, had been sympathetic to the prophetic movement, seeing in it opposition to Gnosticism, and understood I Corinthians 11 to refer to both men and women prophesying in the assembly. And Tertullian, representing the Montanist position, saw it the same.[40] Yet Tertullian, and later Cyprian of Carthage, were clear in their denunciation of women speaking in public.[41]

However, as Ruether points out, throughout church history the concept of prophecy continues to have a close relationship with the renewal of women's ministry in the church. As late as the twelfth century the Waldensians included women in public preaching, based on their belief that preaching and prophecy were the same thing.[42]

Therefore, whatever official roles women may have played in the first century church very quickly became issues of heated controversy and remained so for the next several centuries. Those female offices which did survive remained clearly under the dominance of males and were considered secondary in significance. Concerning prophetesses, what appears to be an acceptable and essential element of the earliest church, and a sign of the New Age, becomes a mark of heresy and apostasy within a few generations. And only a few marginal groups in the Church were able to see the significance of first century female prophecy in terms of participation of women in public ministry and evangelism.

III. Development of Roman Catholic Tradition

A number of factors were at work during post-apostolic Christianity which helped to shape the interpretation of early Christian writings and influenced the thinking of church fathers, particularly concerning women. One of the strongest influences in the development of Christianity was the continual threat of persecution, which helped intensify the eschatological expectation under which Christians lived daily.[43] Another was the threat of heresy, principally from Gnosticism and Montanism.[44] There was undoubtedly also an earnest desire to hold onto those elements of the primitive Christian community which seemed to give it its power. But at the same time, church tradition was shaped by a variety of factors, external and internal, which were not in accord with the tone of the Gospel and the spirit of the primitive church. Over several centuries a number of concepts concerning women developed in an interrelated pattern, and must be noted in tracing the roots of our modern theological dilemma.[45] All of these factors combined to produce a slow and convoluted syncretization of doctrines and traditions concerning femininity. The following are key factors and developments spanning the period from the second century to the Reformation.

Anti-feminism in Canonization and Early Textual Transmission

Preservation and perpetuation of Christianity necessitated the long and arduous process of canonizing works deemed suitable for recognition, and the formulation of creeds and definitive traditions. Under these circumstances early church fathers had to take into account three sets of principles: first, the tone of the Gospel, with all its ideals and spiritual implications, such as love, equality, desire for spiritual fulfillment; second, the current interpretation of apostolic teachings in terms of church doctrine, creedal definition, organization and liturgy; and third, the realities of secular world, including legal status of women, familial patriarchy, slavery, persecution, poverty, and death. In many cases the second two factors won out over the first. As has been suggested earlier, works such as *Acts of Paul and Thecla* were excluded, not because they contradicted the earliest apostolic doctrine but because the were out of step with predominant thinking. And in order to combat trends such as female evangelism, works clearly supporting traditional patriarchy were both promoted and associated with Pauline tradition.[46] Therefore there is ample reason to conclude that attitudes toward women played a prominent part in the selection of works to be recognized by the church as canonical.

Many scholars have observed another significant factor very early in the church in the form of "anti-feminist" editors of the New Testament text, particularly the Western text of Acts represented by Codex Bezae.[47] Menoud indicates that the "anti-feminist" trend in D was more or less general in the last decades of the first century, but was not among the major concerns of the Western recension as a whole.[48] Others see no trend at all.[49] But the occasions are too numerous to take lightly. Among the various texts of interest is that of Acts 17:12 where the editor gave a smoother reading, lessening any importance given to women in the Lukan account of conversions at Berea. In the case of Priscilla and Aquila the Western text tends to reverse the names to place Aquila first,[50] and elsewhere makes various alterations including the insertion of the name Aquila without including Priscilla.[51] It cannot be stated that the New Testament was greatly distorted by such efforts. But the fact that the subordinate status of women was being defended by Christian scholars by devious means is significant.

Interpretation of Scripture

Another matter of significance is the approach the church fathers took to interpreting scripture, both the Old Testament and those New Testament works that had been canonized. Grant stresses that these factors determined much of Catholic tradition.[52] It is almost axiomatic that once a collection of Christian works were accepted as authoritative for church doctrine, the Pauline concept of female subjection would become irrevocable tradition. Such was the case.[53] As Keane points out, the church fathers strongly resisted the leadership of women and interpreted scripture in direct opposition to the spirit of the earliest Christian community.[54] Had the church not adopted the Jewish hermeneutical method with its authoritative view of scripture, patriarchal thinking might not have been incorporated into Christian tradition.

Whether there was an exegetical school of thought in Alexandria is still debatable, but it is clear that Philo, Clement and Origen were advocates of an allegorical approach, which would allow for a variety of interpretations of both Old and New Testament passages. Origen saw scripture as a revelation of "intellectual truths" rather than a factual record of historical events, and the Genesis story of Creation to him was highly symbolical.[55] This entire concept was opposed by the School of Antioch, represented by Theodore of Mopsuestia, John Chrysostom of Constantinople and others, in favor of a literal-historical method. Theophilus of Antioch also stressed adherence to a Jewish exegetical methods as far as the Old Testament was concerned.[56] This lent support to the earlier authoritative and rigorous approach of Tertullian, which robbed the community of any liberty in interpretation and set the stage for both dogmatism and traditionalism.

Augustine of Hippo (A.D. 354–430), recognized as the premier systematic theologian during the early period of church history, followed this approach also. Many scholars are convinced that Augustine was converted to Neo-Platonism rather than Christianity, and that his doctrine after ordination was infused with elements of Greek philosophy which were not parallel to the earliest Christian message.[57] It seems also that Augustine constructed a twofold view of authority, placing the tradition of the church by the side of scripture and formulating a synthesis of Christian doctrines which formed the basis of future theological development. His thinking was normative during the greater part of the Middle Ages. Building on the "Augustinian synthesis" in A.D. 434, Vincent's *Commonitorium* set forth the principle which became the final exposition in the Roman Catholic Church for the interpretation of scripture; namely, that the prophets and apostles must be interpreted in accordance with the tradition and norm of the church.

This has direct bearing on the status of women in that the Jewish interpretation of the Genesis Creation and various allusions to it in the New Testament become the foundation of the church's official position. Had the allegorical method of Alexandria prevailed, the entire tradition of the church would have been altered.

Myth of Feminine Evil

The church's hermeneutical reversion to Old Testament institutions and ideas also contributed to the incorporation of the myth of feminine evil into Christian tradition. Dionysius the Great (A.D. 190–264), Origen's second successor at the school in Alexandria, taught that women, during their menstrual period, should be prohibited from approaching the Table of the Lord and partaking of his Body and Blood, since they are in that state physically impure.[58] This was precisely the view of women by which they were excluded from participation in the cultus of Israel. Such myth would become paramount in the thirteenth and fourteenth centuries, lending support to the popular association of women with other forms of evil and heresy, such as demons and witchcraft.[59] Witherington points out that this was a step backwards and away from the picture painted by Jesus of women in the New Temple.[60] But it is clear that such notions survived even into the twentieth century, forming part of a large body of prejudicial polemic against the ordination of women in both Catholic and Protestant tradition.

It is quite clear also that church fathers consistently viewed woman as the cause and root of sin. Chrysostom wrote: "Among all the savage beasts none is found to be so harmful as woman."[61] Jerome in fact attributed to women the responsibility for all heresy in the church.[62] This view, without a doubt, had its source in the Genesis account of the Fall, giving rise to the myth that all women were insidiously linked to the sin of Eve. In the words of Tertullian:

> You give birth, o woman, in pains and anxieties; and your desire goes to your husband, and he will lord it over you. And do you not know that you are Eve? God's judgment over this sex continues in this eon; its guilt must also continue. You are the gate of the devil, the traitor of the tree, the first deserter of divine Law; you are she who enticed the one whom the devil dare not approach; you broke so easily the image of God, man; on account of the death you deserve, even the son of God had to die.[63]

Tertullian also believed the "sons of God" of Genesis 6:1ff. to be fallen angels, who he said taught women the art of make-up and seduction.[64] This also explains why in Tertullian we see an obsession with dress and adornment, and the symbolic attempt to cover the female form from public view.[65]

The Rise of Monasticism

There is very little evidence of attitudes and teachings on the subject of human sexuality during the early Ante-Nicene period. Those writers who discuss the evils of sex speak primarily of adultery and fornication.[66] However, Paul's teaching on voluntary celibacy quickly gave rise to a new theology which came to dominate discussions on human sexuality for the next several centuries. Prudence under threat of persecution also rendered marriage and family somewhat impractical, and various church fathers exalted virginity and celibacy as a more spiritual level of consecration to God. Consequently it came to be commonly accepted that anyone who is truly devoted to God and mature in faith will vow to live in chastity.

The Montanists believed that it was possible for a couple to live together as husband and wife without benefit of sexual intercourse, thereby fulfilling their celibate vows.[67] Such a spiritual marriage was highly suspect, needless to say, among those of a more rigorous doctrine. There were occasional movements among ascetics in which unmarried priests, deacons and even bishops shared their beds with women consecrated to virginity, claiming no wrongdoing, but this practice was condemned by leading church fathers.[68]

Tertullian was Bishop of Carthage during the early third century and was a Montanist during the latter portion of his writing. Concerning his approach to life and Christian doctrine, he is best described as a rigorist. He viewed marriage as a holy estate and frequently elaborates on the beauty of marital unity. But his strict doctrine on the conduct and moral purity of virgins epitomizes the excessive concern of many of the earlier fathers with almost a cultic quality of maintaining sexual purity. However, Carnelley is convinced that his rigorism resulted from his intense concern for saving women and does not reflect a hatred for them.[69]

Anthony of Egypt (A.D. 251–356) is commonly called the father of monasticism. After the third century, when a special priesthood had developed, celibate life for this class became the norm for both men and women. The earliest mention of virgins as a special order in the church is the *Apostolic Constitutions*, where they are listed with deaconesses and widows and worthy of special honor.[70] Female asceticism was in its own right an expression of liberation within the framework of classical religion. In nunneries during the fourth century women had access to educational experience, higher self-development, and greater spiritual recognition than attainable by women outside.[71] Therefore, this station offered admiration and respect. But this only served the purpose of controlling the female in the interest of male domination.[72] Brennan is convinced that the concept of the cloister, or enclosure, as far as women were concerned in the medieval church was a basic means of institutionalizing the invisibility of women. Women were seeking active expression of Christian devotion, but were thwarted by prevalent andocentric traditions. To appease them the church found ways of granting recognition of service, but at the same time keeping "the temptress" away from the eyes of male celibates and keeping "the inferior female" from any role of recognized authority.[73]

Basilius of Ancyra (A.D. 366) was a medical doctor who offered an extensive analysis of human sexuality, suggesting that the difference was not only physical but spiritual as well. He believed that woman has an innate eroticism about her which lures man to evil, and the polarities of the sexes and yearning for each other is the major distraction which affects spirituality. He concluded that souls are equal in both dignity and structure, and can only find their ideal by mortifying the flesh.[74] Thus Basilius changed the focus from the Parousia to the ambition of achieving total spiritual freedom on earth through the virginal life. This concept is also elaborated by Methodius, bishop of Olympas in Lycia between A.D. 260 and 312, in a very significant treatise on virginity.[75]

John Chrysostom, writing around A.D. 381–398, was a defender of the dignity of marriage but was also enthusiastic about virginity for the truly dedicated. He states resolutely that marital sex can only serve for the suppression of licentiousness and debauchery, since the world is already populated enough.[76] In contrast, Chrysostom and Gregory of Nyssa deal at length with the practical problems of marriage. Chrysostom was at times savage in indicting certain evils such as remarrying once free, which to him was a certain indication of one's spiritual immaturity. But he and most others of their day recognized that the ascetic life was not the sole objective, but spiritual purity and the marriage of the soul to Christ.

Condemnation of Marriage

Various forms of Gnosticism as well as numerous purity sects up to the fourth century, all duly catalogued as heresy, had a dramatic influence on attitudes toward marriage.[77] But the battle against heresy also provoked certain reactions in favor of marriage, of which various works of Clement of Alexandria (A.D. 150–215) are an example.[78] Clement represents certain elements of Greek philosophy, acquired no doubt through Philo and the neo–Platonists. These thinkers saw woman as a very necessary part of man, drawn in part from physiological arguments that woman was half a man's body. Here the Gnostic influence on Christian tradition was significant. From excerpts from Theodotus came the *syzygic* mystery of the inclusion of the female in the male, and their essential return to paradisiac unity in the Messianic kingdom.[79]

Based on this notion, Clement adopted the androgynous view of the original human, that Adam was created with the total elements for humanity, both male and female, and that Eve was only the female component of that whole. In time Clement came to recognize that sex was an essential element of humanity, and defined the temporal destiny of woman in social terms. Her lot was dedication to her husband, to moral purity and to discretion in dress and behavior.[80]

However, it seems that in his attempt to refute Gnosticism, Clement displays certain distinct Gnostic tendencies, and for this reason works attributed to him are as difficult to harmonize as some teachings traditionally ascribed to Paul. Witherington discusses statements in the spurious *Exhortation to the Greeks* where Clement theorizes original sin to be pleasure, embodied in woman.[81] In *Stromata* he links marriage to lust and evil, and describes it as an essential concession to "the disease of the body," meaning the human appetite for sex. Yet he never overtly states that marriage is evil.[82]

Origen (A.D. 185–254) was a student of Clement and his successor as head of the school in Alexandria. To him sex was a consequence of sin and woman a symbol of weakness and evil. Marriage was simply a lesser evil than fornication, a *remedium concupiscentiae*.[83] His self-castration, prompted by a literal interpretation of Matthew 19:42, indicates the fanaticism by which he urgently exalted celibacy as an ideal state. A century later, Jerome (A.D. 340–420) concluded that if is "not good" to touch a woman (sexually) then it is in fact "bad" to touch a woman, and therefore sex, even in marriage, is essentially evil.[84]

Augustine had an intense awareness of the duplicity in a spiritual male's attitude toward woman. On the one hand he loves the female creature of God and desires to see her transformed and renewed. On the other, he hates in her the corruptible and mortal conjugal connection and everything in his relationship to her as husband and wife. Augustine therefore came to view sexual intercourse for pleasure as sinful, although venially so.[85] This seems to have created an inordinate sense of guilt, an excessive sin consciousness, among the married laity in subsequent church history. Church doctrine led men and women to feel that a marital relationship was at best a state of tolerable sinfulness, and their only hope for salvation was reliance upon the mediatorial efforts of the truly spiritual celibates who administered the sacraments and offered prayers and absolution on their behalf. Augustine's *Confessions* reveal an intense struggle to control his own sexuality, which accounts for the transference of guilt and responsibility for sexual temptation onto women.[86]

Despite the endless discourses on the spiritual excellence of celibacy, a few church fathers were concerned for the social inequity which persisted in their world. In this regard the inegalitarian marriage structure was a focus of attention, although little was written that truly challenged tradition. However, Gregory Nazianzen (circa A.D. 380) condemned the legal injustice in Constantinople that permitted a husband to be unfaithful to the wife while punishing her for the same misconduct.[87] In this he urged for fairness and equality of moral accountability.

Ontological Inferiority

A crucial aspect of traditional thinking is the notion of ontological inferiority of women. It appears to be the ultimate explanation of all other aspects of traditional female subordination and exclusion from positions of authority in the church. Origen taught that the interior man consisted of a spirit (*spiritus*) which is male, and a soul (*anima*) which is female. The female part tended toward the natural senses and passions and was inferior, whereas the male part was both more rational and moral.[88] Augustine later attempted to affirm the bisexual physiology of the original human, with Adam possessing the higher spiritual image of God. Eve, having been fashioned from Adam's physical body, was corrupted by the flesh and therefore constituted the lower corporeal nature.[89]

Philo Judaeus, writing in the late first century, had already introduced the idea that *imago dei* referred to the nature of the human spirit, and not the nature or appearance of the body, a position not finding acceptance until Thomas Aquinas.[90] But with the complex debates surrounding the spiritual status of women two centuries later, it became necessary to define the bisexuality of humanity in a monistic way so as not to find the nature of God reflected exclusively in the male. This development in tradition came from the Greek father, Gregory of Nyssa (A.D. 350).[91] He explained that the redemptive process restores males and females to a sexless angelic state, and therefore in the resurrection there is neither "male nor female."[92] The monk, one vowed to a life of celibacy, is a soul redeemed from the duality of bodiliness to return to the monism of the spiritual world.[93]

Chrysostom believed that woman's subjection to the authority of men was an element of divine providence and wisdom, largely because in the fall woman proved that she cannot function responsibly unless under supervision.[94] She was created equal, but lost that status. It does seem, however, that he believed the "headship" motif in I Corinthians 11 to be that of unity, not hierarchy or authority.[95] But the general consensus was that woman was designed to find her relationship with God in her subjection to a man.[96] Augustine believed that God designed marriage to work best if one leads and the other follows, and these roles are determined by sex.[97] Augustine understood both Genesis and Paul to suggest that the purpose of woman as man's helper is summarized in procreation, and that this is God's authoritative order for all time.[98] A syncretism of all these views was passed down through church tradition to Thomas

Aquinas. This thirteenth century theologian subscribed to the Aristotelian view that woman's mind is not rational, and argued that her inferior spiritual nature demands her subjection to man.[99] He agreed with Aristotle that the female is essentially a defective human resulting from an accident in the sperm.[100] It was this line of reasoning which led to the predominant conclusion that woman is essentially naive and intellectually inferior, unworthy of education and highly susceptible to heresy.[101] Thomas also viewed marital sex as a concession to lust, and resulting from the Fall.[102] However, Thomas reinterpreted patristic doctrines to a degree, transforming them into the form inherited by the modern church. He departed from Augustine in that he saw the female as equally the image of God, and her body valuable and good as long as it serves the end of good.[103] But this was defined in terms quite in keeping with tradition. He upheld the stereotypy of roles in marriage and denied the right of women to ordination.[104]

Becoming Male

A problem the early fathers had to contend with was how a woman could take part in salvation if she was essentially evil and possessed only an inferior soul. For this reason the *Gospel of Thomas* attributes to Jesus the logion "every woman who makes herself a man will enter the Kingdom of Heaven."[105] Clement of Alexandria was one of the earliest to address the issue, arguing that a woman would have to deny her fleshly nature to become like a male, and that is not sensible. He said that women are capable of virtue and discipline, as much so as men, and as Christians become images of Christ and models of excellence.[106] In the salvation process woman spiritually becomes equal to man in the sight of God, but Clement did not argue that only in that capacity is woman capable of receiving salvatory grace.[107] Clement rejected the Gnostic position that in Christ some are illuminated and some are natural, arguing that all are equal in Christ.[108]

Elaine Pagels, in her book *The Gnostic Gospels*, attempts to trace the roots of true Christianity through the feminine *sophia* of Gnosticism.[109] It is true that women in many Gnostic communities enjoyed considerably more prominence than those in orthodox Christianity, which may have been one reason Gnosticism was denounced as heresy and fought against so vigorously. But Susanne Heine points out that there was no unity among Gnostic groups, and many were strongly misogynist.[110] Epiphanius had been a member of a Gnostic group in Egypt, and wrote of sexual abominations practiced among them.[111] Yet so strong were the reactions against doctrines denying the fundamentals of Christianity that orthodoxy found itself retreating to standards of the world for the good of its reputation. Therefore, in spite of reactions against it Gnosticism may have had a greater influence upon developing church doctrine that we have thought. Kari Vogt sees this metaphor as common among Christians and non–Christians of the second and third centuries, referring to the development of an individual from a lower to a higher state of moral and spiritual perfection.[112] But she acknowledges that Clement's use of the metaphor did not imply inferiority of women. Rather, both males and females seeking to be united with God must free themselves of the desires associated with the flesh and seek to become the "perfect man." To Clement this perfect man is the true gnostic, either male or female, who like the angels has transcended earthly sexuality.

A similar anthropology is found in Origen, who saw the inner man (*homo interior*) as consisting of the superior male spirit (*spiritus*) and the inferior, sin-oriented female soul (*anima*).[113] The struggle for spiritual progress, or to become spiritually mature, involves overpowering the female aspect of one's being and to become a true male. In later monastic literature the concept develops so that a woman who attains a holy estate is considered "a manly woman." Sexuality being neutralized, such dedicated Christians could work together and enjoy social relations as "brothers" and "sisters," women being considered no longer as women, but men.[114] Jerome, for example, speaking of the relationship between Lucinus and Theodora, states that she was changed "from woman to man, from subject to equal," and that she was not just a sister but a brother.[115]

Woman as a Symbol of the Church

The concept of the *ekklesia* as the bride of Christ in early Christian literature gave rise to much fanciful elaboration. The four visions of the Shepherd of Hermas involve an old lady in shining garments, identified as the Celestial Church.[116] A woman named Rode, perhaps a symbolic name for Rome, also features in the series of visions and represents the encratic elements in early patristic writings.

Origen exploited the bridal analogy and applied it to the union of Christ and the Church, and to the union of Christ and each faithful soul. Thus womanhood, in its ideal and purest form, was a vision of the great spiritual body united with God.[117] This motif, however, seems to have had no bearing on the practical elements of the status of women within the church. Tavard finds this significant as a further reversion to Jewish theology, reflecting the paradoxical picture of woman in the Old Testament: first that she is in a cursed condition inherited from the origins of humanity; yet, she is the type of the heavenly wisdom which presided over the foundations of the world and was embodied in Israel as the bride of Yahweh.[118]

Veneration of Mary

Fixation on Mary's role as mother of the Savior and on her virginity appear as early as Ignatius.[119] Among the better known apocryphal works, the *Protoevangelium of James* is significant in that it was written toward the middle of the second century and clearly designed for the glorification of Mary.[120] Belief in her bodily assumption after death is traceable to Ephraem of Syria, although some have thought it to have originated in Egypt in the fourth century.[121] During this era also Christianity was flowering with cultural imagery related to spiritual femininity, and a variety of literature was constructed around woman as a nurse, seer, revealer, and giver of life.[122] From these roots there grew up an entire doctrine surrounding the person of Mary as the mother of God, including her sinlessness and immaculate conception.[123] Her perpetual virginity seems to originate with Gregory of Nazianzus in his sermons on the martyrdom of Cyprian.[124] All of this occurred against the appeal by Epiphanius that she not be adored as should be the Father, the Son and the Holy Spirit.[125]

One of the ironies of the development of this tradition is that while woman in general was being demonized and degraded, Mary was being elevated to a status of Divine. This served a useful purpose in perpetuating male dominance, in that it offered a patronizing exaltation of womanhood on a spiritual and fantasy level, and diverted attention away from the degradation of women on a social level.

Justin of Rome (circa A.D. 165), in his *Dialogue With Trypho*, suggested the parallel between Eve and Mary as women and virgins, with virginity itself containing the possibilities of death and life. Irenaeus drew a different parallel between Eve and Mary, finding in them a typology similar to Pauline references to the "second Adam." As Adam is the type of Christ so Eve becomes the type of Mary, and what one pair causes in the human spiritual condition the other reverses.[126] Therefore, Mary's role in bringing salvation was elevated to a station near, if not equal to, that of Jesus Christ.

Interest in Mariology intensified in the eleventh and twelfth centuries, especially in the West. A number of factors may have influenced it, particularly negative developments among monastic orders.[127] There developed a more human Mary, frankly erotic in many instances, and more accessible to the laity.[128] But this phenomenon was not indicative of any degree of elevation of the status of women in the medieval Catholic Church. Instead, the cult of the Virgin displayed at every level, theological and popular, an andocentric bias that underlined the weakness, inferiority and subordination of females.[129] Landman states that the cult had an "all male public relations mechanism, which, by stressing Mary's fertility, kept women enslaved through the ideal of blissful consistent pregnancies."[130]

Sacramental Exclusivity

After the Synod of Orange in A.D. 441 the Roman Catholic Church allowed men only to receive ordination. But the roots of this decision are traceable to John Chrysostom, who strongly opposed women teaching or preaching. Reacting to the Montanists, and the leading role of prophetesses in that movement, Chrysostom condemned women's proclivity for teaching heresy.[131] He went so far as to suggest that women were simply too prone to vice, such as drinking too much wine, to be reliable church leaders.[132] There is, however, a certain paradox in Chrysostom, since he was in certain ways supportive of female dignity. He understood I Timothy 2:9 to deal with female dress and deportment is the specific context of public prayer, although whether he believed they could lead such prayers in unclear:

> In like manner, he (Paul) says, "I will that women approach God without wrath and doubting, lifting up holy hands...." Paul however requires something more of women; that they adorn themselves "in modest apparel, with shamefacedness and sobriety."[133]

It appears that in his time many women sought the right to serve as priests, and this he opposed vigorously.[134] Therefore, by the completion of the *Apostolic Constitutions*, it was considered "illegal" and "impious" for a woman to perform sacramental acts such as baptism, a duty that could only be assumed by a male.[135]

Nearly ten centuries later, Thomas Aquinas reasoned that this rule is derived from the nature of a sacrament. A woman can receive blessings but cannot be a vicarious instrument to transmit them to others because of her innately inferior status and state of subjection.[136] So also Bonaventure contended that not only can a woman not be ordained *de jure*, but not *de facto*, since the mediatorial role of a priest, a vicar of Christ, can only be played by a male.[137] Such arguments are without theological merit, but given the historical background and complex church tradition which define the perspective of these scholars, their conclusions are quite understandable.

IV. The Reformation

The Protestant Reformation had a profound impact on Christianity as a whole, and specifically on attitudes toward sexuality. Whereas the ancient church fathers had extolled virginity and celibacy, the reformers redirected the focus of spirituality on common people and daily living. They rejected the double standard of celibacy for those who were truly dedicated to God and marriage for those who were less committed. The universal call of all believers to commitment in routine living led to an exoneration of family and work. The home replaced the monastery as the center of Christian virtue, and marriage was granted a status of dignity, even for the clergy.[138]

But in terms of the social status of women and a formal theology of womanhood, the Reformation changed little. A principal charge of Reformers against Catholicism was its failure to recognize the value of human rights as an essential element of Christian doctrine. But the reformers themselves failed to see the implications of their charges in the area of women's rights. Landman comments that the Reformation gave women back their sexuality, but not equality.[139] This was due in part, no doubt, to the traditional concept of the authority of scripture on which all church doctrine ultimately rested. And when one looks at the focus of Protestant leaders on sin and justification, the contrast between works and grace oriented concepts of justification, their failure to address womanhood in a more critical fashion is understandable.

In this mode of thinking, the role of Christian mother became a special vocation. Raising and teaching children, keeping house, and all the duties of domestic life became a special form of martyrdom. By eliminating the option of sisterhood, specifically serving God as a nun according to Catholic tradition, they reduced the definition of a godly life style for a faithful Christian woman to one—marriage. A spiritual woman was either married to a husband or to Christ.

Martin Luther's picture of woman is full of paradoxes. His focus on divine sovereignty, with God as essentially good and wise and man essentially evil, led to a basic acceptance of traditional models of the status of women. Luther saw Adam as a beautiful creature, requiring sex in Paradise purely for procreation. But in man's fallen state, corrupted by sin, woman becomes a needed entity, a companion in his mundane pursuits and a manager for his house. Sex is associated with the lower human nature. Luther considered intercourse to be man's medicine. He also thought of woman as weaker than man and full of vices, but the good evident in her childbearing capabilities compensates for it all.[140]

Concerning the Genesis Temptation and Fall, Luther believed that Satan attacked where humanity was the weakest. He wrote: "I believe that had Satan first tempted the man Adam would have gained the victory."[141] Woman, then, bears the brunt of God's curse for sin, placed under man's power and compelled to obey him.[142] Therefore, true to tradition, Luther defended the myth that man's rightful role is to rule, wage war, till the soil, build, plant and defend his possessions, while woman, by God's design and command, must submit to male domination. Lacking the ability to administrate affairs outside the home, and those which concern the community, she should devote her energies to her husband and children and not venture beyond her proper place. He also thought it natural for women to rebel and complain against this order of things.[143] Luther speaks representatively of those views on sexual typology that survived Roman Catholic tradition and multiplied through all Reformation denominations:

> Men have broad and large chests, and small narrow hips, and more understanding than women, who have but small and narrow chests, and broad hips, to the end they should remain at home, sit still, keep house, and bear and bring up children.[144]

John Calvin also failed to offer any challenge to the medieval concept of womanhood, except for stressing certain ethical responsibilities of husbands toward their wives. In reaction to the moral decadence of the Renaissance, Calvin proposed high ascetic ideals, in fact imposing them upon the citizens of Geneva. He taught that woman was intended to be man's companion, and not merely a mechanism for sexual release. He saw Adam as being completed in Eve, and in marriage a male and female become symbolically one body and one soul. But he still viewed the wife's role as subordinate to the husband. And while both he and Luther felt that husbands and wives had a mutual obligation to fidelity, in his commentary on the Mosaic law he reveals a clear assumption of male superiority. He readily justified the ancient practice of killing an adulterous wife by stoning, while an unfaithful husband received lesser judgment. This to Calvin was justifiable because of the dishonor an unfaithful wife brought to her husband's name, and the possibility of defiling his posterity.[145]

Among the significant benefits the Reformation did provide for women, that of public education is probably the most significant.[146] Changes in marriage laws also granted women the right to divorce on grounds of adultery, although remarriage was frowned on.[147] But in reality the Reformation, although directed at plight of common people, did little to elevate the status of women. In fact, in certain ways it may have aggravated the situation. Eleanor McLaughlin believes that the Anglican church and Protestantism actually had a negative effect on the religious life of the church by depriving the community of the dynamic female service maintained for centuries in the pre–Reformation church:

> One must insist that we miss the innovative, formative and reforming roles taken in the community by women like Hulda of Whitby, Brigid of Sweden, Joan of Arc, Catherine of Siena, Teresa of Avila, Angela of Merici (founder of the Ursulines) and Madame Guyon, the controversial seventh century French mystic.[148]

The Reformation destroyed, she insists, the one structure within the institutional church where men and women functioned as equals before God, the monastic life, leaving the church to be led by an all-male clerical order.

At least one Reformer, John Knox the Scot, was very critical of women's involvement in politics, although it appears that various factors gradually increased this possibility.[149] Knox believed that women are by nature: "weake, fraile, impacient, feble and foolishe; and experience hath declared them to be inconstant, variable, cruell and lacking the spirit of counsel and regiment."[150] The stigma of evil and inferiority which women had carried throughout the ages remained upon them as an integral part of Restoration doctrine. John Donne expressed it poetically:

> We are borne ruinous. For that first marriage was our funerall; One woman at one blow, then kill'd us all.[151]

The treatment of women who attempted to break this pattern often was extremely harsh. Lysken Dirks, for example, was an Anabaptist imprisoned for her faith in Antwerp in 1550. Monks asked her why she meddled in scriptures instead of sewing as a woman should. Her reply: "Christ commands us to search the scriptures, and Christ should be obeyed rather than man." For her answer she was drowned.

Summary

The increasing stress on asceticism and deprecation of human sexuality during the second and third centuries led to a significant attenuation of the status of women in the church by A.D. 325. Factors such as selective historical record, antifeminism in textual transmission, and selective canonization of Christian literature all combined to strengthen traditional patriarchy in society and in the church. Witherington sees this as a clear regression to an Old Testament image of both the church and ministry, and to patterns of secular culture.[152] In addition, various elements of ancient Roman law and culture, coupled with Aristotelian hierarchical social structure, passed forward into the Roman church, solidifying the ancient view of woman as naturally weaker and therefore subordinate to male authority.[153]

In some sense, later Catholic scholars appreciated the inconsistency of their doctrine, but had no choice but to defend it. John Duns Scot, Franciscan and Oxford professor in the early fourteenth century, clearly stood in Catholic tradition that sin could not be attributed to the church, arguing that a judgment against women consigning them to an inferior and more burdensome role is a great crime against them. But such is their station in tradition. Therefore, he said, it could not have come from the church but from Christ Himself, and what appears to be a gross injustice falls under the inexplicable Sovereignty of God.[154] In the main, the status of women in the church during the Dark Ages remained the same as that of most ancient cultures. Equality with men was claimed only for a small number of the ascetic elite, and that was curtailed by the rigors of ascetic life. But the true implications of New Testament equality could not be satisfied as long as the emancipation of women was tied either to virginity, as an ascetic reversal of nature, or to the spiritual symbolism of Eve and Mary in the fall and redemption of humanity. An increasing synchronization of andocentric beliefs throughout medieval history created a self-perpetuating ecclesiastical order in which the subordination and silence of women was assured.

While the Reformers eliminated the veneration of Mary and the mediatorial role of the priesthood between God and the laity, the ancient paradigm of patriarchy lived on.

Chapter Five Notes

1. J.P. Kirsch, "Thecla, Saint," *Catholic Encyclopedia*, Vol. 14 (New York: Encyclopedia Press, 1912), p. 564. Hoy Ledbetter, "The Prophetess," *Integrity* (June, 1973).

2. W.M. Ramsay, *The Church in the Roman Empire*, eighth edition (London: Hodder and Stoughton, 1904), pp. 375–428; *Asiatic Elements in Greek Civilization*, The Gifford Lectures in the University of Edinburgh, 1915–16 (London: John Murray, 1928), p. 269.

3. Elisabeth Schussler Fiorenza, *In Memory of Her: A Feminist Theological Reconstruction of Christian Origins* (London: SCM, 1983), pp. 173–5.

4. Eusebius, *Ecclesiastical History*, V:1, 17–20 (*LCL*, V, p. 415).

5. Marie-Henry Keane, "Women in the Theological Anthropology of the Early Fathers," *Journal of Theology for Southern Africa* (1987), p. 9. See *Acts of the Martyrs*, "Passion Perpetua et Felicitatis."

6. Rosemary Rader, "The Martyrdom of Perpetua: A Protest Account of Third Century Christianity," *A Lost Tradition: Women Writers of the Early Church*, Patricia Wilson-Kastner, ed. (Washington: University Press 1981), pp. 1–32.

7. Letha Scanzoni and Nancy Hardesty, *All We're Meant To Be* (Waco: Word, 1975), p. 174.

8. George Tavard, *Women in Christian Tradition* (Notre Dame, Indiana: Notre Dame Press, 1973), p. 91.

9. Tavard, p. 91.

10. Everett Ferguson, *Early Christians Speak* (Austin: Sweet, 1971), pp. 229–235.

11. Suzanne F. Wemple, *Women in Frankish Society: Marriage and the Cloister, 500–900* (Philadelphia: University of Pennsylvania Press, rep. 1990), pp. 142–62.

12. Dale Pauls, "Women in European Middle Ages," *Essays on Women in Earliest Christianity*, Vol. 2, Carroll Osburn, ed. pp. 382–3.

13. Adriana Valerio, "Women in Church History," in "Women: Invisible in Church and Theology," Elisabeth Schussler Fiorenza and Mary Collins, eds., *Concilium: Religion in the Eighties* (Edinburgh: T & T Clark, 1985), p. 63.

14. Pliny, *Letters*, X, 96 (*LCL*, II, p. 405).

15. Clement, *Stromata*, III: 6 (*ANF*, II, p. 390–91); G.W.H. Lampe, *A Patristic Greek Lexicon* (Oxford: Clarendon, 1968), p. 353.

16. *Apostolic Constitutions*, II, 4:29–33 (*ANF*, VII, pp. 411–12). See J. Stephen Sandifer, *Deacons: Male and Female?* (Houston: Keystone, 1989).

17. *Apostolic Constitutions*, VIII, 2:17–21 (*ANF*, VII, p. 492).

18. Philip Schaff, *History of the Christian Church*, Vol. I (Grand Rapids: Eerdmans, rep. 1968), p. 500.

19. *Apostolic Constitutions*, III, 3:18–20 (*ANF*, VII, p. 492).

20. *Ibid.*, III, 2:16 (*ANF*, VII, p. 431).

21. *Ibid.*, II, 7:62 (*ANF*, VII, p. 424); II, 4:26 (*ANF*, VII, p. 410); III, 1:7 (*ANF*, VII, p. 429).

22. *Ibid.*, VII, 2:31 (*ANF*, VII, p. 471).

23. *Ibid.*, VIII, 3:19, 20, 28 (*ANF*, VII, pp. 492–3).

24. Chrysostom, *Homilies on Timothy*, XI (*NPNF*, XIII, p.441).

25. *Apostolic Constitutions* I, 3:8 (*ANF*, VII, p. 394). This may not have applied to deaconesses if they were required to be either a virgin or a widow.

26. *Ibid.* I, 3:9 (*ANF*, VII, p. 395).

27. *Ibid.* III, 1:9 (*ANF*, VII, p. 429).

28. Elsie Thomas Culver, *Women in the World of Religion* (Garden City: Doubleday, 1967), p. 71.

29. A. Vermeersch, "Nuns," *Catholic Encyclopedia* Vol. 11 (New York: Encyclopedia Press, 1911), pp. 164–8.

30. B.B. Thurston, *The Widows: A Women's Ministry in the Early Church* (Minneapolis: Fortress, 1989).

31. Ignatius, *To the Smyrneans*, (*ANF*, I, p. 92).

32. Polycarp, *To The Philippians*, 4 (*ANF*, I, p. 34).

33. Justin Martyr, *First Apology*, 67 (*ANF*, I, p. 186).

34. Lucian, *Death of Peregrinus*, 12 (*LCL*, V, p. 13).

35. Tertullian, *On the Veiling of Virgins*, 9 (*ANF*, IV, p. 33).

36. *Apostolic Constitutions*, II, 4: 25 (*ANF*, VII, p. 397, 408); III, 6:7 (*ANF*, VII, p. 428).

37. Schaff, p. 374.

38. J.B. Lightfoot, *The Apostolic Fathers*, Part II, Vol. II (London: Macmillan, 1890), p. 322.

39. Hippolytus, *Philosophoumena* VII:12 (*ANF*, V, 9–153); Epiphanius, *The Panarion* VII, 1:6 (*NHMS*, XXXVI, p. 621).

40. An excellent survey of patristic opinion on women, Charles Caldwell Ryrie, *The Role of Women in the Church* (Chicago: Moody, 1958), pp. 97–137.

41. Tertullian, *On Baptism*, 17 (*ANF*, III, p. 677); Cyprian, *Treatises* III, 46 (*ANF*, V, p. 546).

42. Rosemary Radford Ruether, "Prophetic Tradition and the Liberation of Women: A Story of Promise and Betrayal," p. 3. A paper read at the University of Natal, Pietermaritzburg, August, 1989.

43. Samuel Terrien, "Toward a Biblical Theology of Womanhood," Ruth Tiffany Barnhouse and Urban T. Holmes III, eds., *Male and Female* (New York: The Seabury Press, 1976), p. 24.

44. Irenaeus, *Against Heresies* (*ANF*, I, pp 309ff.).

45. Tavard, pp.48–121.

46. The Pastoral Epistles with their clearly defined church order are a prime example.

47. B.M. Metzger, *A Textual Commentary on the Greek New Testament* (London: United Bible Society, 1971), p. 454; James Hardy Ropes, *The Text of Acts*, F.J. Foakes Jackson and Kirsopp Lake, eds. *The Beginnings of Christianity: Part I, The Acts of the Apostles*, Vol. III, p. 162ff. Ben Witherington, "Anti-feminist Tendencies of the Western Text in Acts," *Journal of Biblical Literature* 103:1 (1984), pp. 82–4.

48. P.H. Menoud, "The Western Text and Theology of Acts," *Bulletin of the Studiorum Novi Testamenti Societies*, II (1951), pp. 30ff.

49. Jeffrey Childers and L. Curt Niccum, "Anti-Feminist Tendency in Western Text of Acts?" *Essays on Women in Earliest Christianity*, Volume I, Carroll Osburn, ed. (Joplin: College Press, 1993), p. 492.

50. Acts 18:18, 26.

51. Metzger, p. 467.

52. Robert M. Grant, *A Short History of the Interpretation of the Bible* (New York: Macmillan, 1963), pp. 75–127.

53. Even allowing for a second century date of the Pastoral Epistles, they were being circulated early enough to find a place in the canon and to have a marked effect on the thinking of major church fathers.

54. Marie-Henry Keane, "Woman in the Theological Anthropology of the Early Fathers," *Journal of Theology for Southern Africa* (March, 1988), p. 5.

55. Origen, *De principiis* IV, 1, 7 (*ANF*, IV, p. 355).

56. This is especially significant in the light of rabbinic thinking evident in Pauline works and traditional Jewish exegetical methods; Grant, pp. 28–41.

57. John H. S. Burleigh, ed. *Library of Christian Classics*, Vol. VI (London: SCM, 1953), pp. 13–15. Robert H. King, "The Task of Systematic Theology," Peter C. Hodgson and Robert H. King, eds. *Christian Theology: An Introduction to its Traditions and Tasks* (London: SPCK, 1983), pp. 4–6.

58. Dionysius, *Epistle to Basilides*, Canon II (*ANF*, VI, p. 96); see Witherington, p. 189.

59. Eleanor Commo McLaughlin, "Equality of Souls, Inequality of Sexes: Women in Medieval Theology," *Religion and Sexism*, Rosemary Radford Ruether, ed. (New York: Simon and Schuster, 1974), pp. 230ff. Other myths which became common in the late Medieval Period were that menstrual blood attracted evil spirits and demons, and that the presence of a menstruating woman could sour milk and kill grass. For this cause in that period menstruating women were forbidden to attend Communion.

60. It seems that during this period the church became increasingly viewed as a "temple," with focus on the structure rather than the people, ministers became viewed as "priests," the Lord's Supper as a "sacrifice," etc.

61. John Chrysostom, *Discourses on Genesis*, II: 54 (*FOTC*, Vol. 74, 82–7).

62. Keane, pp. 4–5.

63. Tertullian, *On the Apparel of Women*, I, 1(*ANF*, IV, p. 14). See Elizabeth Carnelley, "Tertullian and Feminism," *Theology*, Vol. XCII (January, 1989), pp. 31–35.

64. Tavard, p. 59.

65. Tertullian, *On Veiling Virgins* (*ANF*, IV, pp. 27–38). Also of interest is the statue of *Mundus* (Prince of this World) in thirteenth century Germany, in a portal of the Strasbourg Cathedral luring foolish maidens to perdition. His face is appealing, but from the rear his body is seen to be eaten of worms, frogs and snakes, symbolizing the mortal reality of worldly pleasure. By the next century the figure had become common, but was changed into a woman, Frau Welt, the embodiment of the seduction and sin. See McLaughlin, pp. 253–4, citing research by Wolfgang Stammler.

66. E.g., Clement of Rome (A.D. 96), Shepherd of Hermas (A.D. 150); see Witherington, p. 184.

67. Donald F. Winslow, "Sex and Anti-Sex in the Early Church Fathers," Ruth Tiffany Barnhouse and Urban T. Holmes, III, eds., *Male and Female* (New York: The Seabury Press, 1976), p. 29.

68. E.g., John Chrysostom, Cyprian, Ambrose; Tavard, p. 92.

69. Carnelley, p. 33.

70. *Apostolic Constitutions*, II, 25, 26 (*ANF*, VII, p. 410).

71. C. Landman, "A Profile of Feminist Theology," *Sexism and Feminism in Theological Perspective*, W.S. Vorster, ed. (Pretoria: University of South Africa,

1984), p. 4. This paper and others in this work were read at the eighth Symposium of the Institute for Theological Research at UNISA, September, 1984.

72. Hays, p. 107.

73. Margaret Brennan, "Enclosure: Institutionalizing the Invisibility of Women in Ecclesiastical Communities," in "Women: Invisible in Theology and Church," Elisabeth Schussler Fiorenza and Mary Collins, eds. *Concilium: Religion in the Eighties* (Edinburgh: T & T Clark, 1985), pp. 38–48.

74. Basilius of Ancyra, *On Virginity*. See H. Musurillo, "Basil of Ancyra," *New Catholic Encyclopedia*, Vol. II (New York: McGraw-Hill, 1967), p. 147. Possibly absorbed into and confused with Basil the Great of Caesarea, *An Ascetic Discourse* (*FOTC*, Vol. 9, pp. 207–9).

75. Methodius, *The Banquet* (*ANF*, VI, pp. 309ff.).

76. Chrysostom, *On Virginity*, 19, Sally R. Shore, trans. *Studies in Women and Religion*, vol. 9. (New York: Edwin Mellen Press, 1983), pp. 27–28.

77. Marcion was one of the earliest to condemn marriage as tantamout to fornication. George Blond, "Les Encratiques et la vie mystique," *Mystique et Continence* (Paris, 1952), pp. 117–130.

78. Clement of Alexandria, *Stromata*, II, 23 (*ANF*, I, p. 328).

79. Tavard, p. 64. This concept was very significant to the Valentinians also.

80. Clement, *Pedagogue* I, IV (*ANF* II, pp. 209–296).

81. Clement, *Exhortation to the Greeks* (*LCL*, p. 236); cf. Witherington, p. 186.

82. Clement, *Stromata* II, 23 (*ANF*, I, p. 328).

83. Witherington, p. 186.

84. Jerome, *Letter* XLVIII:14 (*NPNF*, VI, p.73); Reuther, p. 178.

85. Augustine, *On Marriage and Concupiscence* 5–17 (*NPNF*, V, pp. 265–280); On the Good of Marriage, 7 (*NPNF*, III, p. 402). See Herbert A. Deape, *The Political and Social Ideas of St. Augustine* (New York: Columbia University Press, 1963), pp. 54–5. Ruether discusses also Augustine's own youthful incontinence, which may have produced in him either guilt, or self-hatred, surfacing in his doctrine of human sexuality. Rosemary Radford Ruether, "Misogynism and Virginal Feminism in the Fathers of the Church," *Religion and Sexism*, pp. 162–3.

86. James A. Brundage, *Law, Sex and Christian Society in Medieval Europe* (Chicago: University of Chicago Press, 1987), pp. 1–123. See Peter Brown, *The Body and Society: Men, Women, and Sexual Renunciation in Early Christianity* (New York: Columbia University Press, 1988).

87. Gregory, *Homily on Matthew*, 37:6 (*NPNF*, VII, p. 339).

88. See Keane, p. 12.

89. Augustine, *The Trinity* 12:1–5 (*LCC*, VIII, pp. 93–4).

90. Philo Judaeus, *Allegorical Interpretation* (*LCL*, I, pp. 167–8).

91. The term *monos* from which the English terms "monastic" and "monk" are derived. Ruether, "Misogynism and Virginal Feminism in the Fathers of the Church," pp. 153ff.

92. Galatians 3:28.

93. Gregory of Nyssa, *On the Making of Man* XVI:1–9 (*NPNF*, V, pp. 404–5)

94. Chrysostom, *Homilies on Genesis* XVII (*FOTC*, 74, pp. 240–1), *Homilies on I Corintians* XXVI (*NPNF*, XII, p. 150).

95. John Chrysostom, *The Homilies of St. John Chrysostom on the First Epistle of St. Paul the Apostle to the Corinthians* (London: F and J Rivington, 1854), p. 351.

96. Hays, p. 100.

97. Augustine, *The Good Marriage*, 27:9.

98. Augustine, *Literal Interpretation of Genesis*, IX, 10–11 (*ACW*, 42, pp. 80–2).

99. Thomas Aquinas, *Summa Theologica*. See also Keane, p. 7.

100. McLaughlin, pp. 216–7.

101. Pope Gregory I (*PG*, LIX, p. 268). See Keane, p. 7.

102. *Summa Theologica*, II–II: 163, 5; *remedium peccati*, to ease the fires of passion. One revolutionary doctrine from Thomas was his emphasis on conjugal duties in marriage; *Summa Theologica, Supp.* 49:2–3.

103. *Summa Theologica*, I: 91, 4.

104. He anticipated modern feminist challenges about the masculinity of Christ, arguing that a sexual being as the saviour was essential in order to relate to humans realistically; and masculinity was essential because the roles of physician, pastor and defender do not fit the subordinate status of women. See McLaughlin, p. 220.

105. *Gospel of Thomas*, 112 (Grant, *The Secret Sayings of Jesus*), p. 197. Tavard, p. 64.

106. Clement of Alexandria, *Stromata*, IV, 7 (*ANF*, IV, p. 420), IV, 19 (ANF, IV, p. 431). Important to Clement was the concept of the "perfect man," *teleios aner*, from Ephesians 4:13.

107. Kari Vogt, "Becoming Male: One Aspect of an Early Christian Anthropology," in "Women: Invisible in Church and Theology," Elisabeth Schussler Fiorenza and Mary Collins, eds. *Concilium: Religion in the Eighties* (Edinburgh: T & T Clark, 1985), pp. 72–83.

108. Clement, *Instructor*, I, 6 (*ANF*, II, p. 217).

109. Elaine Pagels, *The Gnostic Gospels* (Penguin Books, 1982).

110. Heine, pp. 106–123. The Nag Hammadi Texts, including *The Gospel of Thomas, The Book of Thomas the Contender, The Paraphrase of Shem*, and *The Dialogue of the Redeemer* speak of the station of women in very disparaging terms.

111. Epiphanius, *Panarion* II, 26:1–8 (*NHMS*, XXXV, pp. 82–6).

112. Vogt, "Becoming Male: One Aspect of an Early Christian Anthropology," in "Women: Invisible in Theology and Church," p. 72.

113. Origen, *Homily on Genesis* I:12–14 (*FOTC*, Vol. 71, pp. 62–8).

114. Vogt, pp. 75–9; E. Clark, "Ascetic Renunciation and Feminine Advancement," *Anglican Theological Review*, LXIII (1981), p. 245.

115. Jerome, *Letters* 71:3 (*NPNF*, VI, p.153), 75:2 (*NPNF*, VI, p. 155).

116. The Shepherd (*ANF*, II, 9–55).

117. Tavard, p. 67–8; also Henri Crouzel, *Virginite et mariage selon Origene* (Paris-Bruges, 1962).

118. Tavard, pp. 27ff.

119. Ignatius, *To the Ephesians* 7:2, 19:1; *To the Smyrnaeans* 1:1 (*Apostolic Fathers, LCL*, I, pp. 181,193, and 253).

120. This work claims her miraculous birth, Davidic descent, and presentation in the Temple, and begins the tradition of her perpetual virginity. Witherington, p. 206.

121. Ephraem, *Hymns* 11–12. See Herbert Thurston, "Virgin Mary; Devotion to the Blessed," *Catholic Encyclopedia*, Vol. XV, p. 460.

122. Hays, p. 107.

123. Stories were embellished by many church fathers, including Clement of Alexandria, Epiphanius and Ephraem Syrus. Although Tertullian took issue with the notion of Mary's perpetual virginity (*Monograms*, 8), this became dominant by the end of the second century.

124. Gregory Nazianzus (*PG*, XXXV, p. 1181).

125. Thurston, p. 460.

126. Irenaeus, *Against Heresies* III:22,4 (ANF, I, pp. 454–5).

127. McLaughlin, "Women in Medieval Theology," pp. 243ff.

128. Following the development of "courtly love," and various elements of courtesy in which special honor is directed by males toward females, largely to emphasize the female role as an object and possession. John F. Benton, "Clio and Venus: An Historical Review of Medieval Love," *The Meaning of Courtly Love*, F.X. Newman, ed. (Albany: 1968), p. 35.

129. First by isolating Mary from true femaleness (perpetual virginity, immaculate conception), and second, by attributing to her theological roles which supported popular misogynism (motherhood, quiet submission, dependency,); McLaughlin, pp. 246–251.

130. Landman, p. 6.

131. Chrysostom, *Homilies on Timothy*, IX (*NPNF*, IX, pp. 435–6).

132. *Ibid.*, *Homilies on Titus*, IV (*NPNF*, XIII, p. 532).

133. *Ibid.*, *Homilies on Timothy*, VIII (*NPNF*, XIII, p. 433).

134. *Ibid.*, *On the Priesthood*, III, 9 (*NPNF*, IX, p. 49).

135. Keane, p. 9; *Apostolic Constitutions*, III, 9 (*ANF*, VII, p. 429).

136. Thomas Aquinas, *Treatise on the Sacraments*, LXVII, 4, D, 2 (*ST*, XVII, p. 129).

137. Tavard, p. 213–214.

138. Jane Dempsey Douglass, "Women and the Continual Reformation," *Religion and Sexism*, R.R. Ruether, ed. (New York: Simon and Schuster, 1974), pp. 292–318.

139. Landman, p. 5.

140. Douglass, p. 297.

141. Martin Luther, *Luther's Commentary on Genesis*, J. Theodore Mueller, trans. (Grand Rapids: Zondervan, 1958), p. 68.

142. *Ibid.*, p. 82.

143. Martin Luther, *Lectures on Genesis*, Jaroslav Pelikan, ed., *Luther's Works*, Vol. I (St. Louis: 1958), p. 115.

144. Martin Luther, *Table Talk* , No. 55, 1531 (*LW*, Vol. 54, p. 8).

145. Andre Bieler, *L'Homme et la femme dans la morale calviniste* (Geneva, 1963); Tavard, pp. 175–7.

146. Also from the fifteenth century onwards, various humanists favoured the education of women in the classics; e.g. Bruni, Domenichi, Elyot, Bercher and Vives. See William H. Woodward, *Studies in Education During the Age of the Renaissance (1400–1600)* (New York: 1965).

147. *Ibid*, pp. 303–4; divorce was seldom granted, and when it was remarriage by either party was viewed as adultery. The Geneva Marriage Ordinances of 1561 granted equal right of divorce to a woman whose husband committed adultery.

148. Eleanor C. McLaughlin, "Male and Female in Christian Tradition," Barnhouse and Holmes, pp. 49–50.

149. Douglass, p. 301. Specifically in reference to Queen Mary of England.
150. Douglass, p. 301.
151. John Donne, *First Anniversary*, *The Complete Poems of John Donne* C. A. Patrides, ed. pp. 95–110. (London: Dent, 1985), p. 331. Donne, a poet and later preacher and religious leader, left the Roman Catholic Church and was ordained a priest in the Anglican Church in 1615.
152. Witherington, p. 210.
153. Norman F. Cantor, *The Civilization of the Middle Ages* (New York: Harper Collins, 1993), pp. 3–5, 480–81.
154. Tavard, p. 215; Scot also held the doctrine of the Immaculate Conception of Mary, against the contrary opinion of Thomas Aquinas.

Chapter Six

ALEXANDER CAMPBELL AND THE AMERICAN RESTORATION MOVEMENT

The Great Awakening in the early nineteenth century motivated certain individuals to return to the simplicity of early Christianity and to reunite the church by rejecting human creeds and returning to the Bible. Among these were Methodist James O'Kelley, Baptists Elias Smith and Abner Jones, Presbyterian Barton W. Stone, and Thomas and Alexander Campbell of the Scotts Presbyterian Church. A number of denominations today claim their roots in this movement, including the United Church of Christ. The Stone-Campbell element of the movement would eventually become the Christian Church (Disciples of Christ), and after 1900 the more conservative Churches of Christ, and eventually also the Conservative (Independent) Christian Churches. As stated in the introduction, focus on this movement serves as an illustration of the complexity of the gender equity issue and its link to other theological concerns.

The earliest major document in this movement is the *Declaration and Address* by Thomas Campbell.[1] In that work Campbell denounced denominationalism as a great evil which divides the body of Christ and urged believers to return to the Bible as sole authority in matters of faith and practice and the basis for unity among believers. However, it was his son Alexander who gave energy to the movement and defined its doctrines. Alexander Campbell was an iconoclast and reformer in the early years of his ministry and was a progressive thinker on issues such as war, education and slavery. His hermeneutical method was shaped in part by British empiricism, and followed the tripartite model formulated by Edward Dering in the late sixteenth century and developed among various groups interested in detailed patterns of church polity.[2] Campbell was also aware of the latest grammatico-historical approaches to biblical studies applied in Germany and Britain, and made every attempt to be scientific in his exegetical and hermeneutical methods.[3] However, his writings from 1830 onward reflect an ardent devotion to biblical literalism which maintains and fortifies a theology of women firmly rooted in traditional androcentricity. His views are primarily contained in articles and editorials in a periodical called the *Millennial Harbinger*.[4]

On the surface Campbell might appear ambivalent on the issue of women, a characteristic some scholars attribute also to the Apostle Paul.[5] But there is within Campbell a dramatic tension between progressive and traditional interests. On the one hand he is a champion of female elevation, asserting that male and female are equal in moral, religious and social aspects through redemption in Christ. Some of his essays and speeches express a clear recognition that the spirit of the gospel is opposed to the injustice and degradation suffered by women throughout history.[6] Therefore the principles of social reform and equity were to Campbell an important element of the Gospel message, and issues such as slavery and the status of women demanded his attention. On the other hand, Campbell's doctrinal position on women in the church and society is unmistakably traditional and stands in stark contrast with the spirit of the Gospel.[7] His interpretation of relevant biblical passages is similar to that of Calvin, Luther, and the majority of his contemporaries, concluding that God designed woman as the helper of man and that her divinely appointed role is secondary, supportive, and subordinate.

The status of women was an issue of rising concern in the middle 1800s. The first women's suffrage convention was held in Seneca Falls, New York, in 1848. There some 300 men and women produced a treatise called *American Declaration of Sentiment*, which advocated female social equality and became the touchstone for later feminist movements.[8] Shortly afterward, in 1851 at a suffrage convention in Akron, Ohio, a black woman named Sojourner Truth made her famous speech, "Ain't I a Woman?"[9] These events are discussed in the next chapter in relation to the rise of modern feminism. During this period also, there was an unmistakable link between slavery and subordination of women as two major forms of social injustice, and it is ironic that both were defended by many conservative Christians on the basis of biblical doctrine. Nevertheless, women began to advance toward equality in both society and the church. In 1853 Antoinette Brown, a Congregationalist, became the first woman in America to become a fully ordained minister.[10] Naturally, questions concerning the status of women were raised in many Disciples churches also.

Other factors added to the tension in Campbell's developing theology. America was on the verge of civil war with slavery as a primary issue, and the Disciples found themselves being divided along lines drawn by various social, political and economic concerns. The publication of Charles Darwin's *The Origin of Species* in 1859 added credence to the new biblical criticism and its challenge of biblical inerrancy. Therefore, the proper interpretation of the Bible relevant to various contemporary issues became the focus of attention among Disciples, and the importance of a literal application of biblical teachings concerning the status of women was questioned. Consequently, Campbell's theology was tugged by many forces, and as Lindley points out, the constant struggle between Campbell's literalism and liberalism is especially seen in his attitude toward the place of women in the church organization. Lindley writes:

> In a day when the spirit of democracy had led to movements advocating women's rights, while Campbell was in the vein of progressive thinking on issues such as education, slavery and war, he was often reactionary regarding the place of woman, not only in society but in the church.[11]

This tug-o-war between conflicting interests arose out of Campbell's hermeneutical presuppositions. He was devoted to restoring true Christianity by means of biblical literalism, or more specifically understanding and applying scripture as propositional and authoritative truth.[12] To Campbell scripture is a blueprint for all matters of Christian life and faith, and the only acceptable basis for unity among believers. Unfortunately, this presupposition prevented Campbell from following through with what appears to be an intuitive sense of female equality and social justice, and resulted in his rejection of the views held by more progressive churchmen and social reformers of his day. In turn his theology became a prescription for the thinking of many Disciples in future generations.[13]

I. Campbell on Female Education and Elevation

Clearly Campbell supported the idea of female education.[14] In the *Harbinger* he often promoted and endorsed various academies, colleges, and seminaries for women. In a review of several newly established institutions of higher learning, he writes:

> These are but mere samples of what, as a people, we are doing and (are) about to do, in this greatest of temporal and evangelical interests to the church and the world.[15]

Campbell regularly published essays and letters submitted by women, and highly respected their views. Sarah H.C. Gardiner was a frequent correspondent and writer for the *Harbinger*. In one editorial note Campbell commends her for her perspicuity, piety, intelligence, good sense and force of style, and comments that her essay "commends itself to the perusal of all our female readers as an example of how they might exert a positive influence in both the church and community."[16] One contributor to the *Harbinger* identified only as Deborah claims to have followed Campbell's publications and theology since before the days of the *Christian Baptist*, and states her conviction that it was always his aim to elevate and exalt female worth and character.[17]

Women were also among the most active and generous financial supporters of Bethany College, as well as various missions and other special projects undertaken by Disciples. In this regard Selina Campbell often submitted notes or letters for publication, either thanking women for their prayers, encouragement and financial support or generating funds for some new project.[18]

During this period the concept of moral superiority of women emerged in Campbell's works. The *Harbinger* abounds in submittals, essays and editorials which extol and venerate the traditional female role, including select biographies that epitomize female dignity and influence on society.[19] Judge Hopkinton states:

> There cannot be a moral society where they are licentious; there cannot be a refined society where they are neglected or ignorant. Upon them depend the earliest education and first impressions of their children. They regulate or materially influence the principles, opinions, and mannerisms of their husbands and their sons. Thus the sound and healthful state of society depend on them.[20]

In a similar submittal Judge Story writes:

> The chamber of the sick, the pillow of the dying, the vigils of the dead, the altars of religion, never missed the presence or sympathies of woman. Timid though she be, and so delicate that the winds of heaven may not too roughly visit her, on such occasions she loses all sense of danger and assumes a preternatural courage which knows not and fears not consequences. Then she displays that undaunted spirit, which neither courts difficulties nor evades them, that resignation which utters neither murmur nor regret, and that patience in suffering which seems victorious over death itself.[21]

In one issue of the *Harbinger* Campbell reviews a speech delivered by English Lord Ellesmere for the Mayor of Boston. Campbell writes that he was charmed by the speaker's "just and appropriate tribute to woman, its felicitous allusions to her moral supremacy over our species."[22] And in his own lecture to the young women of Hopkinsville Female Institute in Nashville, Campbell clearly affirms that while women are perhaps physically weaker than males, they are at the same time stronger morally and religiously, and in times of stress more constant, firm and devoted.[23] In 1849 Campbell delivered the opening address at a symposium in Louisville, Kentucky, titled "On the Amelioration of the Social State." In that speech he declares that woman is the quickening, animating and conservative element of society, created from the side of man to sit at his side, not at his feet. He praises woman for her influence in history, naming literally dozens of notable women in history who stand as models for female excellence. And he forcefully declares that as society moves toward maturity, which no doubt he envisioned in terms of the millennial kingdom of Christ, woman would play a leading role of guidance and nurturing:

> Society is not yet fully civilized. It is only beginning to be. Things are in process to another age, a golden, a millennial, a blissful period in human history.... Woman, I believe, is destined to be the great agent in this grandest of all human enterprises, an effort to advance society to the access of its most glorious destiny on earth.[24]

In that speech Campbell goes on to focus on female education as a means of assisting women to achieve this noble task. On the surface Campbell appears to lend credence to the trend toward female elevation, but in reality he merely placates advocates of women's rights without compromising the status quo. It is evident that his carefully chosen words speak only of motherhood and childrearing, with no suggestion or support of true female equality.[25] And as a rule, modern feminists reject this type of suggestion of female supremacy as mere eloquent patronization, a chauvinistic ploy to maintain dominance in a traditionally male oriented society.[26]

II. Campbell's Patriarchal Conviction

There is another side of Campbell that reacts at the implications of social trends in his day. Especially when confronted with questions and issues addressed by express biblical passages Campbell stands with tradition, arguing that woman's place is in the home and that her divinely appointed status is one of subjection to the man. In one issue of the *Harbinger* Campbell reflects on a speech he heard in Indianapolis by Robert Dale Owen, the son of his old antagonist Robert Owen. The subject was, in Campbell's summary, "the quest for a new order of society, adapted to man without religion and its conscience." In that speech Owen discusses the rights of women, supporting their equality in society and their equal partnership in matrimony. This view Campbell dismisses as "eccentric" and "whimsical," the "visionary and imaginative aberrations" of men with little understanding of the true will of God for the family or society. Campbell does not deny that women have throughout history suffered indignity and injustice. But he implies that such injustice is generally exaggerated, and he is cautious about lending support to any notion of true gender equality. He comments concerning the trend to "redress these nameless wrongs by a correct theory of woman's rights," an effort he suggests is commendable and leans on the side of virtue, but at the same time is misguided and counterproductive.[27]

In 1848, drawing from Blackwood's magazine, Campbell denies that woman's proper place and purpose on earth includes making laws, leading armies and governing enterprises, or to function on an equal plane with males.[28] She is rather a subordinate to the man, designed by God to play a secondary and supportive role in a world where the male is the glory and supreme reflection of the Creator. Campbell consistently finds what he considers the true and correct paradigm for both the home and society in scripture:

> We have but one infallible standard on this subject; and indeed, being a subject of such transcendent grandeur and importance, it merits just such an infallible standard as God himself has ordained. Well, the question first to be propounded is, What says God's grand institute of woman's rights or wrongs? They are summed up in a few leading particulars. The first great fact is that Adam was first formed, then Eve. Hence the man is not of the woman, but the woman is of the man. He is first and she is second. He is senior and she is junior. They are, therefore, neither equal in rank nor in age.[29]

Campbell's bondage to biblical literalism is nowhere more evident than in his views of the proper role and status of women. In his writings both female subjection and ontological inferiority are founded upon numerous relevant passages in the New Testament, several of which in turn lean heavily upon the Creation Narrative in Genesis.[30] Following the perspective of both Jewish and Christian tradition, Campbell believed Adam and Eve to be literal figures, fashioned by God and placed in the Garden of Eden at the beginning of human history. The biblical account, in Campbell's mind, provides a universal paradigm for social and marital gender stratification. Certain facets of woman's lot in life are fixed by creation and others result from Eve's sin and the fallen state of humanity.

But woman's station as a whole is divinely determined. Woman's rightful place, by God's design, is in the home.[31] Campbell states that man's office is earthwide, but woman's is housewide.[32] Those occasions where women have ascended to the level of national queens, whether in contemporary England or ancient Israel, he considers to be endured by God as a choice of lesser evils in the absence of a suitable king, exceptions rather than a precedent for female ambition. In Campbell's view woman is constitutionally, legally and religiously inferior, whose place is to be "modest and retiring in the presence of him whom God made first."[33]

In the February 1833 issue of *Harbinger*, Campbell includes a lengthy dialogue which also clearly presents his own views.[34] Mr. Goodal is a dignified family patriarch living with his family in the village of Newton Fields near Earl Moira's Castle. On New Year's Eve, 1800, over dinner he poses a question concerning the origin of the custom of eating with the head uncovered. A guest, Mr. Reed, answers that the custom has its roots in early Jewish-Christian practices. Mrs. Reed supports this response, appealing to I Corinthians 11:9–10. Ensuing comments from Mrs. Goodal, Mrs. Reed and others tend to support the common view of marriage which has been perpetuated throughout mainstream Christian history, namely that the husband is the head of the household, and both head and lord over the wife, a hierarchy traditionally founded both in logic and scriptural authority. The covering of the woman's head, they state, is necessary because of the angels.[35] The husband is both a brother and master to the wife. Her veiled head symbolizes her subordination to her husband's authority, given by angels to Eve and reiterated at Mt. Sinai in the Mosaic Law.[36] The dialogue also suggests that because of the redemptive work of Christ as well as the impact of his teaching on the world, woman's lot has been significantly elevated.[37]

In a later issue Campbell employs a fictional dialogue, similar to the one mentioned above, titled "Conversations at the Carlton House" in which he offers instruction on family culture.[38] Mr. Carlton, the father and head of the household engages, his children in a rather formal and awkward conversation about various religious topics, including the origins of certain Christian customs and values. Eliza declares that woman was created second, as a companion for Adam. Mary adds that Satan, whom she identifies as "the Adversary" and calls him "a liar and murderer from the beginning," entered into the serpent as an instrument of his evil interests and deceived "our mother, who believed a lie rather than the truth of God, obeyed her enemy, and included her husband with her in the catastrophe."[39]

Campbell does not belabor the issue of woman as the root of sin and the cause of the Fall, either in this dialogue or elsewhere in his writings. However, in a lecture to young ladies at Hopkinsville Female Institute, he affirms that each of the characters in the Creation Story stood alone and bore the consequences of his or her own deeds. Adam was responsible for his own sin, his own condemnation and his own punishment. Likewise, Eve and the Serpent bore the responsibility for their own choices.[40]

Campbell clearly opposed female leadership in the church. In 1840 a reader submitted a question to the *Harbinger* concerning whether women, referring to them as sisters, have a right to teach and deliver lectures, exhortations and prayers in the public assembly of the church of God. Campbell's reply consisted of a quotation of I Timothy 2:12, and the added comment, "I submit to Paul and teach the same lesson."[41] In a later issue he quotes segments of Macaulay's History with reference to the Queen, comparing her sacerdotal role in the Church of England to that of the Pope to the Roman Catholic Church:

> Well might the dissenters of that age and all reasonable men of this, ask whether it is not monstrous that a woman should be chief Bishop of a church in which an Apostle had forbidden her even to speak.[42]

A more poignant statement of Campbell's position is found in an 1854 editorial where he offers a summary of several relevant New Testament passages:

> Nor would an apostle, who commanded and importuned them to be chaste, keepers at home, obedient to their own husbands, to adorn themselves with modest apparel, with good works, with a meek and quiet spirit; who commanded them to marry, to raise and educate children, and to teach the junior women to follow their example in similar pursuits, contradict himself and stultify his own wisdom and discretion, by telling them, at the same time, that they had political and civil rights and duties, incompatible with this, calling them off into the busy circle of the forum, or the battlefield, or the tumultuous cabals and contrivances of men.[43]

Campbell's conclusion is not surprising. If therefore Paul silenced garrulous women, prohibiting them from even asking a curious question in the religious assembly, it is certainly a shame, rather than a right or an honor, for them to speak out, teach or preach.[44]

> What, says he, women, came the word of God out from you, or did it come only to you? Did God send women to illuminate the world by making them depositories of his truths or the oracles of salvation

to mankind? If he did not, why should the church send them, and
still, less why should they send themselves?[45]

To conclude, Campbell quotes Mrs. Sigourney, a contemporary Christian poet and author whom he describes as "a distinguished lady," who
extols women to avoid contention for power, rather joyfully and grate-
fully submitting to the traditional role God designed: "a helpmeet, such
as was fitting for man to desire, and for woman to become."[46]

In 1856 Campbell addressed a large assembly of young ladies at
Henry Female Seminary in New Castle, Kentucky, and subsequently published the entire address in the *Harbinger*.[47]

In his characteristic eloquence he contrasts the grandeur and perfection of Lady Eve, the mother of all living whose very name means
life,[48] placed in the ambrosial bowers of Eden's Paradise, with Lord Adam
for whom she was fashioned as a suitable helper.

> Woman was created to be a companion, perfectly suitable to man;
> hence it is equally her duty, her honor, and her happiness to accom-
> plish herself for this high and dignified position.[49]

Indeed, Campbell argues that woman is man's better half "in
delicacy of thought, in sensitiveness of feeling, in patient endurance,
in constancy of affection, in moral courage, and in soul absorbing devotion."[50]

> She holds a great and mysterious power to influence the course of
> history. Every distinctive element of her sex was conferred upon her
> in order to her accomplishment for the great work of forming and
> molding human nature in reference to human destiny.[51]

However, this noble task Campbell defines in terms of a divinely ordained
hierarchy where woman's purpose and duty is to support the enterprises
of man. While on the one hand the dignity and significance of womanhood is apparent in Campbell's thinking, it is nonetheless embraced by
the traditional paradigm of male dominance. Woman is clearly a secondary entity in creation whose role is to support man and influence the
world for good only through clearly defined maternal and domestic tasks,
including ministry to the poor, the sick, the wounded and the dying. It
has been noted that Campbell favored and promoted female education.
However, in his mind the purpose of such education is to better equip
women for their maternal and domestic tasks.

She was an extract of man in order to form man; in order to develop, perfect, beautify, and beatify man. And hence these four terms comprehend the whole duty, honor, dignity and happiness of woman; consequently, her education should be equal to her mission.[52]

There is no need, Campbell contends, for women to preach or teach publicly in order to fulfill their purpose and mission. To support this point he appeals to I Corinthians 11 on the veiling of woman's head and face from "staring sensualists," and "green striplings of pert impertinence" who gaze lustfully at women with ogling glasses. While Campbell did not appear to require headcoverings for females in his own churches, he argues that if Paul required such of women to maintain modesty in the church assembly, he would never have encouraged women to take on authoritative roles in the church nor would he have sent out women as missionaries.[53]

Concerning modest feminine attire Campbell defers to an essay by a Baptist missionary, who draws from both I Peter 3:3–4 and I Timothy 2:9–10 to support his conservative and traditional posture.[54] Of particular concern to Judson is "the appalling profusion of ornaments" worn by some Western women, both by visitors to Burma and by those he witnessed during brief furloughs at home, which he attributes to a "demon of vanity laying waste the female department."[55] He specifies ankle bracelets, necklaces, earrings, braided hair, rings on the fingers, arm and wrist bracelets, and other such vanities which he declares are strictly forbidden by the New Testament. Judson states that as a missionary he had refused to even baptize or administer the Lord's Supper to local Karen women unless they abandoned such vain and gaudy adorning, not as if it represented their former religious beliefs but because it violated the specific commands of the apostles.

After the death of Thomas Campbell in 1855, Alexander experienced a decline in mental acumen, and his work as editor of the *Harbinger* suffered.[56] For this reason his son-in-law, W.K. Pendleton, began to assume responsibility for the paper. From 1857 material in the *Harbinger* on the subject of women came largely from Pendleton, but there is little doubt that Pendleton's views reflect the theology of Alexander Campbell.[57]

Addressing the specific question, "Can a Christian wear gold jewelry?" Pendleton states that dress is the outward expression of the inward spirit, and addressing Christian women specifically he quotes I Peter 3:4. On another question, "Do sisters have a right to vote for those who rule over them (elders) in the church?" Pendleton writes that they have as much right as they do to select their own husbands. He adds that in this regard there is neither male nor female.[58]

A more volatile issue gaining momentum at this time was female leadership in the church, suggested in the question submitted by a reader: "Do the Christian Scriptures authorize females to lead in prayer, or to engage in exhortation in the meeting of the church for worship?"[59] Pendleton's lengthy response is based on I Corinthians 14:33–35 and I Timothy 2:8–12. First he distinguishes between public worship and small private gatherings, the latter of which he concedes might be an acceptable venue for women praying even if men are present. But on the general topic of women addressing a church assembly, he writes:

> We cannot see how a prohibition could be more explicit or universal. It is said they must keep silence; that they are not permitted to speak in public; that they may not even so much as publicly ask a question, but must wait and ask it privately at home; that it is disgraceful for them to speak publicly in the congregation; and that they must learn in silence, with entire submission. What could the apostle say more explicit than this?[60]

In his discussion of I Corinthians 11:5 Pendleton argues that Paul addresses custom, but in no way condones women prophesying or praying in the assembly. Instruction on this matter is left until later (I Corinthians 14) when Paul forbids public praying and prophesying by women altogether. Pendleton concedes that some women in the Corinthian church possessed gifts of prophecy, but insists that Paul forbade the practice in the assembly. Pendleton rejects all "farfetched arguments" to justify women preaching, and concludes by quoting patristic writers such as Tertullian, Chrysostom and Epiphanius to say that women were never ordained to offer sacrifice, hold office, teach men or perform any solemn service in the church, and should not be today.[61] In reference to I Timothy 2 he refers to the grave danger of "self deception in the weaker sex."[62]

Challenges of Pendleton's position were submitted by R. Faurot of Philadelphia and appear in various issues of the *Harbinger* in 1864, but Faurot limits his contentions to women praying in a public assembly and published rebuttals are brief and reflect little scholastic depth.[63]

Summary

These materials represent perhaps the most significant voice among Disciples of Christ immediately preceding the debate on ordination of women which took place in 1880 to 1881 and in a second bout from 1891 to 1893, presented largely in the *Christian-Evangelist* and the *Christian*

Standard.[64] Campbell certainly envisioned a trend toward female elevation in society and he supported such in terms of education, influence, respect, and dignity. But on the more fundamental subject of female status in the home, in the church, and in the social hierarchy, he remained firmly traditional. And it is Campbell's biblical scholarship which forms the hermeneutical tradition followed by most Disciples in successive generations.[65]

It is ironic that the conflict in Campbell's views of women parallels a similar conflict within Pauline works, which compose the major "proof texts" for the traditional Christian doctrine on women.[66] Another irony is the fact that both Campbells viewed the Old and New Testaments as having different levels of importance in terms of their constitutional authority for Christians. Yet following the lead of the Apostle Paul and other writers in the Pauline tradition, Alexander Campbell unwittingly rooted his theology of womanhood in the Genesis Creation myth and thereby perpetuated among his followers a gender hierarchy inherited from ancient Judaism.[67]

Those Disciples who supported the nineteenth century elevation of female status in fact did so by rejecting the traditional interpretation of relevant biblical passages, and in turn by rejecting the biblical literalism of the Campbell tradition. Conversely, later generations of Disciples who rejected female equality did so primarily because of their allegiance to the biblical literalism of the Campbell tradition. These would be known as the Conservative Christian Churches and Churches of Christ, whose views entering the twenty-first century remain largely those of Alexander Campbell.

Chapter Six Notes

1. George C. Bedell, Leo Sandon and Charles T. Wellborn, *Religion in America*, (New York: Macmillan, 1982), pp. 463ff.

2. Scottish Presbyterians, English Puritans, and various Reformed and Independent Churches. See Theodore D. Bozeman, *To Live Ancient Lives* (Chapel Hill: University of North Carolina, 1988), p. 70.

3. Thomas H. Olbricht, "Alexander Campbell in the Context of American Scholarship," *Restoration Quarterly* (Vol. 33, 1991), pp. 13–28.

4. Alexander Campbell, editor, *Millennial Harbinger* 1830–1870 (Joplin: College Press, reprinted edition, 1987); hereafter *MH* with abbreviated references by year and page.

5. Kenneth H. Maahs, "Male and Female in Pauline Perspective: A Study in Biblical Ambivalence," *Dialogue and Alliance* 2, No. 3 (Fall, 1988), pp. 17ff. See also Ben Witherington III, *Women in the Earliest Churches*, Society for New

Testament Studies, Monogram Series 59 (Cambridge: University Press, 1988), pp. 24–5.

6. *MH* (54:204–9; 55:149; 56:314).

7. Krister Stendahl, *The Bible and the Role of Women: A Case Study in Hermeneutics*, Emilie T. Sanders, trans. (Philadelphia: Fortress, 1966), pp. 32–4.

8. Janet Riley, "The Ordination of Disciple Women: A Matter of Economy or Theology?" *Encounter*, Summer, 1989 (50:3), p. 222; Carol P. Christ and Judith Plaskow, eds., *Womanspirit Rising: A Feminist Reader in Religion* (San Francisco: Harper and Row, 1979).

9. James Loewenberg and Ruth Bogin (eds.), *Black Women in Nineteenth Century American Life* (University Park: Pennsylvania State University, 1976), p. 235; Shirley J. Yee, *Black Women Abolitionists: a study in activities, 1828–1860* (Knoxville: University of Tennessee Press, 1992), p. 141. All accounts of the role of Sojourner Truth in the early feminist movement rely on Elizabeth Cady Stanton, Susan B. Anthony and Matilda Josleyn Gage, *History of Woman Suffrage*, Vol. I (Rochester, N.Y., 1881).

10. September 15, 1853, at South Butler, New York. See David A. Jones, "The Ordination of Women in the Christian Church: An Examination of the Debate, 1880–1893," *Encounter*, Summer, 1989 (50:3), p. 200. See also Barbara Zikmund, "The Struggle for the Right to Preach," *Women and Religion in America, Volume I, The Nineteenth Century*, edited by Rosemary Radford Ruether and Rosemary Skinner Keller (San Francisco: Harper & Row, 1982), p. 214.

11. D. Ray Lindley, *Apostle of Freedom* (St. Louis: Bethany, 1957), p. 173.

12. Mark G. Toulouse, *Joined in Discipleship* (St. Louis: Chalice, 1992), pp. 54–55.

13. Toulouse, pp. 66, 155.

14. *MH* (38:143).

15. *MH* (52:531).

16. *MH* (39:424–6).

17. *MH* (45:39).

18. Alexander's second wife; *MH* (56:119; 57:383, 415; 58:652).

19. See *MH* (45:283–8) for a lengthy biographical tribute to the Honorable Seliva, Countess of Huntingdon, extolled as a lofty model and example to women for her benevolence, godliness, and mission zeal. She constructed numerous churches and opened a college at Brecknockshire in 1768. See also *MH* (45:349) for a tribute to Princess Elizabeth of the Rhine, eldest daughter of Frederick V of Bohemia in 1620, and Lady Rachel Russell, daughter of the Earl of Southampton in the early 1600s. There is nothing in these biographies which either supports or refutes the traditional paradigm of female subjection.

20. *MH* (44:237–8). See also a submittal by H.H.H. on Woman's Mission, in which the writer states that on her "falls the duty of imparting to the child the first religious instruction." *MH* (52:675–7).

21. *MH* (32:418).

22. *MH* (53:511).

23. *MH* (55:146–54).

24. Lester G. McAllister, ed. *An Alexander Campbell Reader* (St. Louis: CBP, 1988), p. 111. From Alexander Campbell, *Popular Lectures and Addresses*, pp. 47–72.

25. See below, pp. 15–16.

26. Debates on the status of women arise early among the church fathers

(e.g. Tertullian, John Chrysostom, Clement of Alexandria, Jerome, Augustine, Thomas Aquinas) and continue through the Reformation (Martin Luther, John Calvin, John Knox). Patronization by exalting motherhood and female subordination, urging women to take pride in their role as man's divinely appointed helper, is found throughout Christian history.

27. *MH* (51:17).

28. *MH* (48:115).

29. *MH* (54:204).

30. The Adam and Eve story (Genesis 2:18–3:24) is the foundation of Judeo-Christian beliefs concerning the origin of humanity and various traditional ideologies concerning the genders. This account also lies at the root of relevant Pauline texts in the New Testament (cf. I Cor. 11:8–12; Eph. 5:31; I Tim. 2:13–15).

31. Titus 2:5.

32. *MH* (54:204).

33. *MH* (54:205). Campbell appeals to Homer's Hector, who on going to battle begs his wife Andromache to remain and keep order at home.

34. *MH* (33:65–8).

35. The precise meaning of this assertion in I Corinthians 11:10 remains a point of debate among biblical scholars.

36. See also *MH* (54:205) where Campbell understands the Apostle Paul to have taught women to veil their faces in the synagogue and wear long hair for a covering in the Christian assemblies.

37. Neither male nor female in Christ; Galatians 3:28. Campbell believed that Christian principles were the impetus for social advancement in general.

38. In January 1840 Campbell prefaced a new series in the *Millennial Harbinger* with a resolution to promote family education. The two part didactic series is written in the form of a dialogue, and is titled "Family Culture; Conversations at the Carlton House." The setting is the household of Olympas Carlton and his wife Julia at Carmel Place, and it is likely that Campbell bases this material on his own household. See *MH* (40:3–4, 8–9, 72–6).

39. *MH* (40:76).

40. *MH* (55:150)

41. *MH* (40:521).

42. *MH* (49:337).

43. *MH* (54:205). See I Corinthians 11:3; Ephesians 5:22–23; Colossians 3:18; Titus 2:3–5; I Peter 3:1.

44. I Corinthians 14:34–37.

45. *MH* (54:206).

46. *MH* (54:206–7).

47. *MH* (56:301-314).

48. A segment of this lecture is published later in the same year; *MH* (56:392). He argues that Adam named Eve "life" because she was the source of all social happiness, joy, pleasure, and a fountain of strength and moral heroism.

49. *MH* (56:305).

50. *MH* (56:308).

51. *MH* (56:312).

52. *MH* (56:312).

53. *MH* (56:314).

54. A. Judson, "Address to Christian Women," *MH* (32:326); (57:495–502).

Judson was a Baptist missionary working in Maulmain, Burma. The essay is dated October, 1831, and appears in the *Harbinger* in part in 1832 and in its entirety in 1857.

55. *MH* (57:495).

56. There were other personal tragedies, such as a fire at Bethany, which may have contributed to his decline.

57. Transfer of the editorship of the *Harbinger* occurred in January, 1864. See Lester G. McAllister and William E. Tucker, *Joined in Faith: A History of the Christian Church (Disciples of Christ)* (St. Louis: CBP, 1989), p. 146.

58. *MH* (57:459); Galatians 3:28.

59. *MH* (64:325–330).

60. *Ibid.*, 326.

61. *Ibid.*, 328.

62. *Ibid.*, 329.

63. *MH* (64:370; 415).

64. David A. Jones, "The Ordination of Women in the Christian Church: An Examination of the Debate, 1880–1893," *Encounter* 50:3 (Summer, 1989), p. 205.

65. Churches of Christ, Independent Christian Churches, and conservatives within the Christian Church (Disciples of Christ). See M. Eugene Boring, "The Disciples and Higher Criticism: The Crucial Third Generation," *A Case Study of Mainstream Protestantism: The Disciples' Relation to American Culture, 1880–1989*, D. Newell Williams, ed. (Grand Rapids: Eerdmans, 1991), pp. 30–31.

66. Elaine Pagels, "Paul and Women: A Response to Recent Discussion," *Journal of the American Academy of Religion* 42:544, 1974. The concept presented in Galatians 3:23, "neither male nor female…" is set in juxtaposition to Pauline doctrine as a whole and to mainstream Christian tradition. Note also the disputed authorship of the Pastorals.

67. Doris Franklin, "Impact of Christianity on the Status of Women from the Socio-cultural Point of View," *Religion and Society*, 32:2 (June, 1985), p. 46.

Chapter Seven

THE ANTI-SLAVERY MOVEMENT AND MODERN FEMINISM

During the seventeenth and eighteenth centuries, the world saw many advances, resulting largely from American colonialism, world exploration, industrialization, and scholasticism. Christianity also experienced a remarkable spread through world missions, and there arose a remarkable diversity of doctrine among Protestant denominations.

I. Sexism and Slavery

Two significant social and theological issues began to surface: slavery and sexism. The evil in both was becoming a self-evident truth among all advanced cultures, and the church found itself in the anomalous role of defending them in the name of God and tradition. Slavery is presupposed in the Old Testament, both as a matter of historical record and by religious sanction.[1] The same is true of the New Testament, specifically letters traditionally attributed to Paul.[2] While New Testament spokesmen, and more significantly Jesus himself, encourage submission to government officials even if they happen to be evil and their form of rule tyrannical,[3] the underlying principles of New Testament theology clearly oppose tyranny and injustice in any form. In time, where these concepts would permeate society they would gradually eliminate various forms of social injustice, although fundamentally the New Testament teaches Christians to tolerate and submit to the less desirable social order.

However, a tenacious adherence to the literal teachings of the New Testament would never allow for the overthrow of slavery or tyranny, and would perpetuate in the name of divine truth an inferior and essentially anti–Christian ideology. Yet through the centuries the church failed to

125

apply Christian principles in such a way as to urge upward social change. It seems that Jesus' teaching of suffering in silence, turning the other cheek, going the extra mile, and such became weapons in the hands of church officials to maintain traditional inequity, just as the Law of Moses became a weapon of the religious elite among the Jews. Even during the Reformation, Luther's intent of placing the Word of God in the hands of the common people did not reach down far enough in terms of practical social justice. This is demonstrated in his response to the German peasants who asserted that priesthood of all believers made them equal to their landlords. In a tract titled *Against the Thievish and Murderous Hordes of Peasants*, Luther urged nobles to use brutal force to quell the peasant rebellion, appealing to Romans 13 as a supportive text. But to the peasants he reiterated Jesus' teachings in the Sermon on the Mount to endure hardship without complaining.[4] Sixteenth century Spanish theologians found it necessary to develop a new theology of inequality in order to justify enslaving the Indians in the Americas. They declared that every person has an appropriate social function, some to work and serve, others to organize and rule. This condition, they suggested, is best for all concerned, including the enslaved. Similarly, Christians in America's colonial South justified owning and trading black slaves. As one nineteenth century churchman said in defense of slavery:

> Our design in giving them the Gospel is not to civilize them, not to change their social condition, not to exalt them into citizens or free men; it is to save them.[5]

The term "save," it would seem, suggests spiritual regeneration, as it typically does among Christians, without the inclusion of benevolence, education, medical care, social elevation, or any other type of ministry related to physical welfare. Having provided slaves some exposure to the Christian religion, they felt they had done them a great favor. But owning them, selling their children, and abusing their bodies was another matter entirely, totally irrelevant to the Gospel. In fact, most Christian slave owners believed human exploitation to be quite justifiable and perfectly in keeping with the Bible. For this reason, many conservative preachers defended slavery as part of God's grand scheme.

Similarly, the church was a strong opponent of assertive women, whether for voicing opinions on slavery or for advocating women's rights. In colonial America Elizabeth Hooten was a Quaker missionary, quite vocal on significant issues of her day. At age sixty she was flogged by locals to improve her theology. When Quaker Abby Kelly spoke out against slavery she was denounced by ministers as the Jezebel of Revelation 2:20. Sarah and Angelina Grimke are also known to historians for their role in promoting abolition in the 1830s and were quite vocal against sexual exploitation of black women. But clergymen issued a letter denouncing them as crude and offensive because of the unspeakable things they had revealed.

At times churchmen have resorted to ridiculous arguments to defend traditional patriarchy and to stop the mouths of advocates of change. Christians were known to argue against the use of anesthesia in childbirth, contending that on the basis of Genesis 3:16 God wants women to suffer pain.[6] And many have opposed the education of women using I Corinthians 14:35 as a divine mandate that women should learn whatever they need to know from their husbands, or from a male familial head. Hays writes that among other absurd arguments against educating women was the claim that blood directed from the womb to the brain in intellectual pursuits rendered women infertile.[7]

All through the great mission movement of the nineteenth century, women were very involved, but against continual opposition from church leaders. More than one hundred years ago a young lady of the Anglican faith wrote:

> I would have given the church my head, my hand, my heart. She would not have them. She told me to go back and do crochet in my mother's drawing room.[8]

Florence Nightingale had to change countries and churches in order to find the training and encouragement she needed to serve God.[9] Today every country and every church would like to claim her.

In recent years the claim that Christianity has done a great deal to elevate the status of women in society has been a persistent shibboleth. But this no more justifies the subordination of women than would the provision of better work conditions justify slavery to a slave or exonerate the master. As one journalist pointed out nearly two decades ago, "Churches are one of the few important institutions that still elevate discrimination against women to the level of principle."[10] Concerning the posture of the church to this point in history Scanzoni and Hardesty write:

> Christians must honestly face the historical fact that the church has erected many barriers—socially, legally, spiritually, psychologically— against women's advancement. By propagating the notion that God ordained women to be passive and dependent, lacking initiative and assertiveness, confined to kitchen and pew, the church has hampered growth and fostered low self-esteem in women. It has not challenged women to recognize their God-given gifts, encouraged them to fully use their talents, or helped them to gain a natural sense of personhood.[11]

And there can be no doubt that in the past century, in spite of periodic surges of growth, the general decline in membership by mainstream churches can be attributed largely to the virtually unanimous position of clergymen on this issue. Resultingly, most Protestant denominations have slowly severed that element which through the centuries has proved the most loyal in support and service, namely its women. According to Martin Marty in *Righteous Empire*, this massive loss has been either to Unitarianism or to fringe Christian groups where they could fulfill their honest and intense desire to serve God.[12]

One of the first to recognize a connection between slavery and sexism was Frederick Douglass, the great abolitionist.[13] He attended the first convention on women's rights in Seneca Falls, New York, in 1848, lending his support to the controversial resolution on women's suffrage. Three years later at a similar convention in Akron, Ohio, a black woman and former slave by the name of Sojourner Truth delivered her now famous speech, "Ain't I a Woman?" Starting at that point western society began to awaken to the realization that sexism and racism were shackled together by human injustice, and that black women were victims of both. Furthermore, it was becoming painfully obvious that mainstream Christianity had not only failed to offer assistance, but had been a chief advocate of traditional injustice. During this era of awakening Professor O.S. Fowler wrote a book on the sexes, vigorously supporting female suffrage, equal pay for equal work, and inclusion of women in the clergy. He recognized that many sincere Christians had been blind to various forms of tyranny, perhaps because the Bible had become nothing more than a guardian of tradition and human prejudice. But social advancement was rapidly tearing off the mask of hypocrisy, revealing the wolf in sheep's clothing. In 1860 Elizabeth Cady Stanton wrote:

> Prejudice against color, of which we hear so much, is no stronger than that against sex. It is produced by the same cause, and manifested very much in the same way. The Negro's skin and the woman's sex are both *prima facia* evidence that they were intended to be in subjection to the white Saxon male.[14]

Fowler made the provocative and prophetic assertion which those denominations which were not willing to recognize this need were retrograding, and would eventually disappear if they did not boldly reassess their position.[15]

II. The Early Feminist Movement

In 1787 Abigail Adams wrote to her husband John, then engaged in the Constitutional Convention of the young Republic called the United States of America, urging him not to allow unlimited power to be vested in husbands. "Remember," she said, "that all men would be tyrants if they could."[16] This sort of generalization is no less mythical than those traditional beliefs about women which are the focus of this discussion. But it does express the sentiments of millions of women who have come to perceive men as their oppressors in a social structure marked by tyranny and injustice. Feminism in recent history is quite simply a radical reaction against centuries of female oppression. This movement, which some have called "womanspirit rising," emerged at a time and place where self-declaration for women at last had become possible.[17]

Modern feminism had its true beginnings with two sources: Women's Suffrage and the Holiness Revivalist Movement, both in America.[18] Nesbitt points out that with the migration of American-European pioneers to the West, and the corresponding diversity of backgrounds and beliefs, there naturally developed a heightened awareness of women's individual worth and contribution to the community in lay and clergy leadership.[19] The issues that arose in this diverse cultural melting pot brought women to the foreground in terms of moral judgment and social direction. In 1840 Lucretia Mott and Elizabeth Stanton were among the women who attended the World Anti-Slavery Convention where they were prohibited from participation and made to sit in the balcony. It was there that these women realized that they could not fight for the freedom of slaves without also freeing themselves. Eight years later in 1848 the first feminist convention was held in Seneca Falls, New York, attended by some 300 men and women who then produced a treatise called the *American Declaration of Sentiment*, which became the touchstone for all later feminist movements.

At a convention in Akron, Ohio, in 1851 one clergyman warned women not to sell their rights of special privileges and concessions for a mess of equality pottage. "What man," he asked, "would help a political or business rival into a carriage, or lift her over a ditch?" It was this question that prompted the famous speech of Sojourner Truth which not only denounced traditional role distinctions between male and female, but also pointed out the inequity suffered by black women, who enjoyed no privileges or concessions at all:

> That man over there says that women needs to be helped into carriages, and lifted over ditches, and to have the best place everywhere.

> Nobody ever helps me into carriages or over mudpuddles, or gives me any best place! And ain't I a woman? Look at me! Look at my arm! I have ploughed, and planted, and gathered into barns, and no man could head me! And ain't I a woman? I could work as much and eat as much as a man—when I could get it—and bear the lash as well! And ain't I a woman? I have borne thirteen children and seen them most all sold off to slavery, and when I cried out with my mother's grief, none but Jesus heard me! And ain't I a woman?[20]

At the same convention another preacher argued against women's equality, and in favor of male privileges, on grounds of the manhood of the Savior. Sojourner's response was a powerful exposure of the bias of traditional arguments: "Where did Christ come from?" she asked. "From God and a woman! And man had nothing to do with him."[21]

Within this early feminist movement a distinction has to be made between suffragists and reformists. The suffragists were interested in gaining for women the right to vote. But they had neither a vision for organizational needs afterwards nor a relationship of their cause to a general ideology. The reformists did. They sought the vote as a means of changing society—to achieve goals such as cleaning up sweat shops, bringing an end to the exploitation of women, stopping liquor traffic, and eliminating child labor. By the time women were granted a voice in government much of this had been achieved.

The feminist movement as a whole did not attack the fact of woman's unique role or the preference of many women for domestic life. Instead, the contention was simply that woman should be given the opportunity to choose her role and compete in man's world on an equal basis. Many highly educated and influential women of this era continued to play a role of exemplary subservience, patronizing the system to protect potential advances for the cause of women. Mary Lyons, head of the Mt. Holyoke Seminary, avoided attending trustee meetings for this reason. Mary Alice Baldwin, leader of the women's college of Duke University, played the role of "Southern Lady" in homage to propriety and as the essential price to pay for women's education. Frances Perkins, the first woman cabinet member in the United States and Secretary of Labor to Roosevelt, often endorsed the myth that in reality she rejected, that woman's place is in the home.[22]

Likewise blacks in America had to play the patronizing role of "Uncle Tom" to appease whites, which included sitting at the back of buses, drinking from separate water fountains, standing with hat in hand when whites passed, and generally presenting an appearance of laziness and lack of ambition.[23] But beneath the subservience was deep resentment of an injustice to which even traditional Christianity was blind. John Stuart Mill wrote in 1869 concerning the subjection of women: "This relic of the past is discordant with the future, and must necessarily disappear."[24]

The charge leveled at society by vocal feminists was not only that of injustice against women, but also that the church had misused the Bible in defense of its tradition and as a weapon against proponents of justice and truth. At the close of the nineteenth century a number of women who were prominent in evangelism became quite influential also in the American temperance movement. Among them were Amanda Berry Smith of the Holiness Movement,[25] and Carrie Judd Montgomery of the faith healing Pentecostals. Frances E. Willard was president of the Christian Women's Temperance Union from 1879 to 1898, and is considered by historians to be the most famous woman in America during that period.[26]

After the turn of the century there was a temporary lull in the advancement of women's rights. Women of the 1920s inherited a legacy of independence, but the political context in which it was born was forgotten for the time. Instead of concentrating on utilizing woman power to solve social problems, attention turned to drinking, smoking and bobbing hair. The '20s became an era of sexual revolution and gratification. There was a surge in academic interests also, suggested by the fact that a greater percentage of PhDs went to women in 1920 than in 1960. The number of master's degrees taken by women peaked in 1930, and bachelor's in 1940. But female education during this era found very little practical application. Then during World War II women by the thousands were recruited to factories to support the massive military effort, as well as to fill posts vacated by servicemen. Under these circumstances a permanent place for women was carved in man's world, and the myth of feminine ineptness in masculine jobs began to crumble.

Protests against feminism continued through all these years in various forms. In the '30s magazine articles depicted career women neglecting their families and marriages falling apart because of feminism. In some states laws were passed prohibiting married women from working. Most school systems forced female teachers to give up their posts when they married.[27] Educated women during the early decades of the twentieth century began to feel extreme disillusionment with roles which were unfulfilling, keeping women from positions where they could apply their training and skills. Many expressed themselves through civic organizations, movements and special interest groups. Others joined social clubs simply to occupy their time. A few wealthy and middle class women took menial jobs just to alleviate boredom. Most, however, continued in the traditional role where the highest station to which a woman could aspire was that of a charming wife and devoted mother. But dissatisfaction and frustration mounted.

In 1940, seventy-five percent of working women held jobs only available to women, such as typing, stenography, and various fields of teaching and nursing. They had a clear place in the work world, but the choice of vocation was limited and for an equal number of hours they earned only half the pay as men. The rationale was that women worked to have something to do, but did not really need the money, whereas men worked to support families. This also was a myth. According to studies by the Women's Bureau of the Department of Labor, during the '20s and '30s some ninety percent of working women did so out of necessity to provide either supplemental or total income for the family.[28]

After the war there was a concerted campaign by mainstream churches in the United States, using the media and political leaders, to encourage women to return to their subordinate roles. It was thought that since women could be described as anchor and spiritual mainstay of the family, some means had to be found to get them out of the factories and back at home, or the whole society would fall into decadence. So the motto was coined: "Women must bear and raise our children and the men must support them." But in spite of it, through the '50s the trend toward equity continued. By 1960 forty percent of all women over the age of sixteen worked, and by 1970 nearly half of all married women in the United States were working outside the home.

In 1963, in *The Feminine Mystique*, Betty Friedan asked, "Who knows what women can be when they are finally free to become themselves?" She represented a resurgence of the spirit of female equality that arose more than a century earlier. Within a year American Congress passed Title VII of the Civil Rights Act banning sex discrimination in employment, and the President's Commission on the Status of Women announced its conclusion that women had indeed been the victims of discrimination in the marketplace. But failure to uphold that Act prompted Friedan and other activists to found the National Organization of Women (NOW) in 1966 to increase pressure for total equality.[29] Other groups also arose, such as Women's Equity Action League in 1970, to apply pressure to the courts, and the National Women's Political Caucus intended to push the issue in political parties.[30]

Rising sensitivity to the plight of women in Third World countries prompted the United Nations to declare the years 1975 to 1985 the Decade of Women, during which time great strides were made in various areas. Conferences were held in Mexico City in 1975, Copenhagen in 1980 and then Nairobi in 1985, of which the last was the most productive.[31]

Although feminism is considered by some to be the most explosive religious issue of the '70s, its cause suffered during that decade from a lack of conventional leadership.[32] Each local women's liberation group took its vitality from the needs of the local community without unified direction or purpose. Women's liberation theorist Jo Freeman warned about the "tyranny of structurelessness," that the deliberate rejection of structure would lead to a few dominating the movement.[33] So for a while no progress was evident.

III. Feminist Liberation Theology

Within mainstream Christianity there have been and continue to be certain factors which prove counterproductive in the struggle to realize some of the most significant goals, the equity of women being a prime example. Chafe points to this perennial problem:

> The entire Judaeo-Christian tradition was premised on the imperfection of human value and the tendency of people, in the absence of external restraints, to seek their own ends. Reliance on collective good wishes without resort to institutionalized checks and balances, tested severely people's ability to withstand the temptation to take advantage of others and impose their own will. Indeed, among some student radical groups, outlasting the opposition provided a basic technique for controlling—and abusing—the process of participatory democracy.[34]

Consequently, there are often opposing forces within the church, each representing a genuine conviction of truth and right, engaged in a tug-o-war over principles and direction. Against rising feminism traditionalists have felt called of God to defend divine truth. So during the '70s church ministers heavily indoctrinated their congregations from Pauline texts on subordination of wives in a desperate attempt to stem the tide. However, even among conservative Christians, as women continued to broaden their perspective in the secular world, there followed an increasing demand for recognition and access to more meaningful roles in church life. In spite of opposition from clergymen, it can be stated that there were strong religious sentiments underlying the drive for reform in church doctrine concerning the status of women.[35] Christian women simply refused to be ignored. Phillida Bunkle writes:

> The identification of women with spirituality in revival religion ... ultimately implied their special responsibility in the drive toward

social salvation ... (which in turn) led to the attempt to realize the ideals of sanctified womanhood in social action.[36]

Women's studies and raised feminist consciousness naturally gave rise to feminist theology, which according to Denise Ackermann was a necessary development when the pain of sexist oppression came to be examined critically and systematically in the light of Christian faith.[37] Various streams of feminist theology have surfaced in the Western world. The "exclusive," or "revolutionary," sees sexism as the key to all social oppression, while the "inclusive," also called "reformist," sees sexism as one of the structures of oppression, along with racism, classism, and other less dramatic forms.[38] The former, of which women such as Naomi Goldenburg, Carol Christ, and Mary Daly are exponents, attacks the symbols, language and paradigms of the Judeo-Christian tradition in favor of a feminine deity.[39]

It is to be expected that many feminists will overreact to traditional beliefs and institutions in their quest for liberation.[40] Radical feminists have been inclined to reject Christianity and Judaism altogether as hopelessly patriarchal and evil. For them stumbling blocks are found in numerous essential elements of biblical theology, including the masculine identity of God, the person of Jesus Christ, and the entire package of masculine theological language.[41] Other feminists, however, like Patricia Wilson-Kastner, have seen that there is a close relationship between feminism and Christian ideals, and that abandoning tradition altogether would prove counterproductive.[42] Virginia Hearn stresses that a switch to female terminology such as "Mother," "She" and "Her" to describe God is no improvement at all since it creates the problem of a totally female oriented theology.[43] The new *Inclusive Language Lectionary* prepared by the National Council of Churches seems a step in the right direction.[44] Its readings are generic, referring to Jesus as the "Child of God" rather than the "Son of God," and amplifying "God the Father" to "God the Father and Mother." Perhaps something like "God, the Eternal Parent" would be less threatening, but there still remains the problem of selecting pronouns. If the neuter "It" is not suitable, scholars may have to coin an entirely new divine pronoun void of all sexual connotations. But this would mean a return to the "Thee-Thou" language which recent generations have rejected because of its archaic and sacrosanct nature.

Also among radical feminists there has been a concern for female self-awareness, and many advocate an innate perception in women of life and the world which is not only unique but deeper, and quite superior to that typically found in males. But this has brought with it a trend of withdrawal from mainstream society, exclusivism, even lesbianism, as a declaration of self-sufficiency and the androgyny of the whole person.[45]

The key concept in the reformed strain of feminist theology is liberation, which with its concern for praxis found impetus in the relatively new field called liberation theology.[46] Although there are also differences in approach in this rapidly developing theology, key areas of concern include both biblical hermeneutics and Christian theological anthropology as a foundation for establishing a theology of partnership, as opposed to the pyramid of domination which has been prevalent in traditional Christianity. Among the principal exponents of feminist liberation theology are Rosemary Ruether,[47] Letty Russell[48] and Elisabeth Schussler Fiorenza.[49]

In the past two decades feminist liberation theology has developed rapidly with a strong force in Third World countries.[50] Efforts are being directed at awakening world theological sensitivity to the "historic sin" of sexism and formulating both a clear theology and a strategy for accelerating social change.[51] Women's rights movements in Third World countries are centered largely in urban areas and among the social elite and well educated, working to elevate and improve the lot of women without imposing their views on rural and poor women as a class. But at present there are large gaps in our knowledge of these movements, particularly the relationship of churches and female status.[52]

In simple terms, the commitment of feminists has been "to end male ascendancy in society and religion."[53] But Fiorenza points out that today the primary interest of feminist theology lies in calling for a general reconceptualization and revision of accepted theoretical assumptions that are based on the experiences and work of men, and in the process to eliminate patriarchal church structures which have marginalized and silenced women throughout the centuries.[54] Therefore, the focus of concern in feminist theology is not simply furthering the cause of women's rights, but formulating a theology from a woman's unique perspective, which thus far in history has not been done.[55] Particularly among Latin American theologians, consideration is being given to woman's position of "poorest of the poor" as well as her close relationship to the life-giving process, her perception of war and violence, and her concept of the future, all of which has far reaching implications for her contribution to theology.[56]

The World Council of Churches has been most influential in recent years as a supporter of human rights and equality of women. In January 1987 the Central Committee decided to launch an Ecumenical Decade from 1988 to 1998, called Churches in Solidarity with Women. During

that period conferences were held in centers all over the world to promote its objectives, which were outlined as:

1. Empowering women to challenge oppressive structures in the
   global community, their country, and their church.
2. Affirming, through shared leadership, decision making, theology,
   and spirituality, the decisive contributions of women in churches
   and communities.
3. Giving visibility to women's perspectives and actions in the work
   and struggle for justice, peace and integrity of creation.
4. Enabling the churches to free themselves from racism, sexism and
   classism and from teachings and practices that discriminate
   against women and
5. Encouraging churches to take action in solidarity with women.[57]

These objectives, and others, are being recognized globally as essential
aspects of human rights toward which all advancing societies must labor,
and remain as important objectives going into the twenty-first century.

Summary

The connection of sexism and slavery in the early feminist movement assisted in drawing necessary attention to the plight of women
worldwide. The contribution of feminists, even those whose theology is
considered radical, has been valuable in awakening the world to various
levels of social injustice and pushing for elevated consciousness of human
rights and dignity. Many churches saw feminism as a social movement
that was irrelevant to their own doctrines and practices, but its relevance
is undeniable and its impact on Christianity as a whole was inevitable.
This was not an issue or a movement that would go quietly into the night.

Chapter Seven Notes

1. Exodus 21:2–6; Deuteronomy 15:12–18; Leviticus 24:44ff. Kitchen states
that generally a more humane spirit breathes through the Old Testament laws
and customs than were evident in surrounding cultures. K.A. Kitchen, "Slavery,"
New Bible Dictionary, J.D. Douglas, ed. (Grand Rapids: Eerdmans, 1962), p. 1197.
    2. Ephesians 6:5–9; Colossians 3:22; Philemon; I Timothy 6:2.
    3. Jesus, "render unto Caesar...." (Mark 12:14); Paul, "Be subject to the higher
authorities...." (Romans 13:1ff.).

4. H. Richard Niebuhr, *The Social Sources of Denominationalism* (Cleveland: Meridian Books, 1957), pp. 34–37; V.H.H. Green, *Luther and the Reformation* (New York: Capricorn Books, 1964), pp. 137–9.

5. Thornwell, "The Rights and Duties of Masters," quoted by Scanzoni and Hardesty, p. 203.

6. A.D. White, *The History of the Warfare of Science and Theology in Christendom*, Vol. II (New York: Appleton-Century-Crofts, 1955), p. 63.

7. H.A. Hays, *The Dangerous sex: The Myth of Feminine Evil*, p. 99.

8. Russell Prohl, *Women in the Church*, p. 77.

9. Scanzoni and Hardesty, p. 178.

10. *New York Times*, May 17, 1970.

11. Scanzoni and Hardesty, p. 202.

12. Martin E. Marty, *Righteous Empire* (New York: Dial Press, 1970), p. 98.

13. James H. Cohn, *For My People: Black Theology and the Black Church* (Johannesburg: Skotaville, 1985) p. 123; Benjamin Quarles, "Frederick Douglass and the Woman's Rights Movement," *Journal of Negro History*, Vol 25, No. 1, Jan., 1940, pp. 35–44.

14. William Chafe, *Women and Equality* (New York: Oxford, 1977), p. 44.

15. O.S. Fowler, *Creative and Sexual Science, Including Manhood, Womanhood and Their Mutual Interrelatedness, Love, Its Laws, Power, Etc.* (Philadelphia, Chicago & St. Louis: National Publishing Co., 1870).

16. Eleanor Flexner, *Century of Struggle* (New York: Atheneum, 1959), p. 15.

17. An expression which aptly describes the thrust of the demand for equality by women; Carol P. Christ and Judith Plaskow, eds., *Womanspirit Rising: A Feminist Reader in Religion* (San Francisco: Harper and Row, 1979).

18. Donald W. Dayton, *Discovering an Evangelical Heritage* (New York: Harper & Row, 1976), pp. 85–98.

19. Paula D. Nesbitt, *Feminization of the Clergy in America: Occupational and Organizational Perspectives* (New York: Oxford, 1997), pp. 19–20.

20. James Loewenberg and Ruth Bogin (eds.), *Black Women in Nineteenth-Century American Life* (University Park: Pennsylvania State University Press, 1976), p. 235.

21. James H. Cone, *For My People: Black Theology and the Black Church* (Johannesburg: Skotaville, 1985), p. 124; all accounts of the role of Sojourner Truth in the early feminist movement rely on Elizabeth Cady Stanton, Susan B. Anthony and Matilda Joseyn Gage, *History of Woman Suffrage*, Vol. I (Rochester, N.Y.: Susan B. Anthony, 1881).

22. Chafe, p. 104.

23. Chafe, pp. 45–78.

24. Mark Chavez, *Ordaining Women: Culture and Conflict in Religious Organizations* (Cambridge: Harvard, 1997), p. 185. Essay by John Stuart Mill, "The Subjection of Women," 1869.

25. Smith was also black. In 1878 she went to England conducting a two year speaking tour. After that she spent two years as a missionary in India, then eight years in Africa. She only returned to the United States around 1890.

26. Carolyn Gifford, "Profiles of Leadership," *Christianity Today*, Insert (October 3, 1986), p. 11–I.

27. Jo Freeman, *The Politics of Women's Liberation* (New York: David McKay Co., 1975), p. 20.

28. Chafe, p. 32.

29. *Christianity Today*, Vol. 30, No. 14, Introduction to Insert on Christianity Today Institute, p. 3–I.

30. Chafe, pp. 92–3.

31. Inge Lederer Gibel, "The Women of the World Have Won," *The Christian Century* (September 11–18, 1985), pp. 802–4.

32. George C. Bedell, Leo Sandon and Charles T. Wellborn, *Religion in America*, second edition (New York: Macmillan, 1982), p. 264.

33. Jo Freeman, "The Tyranny of Structurelessness," *Berkley Journal of Sociology: A Critical Review* 17 (1972–3), 51–64; Chafe, p. 127–8.

34. Chafe, p. 127–8.

35. Chafe, p. 24.

36. Phillida Bunkle, "Sentimental Womanhood and Domestic Education, 1830–1870," *History of Education Quarterly* (Spring, 1974), pp. 13–30.

37. Denise Ackermann, "Feminist Liberation Theology," *Journal of Theology for Southern Africa* (52: 1985), p. 15.

38. Denise Ackermann, "Liberation and Practical theology: a feminist perspective on ministry," *Journal of Theology for Southern Africa* (52: 1985) p. 33. Sally McFague, *Metaphorical Theology: Models of God in Religious Language* (London: SCM Press, 1982), p. 152.

39. McFague, p. 156.

40. Such a tendency in social revolution is perhaps rooted in Hegelian philosophy. In Christianity it might be seen also in those who become atheists in the struggle to harmonize science and scripture.

41. Mary Daly, *Beyond God the Father* (Boston: Beacon Press, 1973); Naomi Goldberg, *Changing of the Gods* (Boston: Beacon Press, 1979).

42. Patricia Wilson-Kastner, *Faith, Feminism and the Christ* (Philadelphia: Fortress, 1983).

43. Hearn, p. 69.

44. *An Inclusive Language Lectionary* (Philadelphia: Westminster, 1983).

45. See Wilson-Kastner, pp. 12–13. On female poetic and asthetic perception, see Carol Christ, *Diving Deep and Surfacing: Women Writers on Spiritual Quest* (Boston: Beacon, 1980). On special perception in life crises and Jungian psychology of the journey of life, see Penelope Washbourn, *Becoming Woman: the Quest for Wholeness in Female Experience* (New York: Harper and Row, 1975), and Ann Belford Ulanov, *Receiving Woman: Studies in the Psychology and Theology of the Feminine* (Philadelphia: Westminster, 1981).

46. Religious and political conservatives tend to oppose liberation theology as Marxist in origin and nature, and supportive of violent revolution in oppressed countries as a Christian endeavor to bring about positive social change. See "Liberation Theology: Truth or Delusion?" *Personality* (January 30, 1989), pp. 18–21.

47. R.R. Ruether, *Sexism and God-talk* (Boston: Beacon Press, 1983).

48. L.M. Russell (ed.) *Feminist Interpretation of the Bible* (Philadelphia: Westminster Press, 1985).

49. E.S. Fiorenza, "Emerging Issues in Feminist Biblical Interpretation," *Christian Feminism: Visions of a New Humanity*, L. Weldman, ed. (San Francisco: Harper & Row, 1984).

50. At the 1985 conference on "Theological Production of Women in Christian Churches" in Buenos Aires attention centered on defining the specificity of

feminine identity. The Ecumenical Association of Third World Theologians has been working largely from the Asian, African and Latin American perspective. See Rommie Nauta, "Latin American Women Theology," *Exchange* 48:7–31 (December, 1987); Leny Lagerwerf, "South Africa- Women's Struggle in Theology, Church and Society," *Exchange* 48: 33–51 (December, 1987).

51. Rommie Nauta and Berma Klein Goldewijk, "Feminist Perspective in Latin American Liberation Theology," *Exchange*, 48, December, 1987, pp. 1–5; cf. Karen O'Brien, "Feminists to Liberation Theologians Challenge Church on Sin of Sexism" *Latinamerica Press* 18 (1986) 2, pp. 5–6.

52. John C.B. and Ellen Low Webster, eds., *The Church and Women in the Third World* (Philadelphia: Westminster, 1985), pp. 1–18.

53. *Womanspirit Rising: A Feminist Reader in Religion*, ed. Carol P. Christ and Judith Plaskow (San Francisco: Harper & Row, 1979), p. 16.

54. Elisabeth Schussler Fiorenza, "Women: Invisible in Church and Theology," Elisabeth Schussler Fiorenza and Mary Collins, eds., *Concilium: Religion in the Eighties* (Edinburgh: T & T Clark, 1985), pp. x–xi.

55. Leny Lagerwerf, "South Africa—Women's struggle in Theology, Church and Society," *Exchange* Vol. 16, No. 48 (December, 1987), p. 36.

56. Elsa Tamez, "Women, Church and Theology," *Ladoc* 14 (1984) 5, pp. 2–5.

57. *Dialogue & Alliance* Vol. 2, No. 3 (Fall, 1988); cf. *Women In A Changing World* 23:4 (June, 1987).

Chapter Eight

CHURCHES AND DIVERGENT PATHS

From the late nineteenth century until the present many churches have been forced to reexamine their views on the status of women, and subsequently many have made significant doctrinal and organizational changes. The process has been driven primarily by female scholars, each having taken on the challenge of justifying change against cultural bias, church tradition, and the prevalent interpretation of scripture.

In this chapter treatment is given first to the various approaches taken by biblical feminists and the resulting changes made by specific denominations. These are contrasted with those churches continuing to hold to tradition against the overwhelming tide of change. Special attention is given to the Disciples of Christ and the Churches of Christ as an illustration of the divergent paths taken by churches coming from essentially the same conservative theological roots.

I. Hermeneutical Approaches

The difference between liberal and conservative theology is typically defined in terms of hermeneutics and views of inspiration.[1] Such a distinction is important in order to understand the means by which scholars or denominations have come to decisions on the status of women. Sakenfeld distinguishes three interpretive styles applied to the Bible by feminists, and therefore the approaches by which change within specific denominations might be justified: first, looking specifically at selective texts and viewing the Bible as an authoritative guide in life and social order; second, viewing biblical texts generally as a guide in overall perspectives on justice and social order; and third, looking at the entire Bible, noting that some texts are not authoritative and have no bearing on life today.[2]

Of these, the first is clearly conservative in that it is based on a rigid devotion to biblical authority and inerrancy. Therefore, biblical feminists are those who favor female elevation, but who are also devoted the authority of scripture and are compelled to reconcile the two. Biblical feminists fall into two major camps. The hierarchialists, or complementarians, insist that females are subordinate to males based on the order of creation and the *kephale* doctrine of Paul. These scholars advocate greater participation by women in activities of the church but contend that woman's role, by the will and design of God, must remain in submission to male authority.[3] Many in this camp argue that this approach promotes true liberation and dignity for women.[4] Diana Hagee, wife of John Hagee of the Cornerstone Church, states that submission is a position of strength for the Christian wife, whose duty is to "kill the will at the cross of Christ and follow out of obedience."[5]

The egalitarians argue female equality before God, and therefore the right of women to serve in churches in capacities equal to those of men, but they still hold to biblical authority. Jewett, one of the earliest biblical feminists, suggested a partnership model from Genesis Creation Narrative based on the nature of God as asexual.[6] Like Jewett, proponents of this model see both male and female as created in the likeness of God, and ministry to human need must therefore be performed by both sexes in order to truly represent God in the world. Some egalitarians, like Hardesty and Scanzoni, arrive at their conclusions by interpreting Paul's use of *kephale* as "source" and thereby removing the notion that the husband is the head of the wife.[7] Others build their model on Paul's suggestions in Ephesians 5 concerning "mutual submission."[8]

However they approach it, the agenda of biblical feminists is to solve the problem and at the same time preserve the authority of scripture. The problem with this hermeneutical approach is that it begins with a questionable presupposition and then attempts to harmonize the Bible with current trends, often at the expense of scholastic honesty and common sense. Of course, conservatives charge that liberal feminists also begin with a questionable presupposition that women are equal, despite tradition and biblical doctrine, and then are forced to denounce biblical authority based on social change. But this is precisely where their paths diverge. The liberal position is not bound to a fixed tradition or to a rigid view of biblical authority, and is willing to adjust and modify church doctrine to respond to human circumstance. This posture does not limit divine activity in human history to one church, or to any current understanding of the biblical message, but readily acknowledges social development as one method or source of spiritual enlightenment. And it is undeniable that the church has been embarrassed repeatedly in history because of its presupposition of the infallibility and authority of scripture. Therefore, while this method has resulted in change in some conservative churches, the change is for the most part superficial and misleading.

II. Churches Abandoning Tradition

The visions of unity among believers held by Thomas Campbell and his son Alexander proved to be illusionary. By the turn of the twentieth century two major groups had parted company, not strictly by name but by their position on doctrinal issues such as instrumental music in worship, missionary societies, the status of women, and others, issues arising out of different views of inspiration and biblical authority. Further division would follow among the more conservative groups. While Campbell, Barton W. Stone and other leaders of the Restoration Movement were essentially fundamentalists, those who would become the Disciples of Christ moved considerably to the left.[9] It is ironic that today the Disciples of Christ are quite proud of their Stone-Campbell roots, but have little in common with Campbell's doctrinal beliefs.

The first woman to be ordained among Disciples of Christ is generally thought to be Clara Hale Babcock in 1888. Although Babcock worked primarily as an evangelist conducting revival meetings in Illinois and Iowa, she also pastored four churches during her 29 year ministry. However, there is evidence that several less known women were officially ordained by Disciples churches before Babcock: Ellen Grant Gustin and Ema B. Frank in or around 1873, and Melissa Garrett in 1867.[10]

Also during this time women's missionary societies were springing up in many denominations.[11] While the very existence of a missionary society in the church was opposed by the conservative element of the Disciples, The Christian Woman's Board of Missions became a strong force in the advocacy of women's leadership in the church and provided an important vehicle of service for women. The CWBM was founded by Caroline Neville Pearre in 1874, supported by Isaac Errett, editor of the *Christian Standard* and president of the American Christian Missionary Society. Marie Butler Jameson was elected the first president.[12]

Additionally, in a controversial service in 1883, three other women were ordained along with their husbands by the General Missionary Society. All of these were surrounded by controversy. During the years 1892–93 an intense debate raged in the pages of the *Christian Standard*, with the majority of the contributors favoring women's ordination.[13] Today Disciples women have free access to any and all positions of leadership in the church, at least theoretically, whether local, area, regional or national. Local boards of elders typically include women, and as suggested in the Introduction of this study, worship services in Disciples churches include women in every area of leadership. However, as in other denominations, female ministers in Disciples churches do not receive equal pay for the same position, and fewer of them are able to enter senior pastorates directly out of seminary.[14] This supports the general assumption that while there is clear and salubrious progress, women have not yet found total equity even among the more progressive churches.

Other denominations that took a progressive stance in the nineteenth century include the Congregationalists. The first woman to be ordained by this group was Antoinette Brown, in 1853. Significantly, in the ordination sermon by Luther Lee, justification for this action was found in identifying "preaching" with "prophecy" in the first century church.[15] The United Church of Christ also began ordaining women in the late 1800s, and today has about a thousand clergywomen among its 1.4 million members.[16] The earliest female leadership in American churches includes Judith Sargent Murray, who was licensed by the Universalists around 1790. Full ordination came later, Olympia Brown probably being the first in 1890. The Unitarians ordained Celia Burleigh in 1869, and 70 others in 1890.[17]

The United Methodist Church approved licensing women to preach in 1919 and ordained them in 1924. In 1956 the final formalities were completed which granted women equality with men as members of annual conferences.[18] Today this church has 1,500 female ordained ministers; two of its 46 bishops are women and one of them is black. Dr. Marjorie Mathews was the first female bishop in history, installed in 1980. The Methodists are also credited with sanctioning women as foreign missionaries very early, and the Women's Foreign Missionary Society, now called the United Methodist Women, has been one of the largest women's movements in history boasting a membership of more than 2 million around the world.[19]

The United Presbyterian Church also voted to ordain women in 1956. But this also was after long debate. Louisa Woosley was denied ordination in 1889, and then endorsed as a lay evangelist half a century later. Today there are more than a thousand women in clerical positions in that church, including executive presbytery, although many churches were reluctant to follow through.[20] The World Alliance of Reformed churches (WARC) has 120 member churches worldwide, including Presbyterian, United and Reformed churches, of which 92 member churches are now ordaining women.[21]

The Episcopal Church (the American branch of the Anglican Church) reinstituted the office of deaconess in 1970 and in 1973 ordained eleven women to the priesthood, although the latter was not sanctioned by the General Convention until three years later. As of June 1, 1987, there were 1,167 ordained women, of whom 371 were deacons and 796 were priests, including 110 rectors. In 1989 Barbara C. Harris, a former civil rights activist, became the first female bishop in the Episcopal Church. Although some bishops continue to oppose it, the church has declared it acceptable and since then several women have been consecrated as bishops, both in the United States and Canada. The issue still is very sensitive among the 120 Episcopalian dioceses and some feel it will end in a split.[22] But generally women are being accepted as effective leaders in the church. At the 1985 General Convention 202 of the 912 Deputies were women, and 11 of the 40 members of the Executive Council are women.[23]

Heated debate continued to rage within the Anglican Church whose tradition, like that of the Roman Catholic Church, holds women to be unfit to consecrate the bread and wine of communion and to give absolution. This priestly role can only be filled by those who, like Jesus Christ, are of the masculine gender.[24] Discussion on this issue in the Anglican Church began more than a century ago.[25] In 1898 a petition signed by 1,100 women was presented to the Upper House of the Canterbury Convocation protesting the exclusion of women from parochial church councils. Charles Gore, Bishop of Oxford (1911–19), gave strong support for the participation of women in the government of the church until such was granted in 1919.[26] But even then opponents contended that eventually it would lead to the ordination of women, to the detriment of the church.

The Anglican Church determines policy by a two-thirds vote in three houses, namely the bishops, the clergy and the laity. In 1986 the ordination of women failed in all three, although it did receive a majority vote. This failure came in the face of the Archbishop of Canterbury Robert Prince's firm declaration that he would support it and his prediction that if not approved now it was certain to come in the future. But it seemed likely also to drive a wedge between the provinces of Canterbury and York, since the Bishop of London, Dr. Graham Leonard, remained a major opponent.[27] In 1988 the Lambeth Conference on women bishops in the Anglican Church, conducted at Canterbury, England, failed to resolve the problem totally, although churches in the United States, Canada, New Zealand, Hong Kong, Kenya and Uganda were accepting women priests. Bishops at the conference voted to respect decisions made by each church body.[28] South African Archdeacon Anthony Kriels said that in his country the church was still not ready to change this deeply rooted tradition.[29] In May and June of 1988 the status of women was the topic of discussion at the 26th Provincial Synod of the Anglican Church in Southern Africa, held in Durban. The author was there. After the failure to obtain the necessary two-thirds majority vote to grant ordination to women, Chris Ahrends, chaplain to the Archbishop of Capetown, Desmond Tutu, asked to be dismissed from the priesthood to serve only as a deacon as an act of solidarity with women.[30] In Australia the issue continued to be hotly debated also, the prevalent view being traditional.[31] However, in November of 1992 the tide turned and the necessary two-thirds vote gave women the right to ordination in the Anglican Church.[32]

The Assemblies of God are, like other Pentecostal groups, considered to be conservative. Following traditional views of marriage, they believe the husband to be the head of the house and the wife subordinate to his authority. However, on the matter of women's role in the church, they have adopted a position which to their satisfaction retains a value for the authority of scripture and at the same time allows for female leadership. The General Council Bylaws state:

> The Scriptures plainly teach that divinely called and qualified women may also serve the church in the ministry of the Word (Joel 2:29; Acts 21:9; I Corinthians 11:5). Women who have developed in the ministry of the Word so that their ministry is acceptable generally, and who have proved their qualifications in actual service, and who have met all the requirements of the credentials committees of the district councils, are entitled to whatever grade of credentials their qualifications warrant and the right to administer the ordinances of the church when such acts are necessary.[33]

One of the shining stars in early Assemblies of God history was Aimee Semple McPherson, whom they ordained as an evangelist in 1919. Denominational loyalties were less rigid in those days, and Aimee was very popular all over the United States and Canada. By 1922 she held some form of official ministry status in numerous Holiness and Pentecostal churches, as well as the Methodist Episcopal Church in Philadelphia and the First Baptist Church in San Jose. The latter was quite controversial and was never ratified by the Baptist Association. Her ability appealed broadly across denominational lines, and her meetings were always ecumenical and interdenominational. Among her successes was a radio ministry out of Los Angeles. She was the first woman to receive an FCC license to operate a radio station. In 1923 she founded the International Church of the Foursquare Gospel, which today claims 24,000 churches and 2.8 million members worldwide. McPherson was mentor to black evangelist Emma Cotton, a woman of great significance in the early years of the Church of God in Christ.[34]

According to Joseph R. Flower, General Secretary for the General Council, the Assemblies of God in 1986 had a total of 3,718 women with ministerial credentials, including 1,588 whom they recognize as ordained ministers. The larger number constitutes nearly fourteen percent of the total credentialed ministers in the Assemblies of God, although only 276 of these women pastor churches. It is also noteworthy that 1,534 of that total are married to credentialed ministers. More than 700 have husbands who are not ministers and 671 are single. Another 728 are widowed.[35]

The Brethren in Christ Church, like the Assemblies of God, continues to uphold the traditional hierarchy of marriage as ordained of God, but has granted the right to women to engage in any form of ministry and to be ordained to positions of church leadership.[36] The Moravian Church has also made changes in spite of internal tension. According to a doctrinal statement adopted in 1981 by the Unity Synod of the Unitas Fratrum, this brotherhood recognizes the call to ordination of women as well as men. Apparently in recent times some congregations were prepared to accept women only as associate pastors, but a statement from the Southern Province of the Moravian Church in America makes it clear that candidates for all positions must be considered without discrimination.[37]

In 1965 the American Baptist Convention adopted a resolution, which was affirmed in 1980, stating that there should be no differential treatment of men and women in the church, family or society, and that there should be equal opportunity for full participation by women in the work of God. To this end churches were urged to engage in study and action that would result in implementation of this resolution internationally.[38] As of May, 1987, there were only 147 women pastors, which is three percent of the total number of pastors in American Baptist Churches. However there were 114 female ministers of education, and 124 women in positions of associate pastor, interim pastor, youth and music minister. More than 200 hundred were serving as missionaries outside the United States, and about forty served as chaplains and pastoral counselors. Ten were classified as educators in colleges and seminaries.[39]

Another group which should be mentioned here are the Evangelicals. This broad range of churches hold a strong commitment to a conservative hermeneutical approach to scripture. Yet Evangelical scholars at a number of seminaries and colleges have published books and articles supportive of broader roles for women in the church.[40] Some have changed their position on female ordination, and others have not.

The Seventh Day Adventists are also undergoing changes in spite of their dedication to following scripture. John C. Brunt, dean of the School of Theology at Walla Walla College, argues that among Adventists a literal and fundamental interpretation of relevant New Testament passages cannot disallow the ordination of women simply because such is not an issue in the literal and historical context.[41] Although this has been controversial, the key role of Ellen G. White in their movement paved the way to a broader and more progressive understanding of the role of women than in most other conservative groups. Today Adventist churches are accepting women in the roles of pastor and elder.

There is diversity among black churches on the issue of gender equality. James H. Cone, professor of Systematic Theology at Union Theological Seminary, points out that black women in the church have carried a burden even greater than the double jeopardy of racism and sexism suffered by black women in general, in fact a "triple jeopardy." From the beginning of women suffrage black churches in America agreed with Sojourner Truth, Ida Wells and Harriett Tubman regarding white racism, but it did not support their views on women's rights.[42] Black attitudes toward women ministers remained similar to that of white denominations, and for similar reasons.[43]

The African Methodist Episcopal church is a prime example. Largely because women were insisting they also had a calling from God, the AME created the offices of stewardess in 1869 and deaconess in 1900. But in spite of its progressive nature, as compared to other black churches, the AME had difficulty in granting women the right to preach. Although some women were granted licenses to preach, this denomination did not make it official until 1884, and even then it was limited to the subordinate office of "evangelist." Bishop Henry McNeal Turner was publicly reprimanded for ordaining a woman, stated clearly by the General Conference in 1888:

> Whereas Bishop H. M. Turner has seen fit to ordain a woman to the order of a deacon; and whereas said act is contrary to the usage of our church, and without precedent in any other body of Christians in the known world; and as it cannot be proved by the scriptures that a woman has ever been ordained to the order of the ministry; therefore be it enacted that the bishops of the African Methodist Episcopal Church be and hereby (are) forbidden to ordain a woman to the order of deacon or elder in our church.[44]

In spite of general opposition, the nineteenth and early twentieth centuries saw a number of outstanding black female preachers, the most famous being Jarena Lee of the AME.[45] Cone asserts that the civil rights struggles of the 1960s and '70s reinforced sexism in the black community, particularly in the church. The attitude of black males remained harshly traditional, suggested by the alleged words of Stokely Carmichael: "The only position for women in the SNCC is prone."[46] Black preachers during that era became strong advocates of women's inferiority. Cone states:

> As some white male ministers began to retreat in the face of emerging power of the woman's movement in the seminary and church, black clergymen laughed at white men's inability to keep women in their place. At the same time they mimicked white antifeminist conservatives by preaching about the value of the American family in which wives are subordinate to their husbands. This was the sanctimonious—supposedly biblical—version of the male revolutionary's demand that black women stand behind their men.[47]

The black movement in the USA was largely controlled by black theologians and ministers. The only woman asked to sign the "Black Power Statement" issued by the National Conference of Black Churchmen in 1966 was Dr. Anna Hedgeman, author and staff member of the NCC commission on race and religion. Black male theology was criticized by a few significant women, such as Pauli Murray, an Episcopal priest and lawyer, and Theressa Hoover, an executive of the board of Global Ministries of the United Methodist Church.[48]

Matters began to change in black theology in the middle 1970s, but only after confrontation. Cone reflects upon his caution in presenting a paper at Union Theological Seminary in October of 1976:

> If my paper can be compared to that of a southern white liberal, the reactions of many black male seminarians were similar to those of most reactionary southern white racists. They quoted the Bible to justify that women should not be ordained, and some even insisted that they should not even be in the pulpit.[49]

Cone was shocked, but his black female colleagues were not. This reaction made clear the need for a black feminist theology, which is developing today under the leadership of women like Pauli Murray, Katie Cannon, Delores Williams, Kelly Brown and Cherl Gilkes.[50]

During the '80s and '90s as black female theologians from the USA encountered women of various Third World Countries, for example at WCC and other ecumenical gatherings, they were struck by the realization that the triple jeopardy of black American women is but a shallow image of the global plight of women, both in and out of the Christian tradition, and which requires a solidarity with all non–European women.

This awakening itself may have helped bring about change. After 213 years of struggle for civil rights, in 2000 the AME elected Vashti McKenzie as its first woman bishop.[51]

It appears that from the early nineteenth century those individuals and denominations who led the way to gender equality were motivated by a broader vision than tradition had allowed coupled with a less rigid view of biblical authority. Conservative churches took longer to change, and generally did so by reinterpreting key passages so as to preserve their view of biblical authority. In 1973 there were around 6,000 clergywomen in all American denominations and in 1995 the number had risen to 50,000.[52] At least eighty Protestant denominations are now ordaining women. In 1986 a woman was elected as the commanding general of the Salvation Army.[53]

III. Churches Holding to Tradition

There are other churches, however, that continue to hold to the traditional position on the status of women, despite social trends, internal pressure, and fervent reexamination of scripture. Among them is the world's largest Christian denomination with more than 62 million members—the Roman Catholic Church. One of the earliest scholarly works on women in Christian tradition was produced by George Tavard, who writes concerning the position of the Roman Catholic Church:

> Although the world of the twentieth century has passed through a series of catastrophes, modern men have not recovered the primitive Christian vision of, and wish for, the swift return of the Lord. Far from longing for the end, they dread it. And recurrent dissatisfaction with material progress is not such as to send them to solitude in whatever deserts are left by the population explosion; on the contrary it has inspired an ever more strenuous search for earthly happiness. The intellectual world did not change in depth between the end of the Roman empire and the beginning of the modern world in the sixteenth and seventeenth centuries. Moreover, since religious institutions are generally of a more conservative bent than secular organizations, the theological mind has evolved more slowly than its secular counterpart. For these reasons, the contemporary ideas about women that are assumed in Catholic theology have preserved substantially the same principles as the theology of Augustine of Hippo and Thomas Aquinas.[54]

Contemporary Catholicism has put forth a couple of what Tavard calls "models" for womanhood to cope with her changing social station.

In October, 1965, during the Second Vatican Council, two American bishops submitted to the relevant commission suggestions concerning the
church's position on women, and their suggestions represent two completely different philosophies.

The late Archbishop Paul Hallinan of Atlanta confessed that the
church has been very slow in denouncing the degradation of women in a
form of slavery, and offered four proposals to help rectify this injustice:

1. That the Church redefine liturgical functions of women to allow
   them to serve certain sacraments, and in essence reestablish the
   ancient order of deaconess.
2. That the scheme include women in the instruments to be set up
   after the council to further the lay apostolate.
3. That women have representation in present and post-conciliar
   agencies and other interests.
4. That opportunity should be given to women, both as sisters and
   laywomen, to offer their talents to the ministry of the Church.[55]

In contrast, Bishop Fulton Sheen offered a perspective which defined
the proper role of women in terms of "purity, protection of the weak,
sacrifice, procreation and the sustaining of human life," all of which cor-
respond to the tender motherly instinct and which he sees as essential in
counterbalancing the masculine administrative rigidity. He then outlined
a broader role for Christian women in the economic, social and cultural
realm which might be thought of as merely an extension of the traditional
role, and concluded that every woman, without exception, is morally oblig-
ated to realize one of these forms of motherhood.

Tavard points out that both of these contributions to the Council
were concerned with promoting women in the Church and the world. But
the first suggests basically an idea the Gospel of Thomas attributes to
Jesus, that "Every woman who makes herself a man will enter the kingdom of heaven;" that equality between the sexes is achieved when a woman
forfeits motherhood and sexuality to live as a celibate male. The other
merely offers a patronizing extension of the female's realm of servitude,
making the world her domicile and society her children, but retaining the
same status of subordination to the male. In neither position is there genuine equality.

A third model is suggested by writers such as Gertrude Von Le Fort,
which seems to have originated in Aristotle and was transmitted into the
Middle Ages through Thomas Aquinas. The image of Mary is spiritually
intertwined in Christian womanhood, wherein there is the dual mission

of protecting virginity, symbolic of virtue in general, and of devoted motherhood. Woman is from design an essentially receptive and passive entity. Her anonymous role in history as the transmitter of life, the passive instrument of nature and man, gives woman a spiritual significance reflective of the Holy Spirit and therefore in a sense greater than that of the male.[56]

A fourth model came from Pope Paul VI, who also extolled motherhood, but admitted that defining woman's role in terms of the home and family is given added significance because of the special social problems of the modern world.[57] Thus, in training of children, teaching religious traditions and guarding social virtue through influence in the home, women are glorified as the shapers of the future. Beyond this, in an address delivered in 1966, the Pope painted a moving vision of womanhood which finds her greatest importance in symbolism.[58] In woman, he stated, is to be seen the purest reflection of the creator in that she is the source of life. She represents ultimate moral purity. In her self-giving she is man's closest companion. She is especially sensitive to cultural and social values, by nature aspiring to be religious, and in all these is both the image and vision of ideal humanity.

More recently, Pope John Paul II has issued perhaps the most passionate espousal of women's equality ever by the Roman Catholic hierarchy. In an apostolic letter titled *Mulieris Dignitatem*, issued September 30, 1988, the pope takes up the language and sentiments of the women's rights movement, going so far as to denounce all prejudice and discrimination against women in everyday life as sinful but reaffirming Catholicism's centuries old ban against women priests. He defines motherhood and virginity as the two major vocations for women. However, the pope does break with earlier Catholic models for womanhood in that he sees the dominion of the husband over the wife as a loss of stability and equality in the ideal marriage union, a problem linked to original sin. Cardinal Joseph Ratzinger, head of the Congregation for the Doctrine of the Faith, described the 120 page letter as a "permanent interpretation" of church teachings, unlikely to be changed.[59]

An essential problem in Catholic doctrine is a theology which renders woman unsuitable for any sacramental function,[60] and incapable of receiving the "indelible character" which their holy orders confer.[61] One Roman Catholic theologian explains it in these terms:

> The reason ... for denying women the right to teach is a reason that is absolute and universal, based on the natural condition of inferiority and subjection that is the position of women.[62]

All the above Roman Catholic models fail to deal with the real issues of inequity. Both Paul VI and John Paul II did little more than patronize, giving woman dimensions of grandeur meaningful only as visions and symbols without compromising the inequity which persists in practical terms.

Some have described Catholic models as openly "schizophrenic," seeing woman as weak and the symbol of evil while attempting at the same time to idealize her as the symbol of transcendent goodness. Persistent efforts to praise and idealize the Virgin Mary are equally contradictory in dealing realistically with modern Christianity. In one way or another all current Catholic models glorify the same sexual polarization, still confining women to traditional roles and viewing them as inferior, subordinate and tainted with evil.[63]

Not only do many Catholics feel that full ordination is in order for women, but they also believe that priests and nuns should have the privilege of marrying. But since Catholicism claims to be the oldest and truest line of the Christian Church, tradition has a solid foothold. Since 1966 the number of Catholic women in religious orders has dropped a full third, from 180,000 to 120,699. According to Sister Marjorie Tuite, a Dominican nun and coordinator for the National Association of Religious Women, a major complaint is that while women outnumber men in offices of the dioceses in the United States, they have no access in the Roman Catholic institutional church structure. "The Pope can talk with Lutheran bishops," she says, "but he cannot sit down and dialogue with women who have given their whole life to the church."[64]

Since Vatican II there has been little progress in the status of Catholic women, except heightened interest and concern among Catholic bishops. But organizations such as the Leadership Conference of Women Religious continue to push for change at every level.[65] One of the most comprehensive statements from the feminist element of Catholicism is a collection of essays titled "Women: Invisible in Church and Theology" in *Concilium.*[66] Marie Zimmermann argues that new code of Canon Law, promulgated in 1983, does not really change the age old Catholic legislation which in practical terms declares women neither suitable for the clergy nor eligible to enjoy all the prerogatives of members of the laity. Within the Catholic Church functional rights and power (*sacra potestas*) belong only to baptized males, whether married or celibate.[67] Furthermore, Margaret Brennan charges that Canon Law is very carefully structured so as to keep women silent, invisible and powerless. The activities of women in ecclesiastical communities, designated as "women religious," remain controlled by means of cloister (enclosure) as they have been for centuries, and are regulated by prescriptions in Canon Law covering Institutes of Consecrated Life.[68] Therefore, the Catholic Church has developed and maintained a complex system of laws and orders designed to protect its tradition and to keep its women under control, with no hint of possible change. Pope John Paul, in his 1994 Apostolic Letter *Ordinatio Sacerdotalis*, stated emphatically that priestly ordination is reserved only for males, it is not subject to debate, and this position is held definitively by all the faithful.[69]

Southern Baptists, the largest Protestant (non–Catholic) denomination, are among the mainstream conservative churches in America's "Bible belt," and represent a major segment of Christians holding to the traditional subordination of women. According to some reports, more than 300 women have been ordained in Southern Baptist churches. But in October of 1986 the Home Mission Board of the Southern Baptist Convention voted to disallow women from official ordination, upholding traditional discrimination against them in the arena of church leadership. Feminists in that group were outraged and defiant. At a meeting in St. Louis the Steering Committee agreed that "Women will continue to answer God's call, and God will continue to choose whomever God wills, regardless of the vote of a board of fallible human beings."[70] Conventions in Oklahoma and California have struck from their membership those churches which have ordained women as pastors or deacons. Jimmy Draper, then president for the Southern Baptist Convention, stated that the issue should not be a test of orthodoxy. And it seems that among Southern Baptists the debate has more to do with whether the Convention has a right to tell a church who it can ordain than whether ordaining a women is theologically sound.[71] The debate has continued, but the official position remained unchanged going into the twenty-first century.

The Free Will Baptist churches in America can be traced to the influence of New England Baptists of Arminian persuasion, as opposed to those holding Augustinian-Calvinistic views on the sovereignty of God. This fellowship of churches allows each other considerable latitude in certain aspects of doctrine and practice, and offers no legislation on the status of women. Throughout the years some women have been ordained, but there seems to be a trend toward a more conservative posture at the present time.[72]

Those churches known as the Plymouth Brethren, an appellation disliked by them, have no formal organization or creed. However, Davis Duggins, publisher of *Interest* magazine and a representative of this group in public relations, says that the subject of women's ministry is currently a major topic of discussion among them. He writes:

> The traditional position has been to interpret the restrictive passages
> of Scripture very literally. Hence, women did not participate vocally

in public meetings, nor hold official leadership positions. In addition, most brethren churches encourage women to wear a head covering during public meetings.[73]

Duggins goes on to explain, however, that in recent years some Brethren churches have modified these positions, and changes are still occurring. They do not have ordination, in the same sense as other denominations do, and only recognize God's individual calling into areas of full-time Christian service. Women might be commended, but their work will never include public preaching or administrative duties usually associated with the traditional concept of minister, pastor or priest.

The Evangelical Free Church has ordained women in the past but now does not. The term "evangelical" can be applied to a large number of churches, many of whom are members of organizations that overtly use that name. Their doctrine borders on fundamentalism though generally evangelicals do not like that label, preferring to see their roots in Barth's "neo-orthodoxy."[74] According to Kenneth Kantzer, president of Trinity Evangelical Divinity School in Deerfield, Illinois, the issue will not be resolved within evangelical circles for at least another generation.[75] Virginia Hearn states that the evangelical feminist movement in North America is still comparatively small. At the 1973 meetings of Evangelicals for Social Action, caucuses were formed to promote feminism, resulting in The Evangelical Women's Caucus formed in 1978. But only a fraction of evangelical churches are associated with it today.[76]

Churches of Christ today number more than 13,000 in the USA, the largest being Madison Church of Christ in Nashville, Tennessee, claiming more than 4,000 members.[77] They have perhaps 3 million members total, although figures are difficult to obtain from outside the United States. Their watchwords, coined by Thomas Campbell, are, "Speak where the Bible speaks and be silent where the Bible is silent." Some of the doctrines which identify Churches of Christ are baptism by immersion for the remission of sins, plural eldership in each congregation, a capella singing, the Lord's Supper each Sunday, autonomy of each congregation, and opposition to written creeds. Members of this group have had the reputation, and deservingly so, for believing that they are the only true church, the restored church of the New Testament, and consequently the only body of saved people among all Christian denominations. Their body of doctrine is thought to be "the faith once delivered" for which they must earnestly contend (Jude 3). Leaders typically take a strong vocal stand against any doctrine they perceive as of human origin,[78] and express their fervor for unity among believers by denouncing "the evils of denominationalism."

An intense sectarian spirit has resulted in a history of feuds and squabbles within and among congregations.

Some members of the Church of Christ recognize that this approach to unity has produced more division than it has resolved. Since their split with the Disciples of Christ around 1900, numerous other splits have occurred over issues like church cooperation (in funding orphans' homes, colleges, and care facilities for the aged), multiple cups in the Lord's Supper, fellowship of divorced persons, Sunday school classes for children, kitchens in the church buildings, headcoverings for women in the assembly, and many others.[79] In each case the divisive issue hinges on whether such a practice is "scriptural" in terms of a fundamental adherence to the New Testament "pattern" for faith and practice.

Among Churches of Christ the prevalent interpretation of biblical passages concerning the status of women is quite traditional.[80] Women are characteristically very active in the life of the church, serving and working in many capacities. But what they are permitted and assigned to do is overshadowed by the principle of subjection to male authority. Interpretation of pertinent scriptures is essentially the same as that of the Plymouth Brethren. Women do not preach, teach mixed adult classes, lead singing or prayers in a public assembly, hold any recognized church office or do anything which might be interpreted as having authority over a man.[81]

As is the case in other churches, the status of women in the Church of Christ presents an obvious conundrum. Many of their women have master's and doctor's degrees, and serve on school boards, teach in universities, hold executive positions in business, and make public addresses in secular or academic assemblies. But in the context of church assembly and organization they are required to take a back seat. The entire problem revolves around the same two concepts which undergird Pauline doctrine: first, the alleged "authority" of men over women; and second, that segment of church life deemed "worship." But how this is applied in practice seems arbitrary and inconsistent. Women generally prepare the elements for the Lord's Supper, but they cannot serve them during the assembly. They may sing as part of the congregation and say "amen" at the end of prayers, but they cannot lead a public prayer, sing a solo, direct a choir or lead the entire congregation in song. They may ask questions in a Bible class, read scripture aloud and even make comments, but they cannot make announcements to the whole congregation or read scripture in the "worship service." Many women hold lecturing and administrative posts in Church of Christ colleges and universities,[82] but are excluded from teaching the Bible or related subjects. Churches of Christ commonly have

secretaries who handle a major part of the office management, and it is
not uncommon for a deacon's wife to assist her husband with his assigned
work, if not do it for him. But these dedicated women are not permitted
to be called ministers or deacons.

It would be unfair to assert that these role distinctions are totally
fixed and enforced by men. Among the women of the Churches of Christ
there has developed a well defined gender-role conscience by which strict
regulations are self-imposed. Most are very sensitive to what they understand to be their proper place and would not lead a public prayer if so
permitted. So much is the case that when a boy of twelve has been baptized, his female Sunday school teacher might feel uncomfortable teaching him and will insist on his being removed to a class taught by a man.
Should a man walk into a ladies' class taught by a woman, she will either
insist on his leaving, or will ask him to teach in her stead. Many women
in the Church of Christ will not pray in front of a man, not even at the
family table; only at their children's bedside.

Change of doctrine among Churches of Christ is exceptionally
difficult. There is no headquarters or general synod where such issues can
be resolved for the entire denomination. The practice of "withdrawal of
fellowship" has provided each congregation a defense against perceived
heresy. Hence anyone who becomes too vociferous on a delicate issue is
either silenced, pressured to leave or is officially disfellowshipped by the
local church, and entire congregations that veer off the traditional path
are repudiated by the rest. Steve Sandifer attests to this fact with regard
to one church attempting to install deaconesses four decades ago.[83] The
same thing has happened more recently, with similar results, and moving
into the twenty-first century there appear to be no churches where deaconesses have been appointed. To do such is to abandon the faith. Therefore, by controlling financial resources and keeping a tight rein on pulpits,
the conservative element of the "brotherhood" manages to maintain a well
defined doctrine without the benefit of a written creed. The practice of
congregational autonomy, with no form of central headquarters or conventions to determine policy, also limits democratic voice and hinders mass
change in policy. Furthermore, local church elders are for the most part
"laymen" with little or no biblical, theological or ecclesiastical education.
Consequently, several generations of leadership in Churches of Christ have
had a very limited grasp of major theological issues or the implications of
their hermeneutical posture. A large percentage of Church of Christ ministers are non-degreed, holding diplomas from church financed schools of
preaching. Comparatively few hold graduate degrees. Consequently, control of brotherhood thinking lies with schools of preaching and various

conservative publications, both of which tend to serve as tools of indoctrination rather than education.[84]

Regardless, today the Church of Christ is experiencing an identity crisis involving a number of issues, all of which hinge upon hermeneutics.[85] The "brotherhood" has suffered considerable internal criticism for its inconsistency both in doctrine and practice, particularly with regard to the status of women. In the mid–1970s Hoy Ledbetter, Normon Parks, Bobbey Lee Holley and a few others were quite vocal on the issue of women in the church, although their message was strongly denounced.[86] Today there is evidence of movement, supported by an academic circle who are more objective than those who write with an agenda of doctrinal apologetics. Carroll Osburn, Professor of New Testament at Abilene Christian University, has edited an exceptional collection of scholarly essays on women in the church, and overall the views of the contributors are anything but traditional. Among them, Frederick Norris concludes that "women in church leadership is biblical."[87] Only time will tell the impact that this research might have on local churches.

There are a few churches taking slow but certain steps away from this exceptionally narrow tradition.[88] Stephen Sandifer, in a thorough examination of deaconesses in Christian history written largely from the standpoint of Church of Christ tradition, urges change and concludes optimistically:

> In years to come, one congregation will have no deacons, another will have deacons, and another will have deacons male and female. Hopefully these congregations will respect the autonomy of each other and the attempts of the leadership to be true to the Word in their ministry for God.[89]

Despite his affinity for change, Sandifer writes from the perspective of traditional female subjection. He advocates the existence of deaconesses in the primitive church and the acceptability of this role of service today, but he is careful to declare that even deaconesses are not ordained officers or evangelists and that they have always been under the authority of men.

Some churches have appointed women to positions called "special servants" or "ministry leaders," which are comparable to deaconesses but with an innocuous title. Others permit women to teach adult classes, serve at the Lord's Table, and lead public prayers and congregational singing.[90] All such efforts are being met with criticism, and large groups of churches have withdrawn fellowship from certain congregations for this kind of practice. But it appears that such actions are no longer a deterrent to churches with positive and independent vision. As worded a decade ago by James E. Howard, minister for the White Station Church of Christ in Memphis: "The next great issue in the church will most certainly be that of the role of women."[91] The status of women may prove to be a test issue that will demand a reassessment of the entire self-definition and doctrine of the Churches of Christ, and if so holds the potential for building bridges of communication toward unity, rather than forcing further division.

Summary

Of the many churches that have accepted ordination of women, there are essentially two categories. Liberal churches made this transition with the greatest ease, since it posed no threat to their theology and represents a significant element of their world view. The other category consists of various conservative churches who managed to dismiss patriarchal doctrines in the New Testament as transitory and irrelevant, or simply reinterpreted them to remove the restrictive impact. But most of these continue to uphold traditional headship of the male in marriage and some maintain an umbrella of male authority in the church.

Among the churches that have resisted change there are also significant differences in theology. The Roman Catholic and Orthodox churches have a similar historical tradition which has constructed a theology of womanhood far more complex than that presented in either Old or New Testaments, and reject female ordination primarily because of the male model of the priesthood in administering sacraments. The conservative Protestant churches that hold to tradition, such as Churches of Christ, have a much less complicated reason. They do so out of allegiance to biblical authority and a literal application of its doctrines. What Paul writes is God's law, for all times and all cultures.

Chapter Eight Notes

1. Bedell, Sandon and Wellborn, pp. 224–284.
2. Katherine D. Sakenfeld, "Feminist Uses of Biblical Materials," *Feminist Interpretation of the Bible*, Letty Russell, ed. (Philadelphia: Westminster, 1985), p. 56.
3. Jack Cottrell, *Feminism and the Bible* (Joplin: College Press, 1992).
4. John Piper and Wayne Grudem, eds., *Recovering Biblical Manhood and Womanhood: A Response to Evangelical Feminism* (Wheaton: Crossway, 1991). Susan Foh, *Women and the Word of God: A Response to Biblical Feminism* (Phillipsburg: Presbyterian and Reformed Pub. 1979).

5. Diana Hagee, *Submission and How I Conquered It*. The Cornerstone Church, San Antonio, Texas, is conservative and nondenominational.

6. Paul Jewett, *Man as Male and Female* (Grand Rapids: Eerdmans, 1975). Virginia Mollenkott, *The Divine Feminine* (New York: Crossroad, 1989). Gilbert Bilezikian, *Beyond Sex Roles* (Grand Rapids: Baker, 1985).

7. Nancy A. Hardesty and Letha D. Scanzoni, *All We're Meant to Be* (Nashville, Abingdon, 1986).

8. Richard C. Kroeger and Catherine Kroeger, *I Suffer Not a Woman: Rethinking I Timothy 2:11–15 in Light of Ancient Evidence* (Grand Rapids: Baker, 1992).

9. The issue of inspiration, in fact, was a major point of division leading to the split between the Disciples of Christ and the Churches of Christ. Randy Fenter, "Do Not Go Beyond What is Written" (Part 2), *Image* Vol. 5, No. 9 (September, 1989), pp. 8–11. Lester G. McAllister and William E. Tucker, *Journey in Faith: A History of the Christian Church (Disciples of Christ)* (St. Louis: CBP, 1989), pp. 361–69.

10. Debra B. Hull, *Christian Church Women, Shapers of a Movement* (St. Louis: Chalice Press, 1994), pp. 28–9.

11. Congregationalist (1869), Methodist Episcopal (1869), Presbyterian (1870), Episcopal (1871), Baptist (1873) and African Methodist Episcopal (1874); Janet Wilson James, *Women in American Religion* (Philadelphia: University of Pennsylvania Press, 1980), pp. 171–190.

12. Hull, pp. 118ff.

13. Mary Ellen Lantzer, *An Examination of the 1892–1893 Christian Standard Controversy Concerning Women's Preaching* (Johnson City, Tennessee: Emmanuel School of Religion, 1990).

14. Karen-Marie Yust, "Women: Remaking Ministry," *Disciple* (June, 1998), pp. 3–6.

15. Rosemary Radford Ruether, "Prophetic Tradition and the Liberation of Women: A Story of Promise and Betrayal," p. 3. A paper read at the University of Natal, Pietermaritzburg, August, 1989.

16. The United Churches of Christ claim early affiliation with liberal theological schools such as Yale, Harvard, Chicago, Union, Andover Newton, and Vanderbilt.

17. Forrest Whitman, "Women Liberal Religious Pioneers" (Boulder: Unitarian Universalist Church, 1991).

18. Melvin E. Dieter, "Women and Ministry in the Methodist Tradition," *The Asbury Seminarian*, Vol. 39, No. 4 (1985), pp. 3–7. Dieter also mentions a number of powerful and influential women in the history of Methodism, including Susanna Wesley, Mary Fletcher, Barbara Heck and Antoinette Brown, the first woman regularly ordained in America. But in 1880 the General Conference of the Methodist Episcopal Church took a drastic stand against the ministry of women in the church, which delayed ordination of women some seventy years.

19. Franklin, *Ibid.*

20. Hestenes. p. 5–I. See Richard and Catherine Kroeger, *Women Elders ... Called by God?* (Presbyterian Distribution Service, 1997).

21. Henny G. Dirks-Blatt, "The Ordination of Women to the Ministry in Member Churches of the World Alliance of Reformed Churches," *The Reformed*

World, Vol. 38, No. 8 (1985), pp. 434–43. Her paper contains a good summary of developments in Reformed tradition from the 1880s.

22. James Bone, "Radical Trailblazer," *Woman's Weekly Supplement to the Natal Mercury* (Thursday, March 9, 1989), p. 2. Also discussed at the Lambeth Conference of Anglican bishops, held at Canterbury, England, 1988.

23. Susan M. Cole-King, "Women Priests and the Episcopal Church in the U.S.A." A paper distributed by the Episcopal Church Center, New York, 1987.

24. Chris Ahrends, "Woman as Priest," *Leadership* (July, 1989).

25. A concise history of women's ministries in the Anglican Church is presented by Mary Tanner, "The Ministry of Women: an Anglican Reflection," *One In Christ*, Vol. 21, No. 4 (1985), pp. 284–292.

26. Alan Wilkinson, "Three Sexual Issues," *Theology* (March, 1988), pp. 124–6.

27. Kenneth Slack, "No Women's Ordination for Anglicans, Yet," *Christian Century* (August 13–20, 1986).

28. The Anglican Church is a loose communion of 28 independent denominations worldwide. *Lutheran World Information*, 28/88, p. 10.

29. *Natal News,* October, 1988.

30. Ahrends, *Ibid.*

31. David Peterson, "The Ordination of Women- Balancing the Scriptural Evidence," *St. Mark's Review* (March, 1986), p. 20.

32. *The Synod Debate: the Ordination of Women to the Priesthood*, November, 1992. London: Church House Publishing, 1993.

33. Bylaws, The General Council of the Assemblies of God, paragraph k; cf. Joseph R. Flower, General Secretary of the General Council, "Does God Deny Spiritual Manifestations and Ministry Gifts To Women?" an unpublished paper.

34. Burgess, Stanley M. and Gary B. McGee, eds., *Dictionary of Pentecostal and Charismatic Movements*, pp. 569–70.

35. Flowers, pp.1–2.

36. So stated in a letter from Glenn A. Ginder, Bishop of Brethren in Christ Church, Midwest Regional Conference; December 18, 1987.

37. *The Ground of the Unity* (Herrnhut, German Democratic Republic, 1981), p. 3; *The Moravian Covenant for Christian Living*, Southern Province, p. 27.

38. American Baptist Church, General Board Reference # 8019: 10/81.

39. Statistics provided by Women in Ministry, American Baptist Churches, 475 Riverside Drive, Room 1700, New York, N.Y. 10115. Cf. Mary L. Mild, ed., *Watchword*, Vol. 9, No. 1 (September, 1985).

40. E.g., Wheaton College, Gordon-Conwell Theological Seminary, North Park Theological Seminary, Regent College, Fuller Theological Seminary, et al.; Hestenes, p. 6–I; Virginia Hearn, "Christian Feminists in North America: The Experience of Evangelical Women," *Dialogue & Alliance*, Vol. II, No. 3 (Fall, 1988), gives a thorough treatment of today's feminist movement from an Evangelical viewpoint, starting in 1974 with the roots of the Evangelical Women's Caucus. Other Evangelical feminist writers include Nancy Hardesty, Judith Steinmetz, Katie Funk Wiebe and Letha Scanzoni.

41. John C. Brunt, "Ordination of Women: A Hermeneutical Question," *Ministry* (September, 1988), pp. 12–14.

42. James H. Cone *For My People: Black Theology and the Black Church* (Johannesburg: Skotaville, n.d.) p. 126.

43. An exception is the Evangelical Lutheran Church of Southern Africa (the Black Lutheran Church), which as of 1980 has ordained women.

44. Jualynne E. Dodson, "19th Century AME Preaching Women," in H.F. Thomas and R.S. Keller (eds.), *Women in New Worlds* (Nashville: Abingdon, 1981), p. 287.

45. Cone, p. 127.

46. Student Non-Violent Coordinating Committee.

47. Cone, p. 132.

48. Pauli Murray, "Black Theology and Feminist Theology: A Comparative View," *Anglican Theological Review*, January, 1978, pp. 3–24; Theressa Hoover, "Black Women and the Churches," Alice Hageman (ed.), *Sexist Religion and Women in the Church* (New York: Associated Press, 1974), pp. 63–76.

49. Cone, pp. 134–5.

50. Cone's work, as well as black feminist theology in America and Africa, is discussed by C. Landman, "A profile of feminist theology," *Sexism and Feminism in Theological Perspective*, W.S. Vorster, ed. (Pretoria: Uiversity of South Africa, 1984), pp. 17–23.

51. *UC News*, July–August, 2000. McKenzie, pastor of Payne Memorial AMC in Baltimore and author of *Not Without a Struggle: Leadership Development for African American Women in Ministry* (Pilgrim Press).

52. Nesbitt, p. 25.

53. Roberta Hestenes, "Women In Leadership: Finding Ways to Serve the Church," *Christianity Today* (September 3, 1986), 4–I.

54. George H. Tavard, *Woman in Christian Tradition* (Notre Dame, Indiana: University of Notre Dame Press, 1973), p. 126.

55. Vincent Yzermans, ed. *American Participation in the Vatican Council* (New York, 1967), p. 202.

56. Gertrude Von Le Fort, *The Eternal Woman* (Milwaukee, 1954); the French text *La femme eternelle* (Paris, 1946); Willi Moll, *The Christian Image of Woman* (Notre Dame, Indiana, 1967); Suzanne Cita-Malard, *Les Femmes dans l'Eglise a la lumiere de Vatican II* (Paris, 1968).

57. *Osservatore Romano*, December 10, 1965; Tavard, p. 147.

58. *La Documentation Catholique*, 1966, no. 1482, col. 1923.

59. The English title is "On the Dignity and Vocation of Women." The letter, issued on the occasion of the Marian Year, carries the authority of church doctrine, but not the infallibility of a papal encyclical. Sarie Gilbert, "Papal Letter..." *Lutheran World Information*, 28/88, pp. 11–12. On the strength of Canon Law in the Roman Catholic Church, see Clara Maria Henning, "Canon Law and the Battle of the Sexes," R.R. Ruether, ed. *Religion and Sexism* (New York: Simon and Schuster, 1974), pp. 267–291.

60. Nicolae Chitscu, "The Ordination of Women," in *Concerning the Ordination of Women*, p. 58; cf. Scanzoni and Hardesty, p. 171.

61. Leonard Hodgson, "Theological Objections to the Ordination of Women," *The Expository Times* 77 (April, 1966), pp. 212–213.

62. Catherine Benton, "Does the Church Discriminate Against Women on the Basis of Their Sex?" *Critic* 24:22 (June–July, 1966).

63. Tavard, pp. 149–50.

64. Roberta Green, "Cutting Across Convention," *United Evangelical Action* (January–February, 1984), p. 6.

65. Mary Luke Tobin, "Women in the Church Since Vatican II," *America* (November 1, 1986), pp. 243–6.

66. Elisabeth Schussler Fiorenza and Mary Collins, eds. *Concilium: Religion in the Eighties* (Edinburgh: T & T Clark, 1985). Writers include Elisabeth Schussler Fiorenza, Mary Collins, Marie Zimmermann, Margaret Brennan, Marjorie Proctor-Smith, Adriana Valero, and Mary Boys, all well known in the Catholic feminist movement and all noted academicians and theologians.

67. Marie Zimmermann, "Neither Clergy Nor Laity," in "Women: Invisible in Church and Theology," pp. 29–37. See *The Code of Canon Law*, English Translation (Grand Rapids: Eerdmans, 1983).

68. Margaret Brennan, "The Invisibility of Women in Ecclesiastical Communities," in "Women: Invisible in Church and Theology," pp. 38–48. See *Code of Canon Law*, III:1.

69. Cf. 1998 *motu proprio, Ad Tuendam Fidam*; Hopko, Thomas, ed. *Women and the Priesthood* (St. Vladimir's Seminary Press, 1999), pp. 251–2. Hopko says strong influence from Protestant and Anglican churches has led prominent Orthodox Church leaders in France, Greece, and Russia to favor female ordination. But he adds that the Orthodox Church has hardly begun to formulate a response to the issue and the task will take years, p. 253.

70. Susan Lockwood Wright, "SBC Women Ministers Break Their Silence," *The Christian Century* (November 12, 1986), p. 998.

71. Green, p. 6.

72. Melvin Worthington, Executive Secretary, National Association of Free Will Baptists, Inc., 1987. Cf. *A Treatise of the Faith and Practices of Free Will Baptists*, revised edition, 1981.

73. Davis Duggins, personal correspondence, December 28, 1987.

74. Milton V. Backman, Jr. *Christian Churches of America* (New York: Charles Scribner's Sons, 1976), pp. 223–6.

75. Green, p. 6.

76. Virginia Hearn, "Christian Feminists in North America: The Experience of Evangelical Women," *Dialogue & Alliance*, Vol. II, No. 3 (Fall, 1988), p. 68.

77. Mac Lynn, *Where the Saints Meet* (Pensacola: Firm Foundation, 1987).

78. For ties with the watchword *ad fontes* of early Renaissance Christian Humanism, as well as Reformation appeal to *sola scriptura* and pattern theology in English Puritanism, see Leonard Allen and Richard T. Hughes, *Discovering Our Roots: The Ancestry of Churches of Christ* (Abilene: ACU Press, 1988).

79. A few groups require a headcovering for women. They, and other splinter groups opposed to certain practices among the mainstream churches, are typically called "Anti churches." They have no fellowship with the mainstream churches, whom they call "liberal."

80. Rejection of deaconesses in early church; Burton Coffman, *Commentary on Romans* (Austin: Firm Foundation, 1973), p. 508; Sees Galatians 3:28 as spiritual equality, Coffman, *Commentary on Galatians, Ephesians, Philippians and Colossians*, p. 66; Rejects possibility of female prophetism or public prayer in the early church, Coffman, *Commentary on I and II Corinthians*, pp. 165–79; David Lipscomb, *A Commentary on the New Testament Epistles* (Nashville: Gospel Advocate, 1935), pp. 216, 264.

81. James O. Baird, "God Assigned a Special Role for Women in the

Church," *Introducing the Church of Christ,* John Waddey, ed. (Ft. Worth: Star, 1981) pp. 121–125; Roger E. Dickson, *International New Testament Study Commentary* (Church of Christ: 1987), p. 454, 465, 593.

82. Abilene Christian University, David Lipscomb, Freed Hardeman, Harding, Oklahoma Christian University, et. al.

83. J. Stephen Sandifer, *Deacons: Male and Female?* (Houston: Keystone, 1989), pp. 160–61.

84. Schools of preaching like Sunset (Lubbock), Brown Trail (Ft. Worth), Bear Valley (Denver), White's Ferry Road (West Monroe). Publications like the *Gospel Advocate, Christian Chronicle, Contending For the Faith,* and *Firm Foundation.*

85. Thomas H. Olbricht, "Women in the Church: The Hermeneutical Problem," *Essays on Women in Earliest Christianity,* Vol. 2, Carroll Osburn, ed (Joplin: College Press, 1993) pp. 545–568.

86. Hoy Ledbetter, "The Prophetess," *Integrity* (July, 1973); Normon L. Parks, *Woman's Place in Church Activity* (Grand Blanc: Integrity, 1975).

87. Frederick W. Norris, "Women Ministers in Constantinian Christianity," Carroll D. Osburn, ed. *Essays on Women in Earliest Christianity,* Vol. 2 (Joplin: College Press, 1993), p. 374.

88. Hoy Ledbetter, "The Prophetess," *Integrity* (July, 1973); Normon L. Parks, *Woman's Place in Church Activity* (Grand Blanc: Integrity, 1975).

89. J. Stephen Sandifer, *Deacons: Male and Female?* (Houston: Sandifer, 1989), p. 193.

90. Bering Drive Church of Christ in Houston, and Stamford Church of Christ in Stamford, Connecticut. See essays by Bill Love and Dale Pauls, *Essays on Women in Earliest Christianity,* Vol. 2.

91. Cover statement, Sandifer, *Deacons: Male and Female?*

Chapter Nine

THE CONTINUING
THEOLOGICAL DILEMMA

Today we live in a world of exceptionally rapid advancement and unparalleled freedom for women, not just in the West but in most developed countries as well. In advanced cultures female elevation is evident in business, science, politics, and education. Although less pronounced in poorer societies, liberation theology is becoming a springboard for the advancement of women's status around the world. In every sphere of life, women are discovering a new identity, with self-expression and acceptance as the equals of men.

However, religion in general, including Christianity, not only has failed to keep pace but has been a major hindrance to women's advancement. Numerous problems accompany the theological dilemma. Craig Bird, features editor for the Southern Baptist Press in Nashville, stated one practical problem succinctly: "You've got a lot of highly educated women coming out with master of divinity degrees, having mastered Hebrew and Greek, and having no place to go."[1] A 1986 survey conducted by *Christianity Today* among evangelical seminaries in the United States revealed that one-fifth of the students were female, and the percentage has increased each year.[2] Many are trained to assume positions their churches are not prepared to give them.

The concept of divine calling is a questionable notion among exact scholars, especially because there is no legitimate means of testing, verifying or denying personal religious experiences. However, some churchmen see the Holy Spirit's call to minister as one of the most powerful legitimizing factors in today's feminist movement in the church.[3] Like the charismata of the first century, the present feminist movement conceivably heralds a new spiritual awakening with the potential to impact the entire world. And who can deny its power? In the words of Seventh Day Adventist John C. Brunt, recalling Peter's response to a similar dilemma, "Can anyone keep these women from being ordained? They have received the Holy Spirit just as we have."[4]

However, even this line of reasoning seems superfluous considering the events of the last 200 years. The "call" of women to various levels of ministry in early nineteenth century America was driven by freedom and necessity, a social phenomenon linked to several other advances in human rights and justice that became "self-evident" truths against the voice of scripture and religious tradition. Whether or not the spirit of God is seen as the driving force, academics agree that the feminist movement is a very significant step in social advancement.[5] It is quite evident that women are gaining more and more ground toward genuine equity, and this will apply persistent pressure on all religions to adjust accordingly. As Roberta Hestenes points out, the rapid advancement in the social status of women, their changing life styles, and increasing pressure from the feminist movement worldwide all have combined to force churches to rethink their official positions.[6] Harold H. Oliver comments that feminism is the greatest challenge ever to confront the church, since it opens the door for serious and radical rethinking of both the religious experience and the entire Christian tradition.[7]

Some argue that the changing position of society on the status of women is irrelevant to theology. Tavard, for example, says that the church unwittingly followed society in restricting women, using scripture as its authority. To reverse its position now, again following society, obliterates its claim to divine authenticity and invalidates its purpose of making known to the world the manifold wisdom of God.[8] The church, he says, should come to conclusions independent of social trends. This position is idealistic, giving the church more credit than it is due for initiating social advances in history. More often than not the church has hindered scientific discovery and social development, fearful of tainting its self-image of doctrinal purity and losing control of its members. Nonetheless, whether churches take the lead in this element of social change or find themselves tagging along behind, the total issue is very much a theological one and must be dealt with on a theological level, as well as a practical and sociological level.[9] Edwards correctly observes that only recently have we come to appreciate the close interrelationship between socio-cultural factors, biblical interpretation and the current doctrine of God.[10] In a variety of ways the Church and Christian tradition have been led to enlightenment by certain positive social trends and through religio-social revolt, beginning perhaps with the Renaissance. Failure to recognize this possibility is the result of human misconceptions concerning divine revelation.

From an overview of the positions being taken in various churches, no line can be drawn to distinguish the kinds of churches that are making allowances for feminism as opposed to those that continue holding to tradition. But certain factors do become apparent. Obviously, the dilemma is most critical among churches with a more sacramental and cultic concept of priesthood, and among those whose doctrines are based on a more conservative hermeneutic.[11] The issue is much deeper than most realize, lying at the very core of the Christian faith and pertaining to the very foundation of all church doctrines and Christian beliefs. Questions concerning the status of women come at a time when Christian theology is undergoing serious self-examination and radical paradigm shifts away from classic systematic, historical and metaphysical approaches toward a religious pluralism and a search for meaning in the God-consciousness of humanity as a whole.[12] This means that feminist theology, and the entire issue of the status of women in the church, is a significant element of a much broader movement in world theology.

Ordination of women tends to be a focal point simply because conclusions reached on this issue represent conclusions on all others specifically related to women in the church and society. As Chavez argues, rules about ordination of women serve as a symbolic display of a broader liberal agenda of recognizing gender equality and institutionalizing individual rights.[13] With some exceptions, churches that are prepared to ordain women will have given up the entire paradigm of male dominance, while those that refuse to ordain women advocate male dominance and deny gender equality. Of course, there are those denominations that assert they are fully supportive of female equality but deny women access to leadership positions.[14] This position is blatant hypocrisy.

The status of women in the church is but a part of the very complex paradigm of patriarchy which has prevailed in most cultures throughout recorded history until the present. It is most evident in the traditional marriage hierarchy, in which the male holds a position of authority and the female a station of subordination and subjection. Therefore it is almost axiomatic that in order to deal with a problem of this magnitude, the church must come to grips with the deeper implications. It follows also that conclusions on this issue have ramifications cutting to the marrow of each specific denominational identity. As Haight suggests:

> Theological reflection should do more than remove theological obstacles to the ordination of women. It should offer a positive theological affirmation that supports the Christian vision of the freedom through liberation and equality through salvation of human beings.[15]

Over the last two decades scholars have generated an enormous body of historical and exegetical research relevant to the status of women. Yet in many churches the position remains firmly traditional. It is one thing to appreciate the degraded status of women in the ancient world, or in church history, or to determine exegetically the meaning of biblical teachings in their original context. But interpreting those teachings in ways meaningful and relevant to the church today is quite another matter, particularly where it involves radical change. Therefore, conclusions to be drawn from this study are numerous, and each presents further problems for future theoretical and practical exploration.

I. No Basis for Female Subordination

First, it must be concluded that there is no legitimate reason for the church to perpetuate the tradition of female subordination in any form. Careful analysis of historical backgrounds, relevant biblical passages, and the history of church doctrine on this issue suggest that female subordination is a social ideology upheld by Judaism and by Christian tradition as a whole, but opposed in principle by the Gospel of Christ. The power paradigm upon which traditional marriages have been structured, as well as the social and religious hierarchy that has relegated women to a secondary and inferior station, are essentially erroneous and unjust. Feminist objections to traditional patriarchy, with all its ramifications, are in general quite valid. Therefore, there is no theological justification for debarring women from ordination, from any other office or ministry, or from filling any role or duty traditionally reserved for men. Nor is there any sound theological basis for perpetuating patriarchy in the home as a divinely ordained paradigm.

These essential conclusions become a major premise for further tasks and conclusions, and force a reassessment of numerous presuppositions which have served as the foundation of earlier conventional ideologies.

II. Rethinking the Inspiration of Scripture

Perhaps the most critical issue underlying the dilemma concerning the status of women is the entire concept of inspiration of scripture.[16] Stated in simple terms, the Bible has been viewed by conservatives as fully and totally "God-breathed," and therefore inerrant and infallible.[17] Accordingly, the Genesis account of creation has been understood as accurate and factual history, and all its implications concerning the station of women have stood as undeniable testimony of God's design from the beginning. Allusions to Genesis 2 in the New Testament are then taken as evidence of the historicity of Adam and Eve and the veracity of the Creation Story in literal terms, simply because it is assumed that inspired writers would not build an argument or base a doctrine on an untruth.[18] Feminist theologians have aligned themselves with mainstream scholarship by following the historical-critical approach to biblical hermeneutics. This means that they reject plenary verbal inspiration and the concept of biblical inerrancy, which is the mainstay of conservative theology. Fiorenza states the position in these terms:

> A fundamental methodological insight of historical criticism of the Bible was the realization that the *Sitz im Leben* or life setting of a text is as important for its understanding as its actual formulation. Biblical texts are not verbally inspired revelation nor doctrinal principles but historical formulations within the context of a religious community.[19]

We have noted that many have tried to deal with the enormous difficulties posed by modern feminism by explaining away any traditional sexist implications in both Genesis and Pauline writings. The purpose has been to defend and uphold the written Word at virtually any cost. But in the end such efforts fail against the obvious patriarchal and andocentric overtones of most ancient literature, Pauline works included. Relevant Pauline texts do in fact represent and defend the ancient patriarchal paradigm, despite its contradiction of the Gospel. Therefore, the unavoidable conclusion is that Paul and other biblical spokesmen were not infallible in their opinions, teaching and writing, and that whatever is by nature inferior or beneath the ideals of the Gospel message should not be interpreted as having any measure of revelatory authority.[20] This means that a solution to the current dilemma over the status of women can only be found in a reexamination of the conservative approach to scripture.[21] In conservative tradition there has existed a clear tendency to elevate the Bible above its claims of itself. In Fiorenza's words, "In maintaining verbal inspiration of all passages, the Church has made the Bible into a fetish."[22]

The conventional conception of plenary-verbal inspiration is seriously challenged by the existence of certain myths within the Judaeo-Christian tradition and within biblical literature.[23] The mythical nature of numerous traditional beliefs concerning women is undeniable. This is not to say that myth is without value. Elizabeth Janeway observes that myth exists entirely in the present. It is essentially the world of our imagination, consisting of beliefs which influence perception of real events.

But it draws from alleged events or concepts in the past which it sees as both sacred and eternal, and their relevance to the present are reinforced by means of ritual.[24] Myth in relation to role behavior is a means of knowing and understanding the structure of our world, the way society creates and maintains itself. Around 1920 Bronislaw Malinowski wrote:

> Myth fulfills in primitive culture an indispensible function: it expresses, enhances and codifies belief; it safeguards and enforces morality; it vouches for the efficiency of ritual and contains practical rules for the guidance of man ... it is not an intellectual explanation or an artistic imagery, but a pragmatic charter of primitive faith and moral wisdom ... a statement of a primeval, greater and more relevant reality, by which the present life, fates and activities of mankind are determined.[25]

The problem in religion is the confusion of myth with truth. Thinking about myth and woman's place requires triple thinking, involving history, values and present facts. As society changes there is of necessity a continual reexamination of its norms and beliefs against demonstrable fact, and thereby myth gives way to enlightenment. According to Janeway:

> Woman's role is a good laboratory example to examine, because it has been the scene of such a struggle long enough for us to note effects and not simply beginnings. Here, roles are changing and even some of the mythology surrounding them has been shifted and replaced.[26]

However, today's misconceptions inevitably will become tomorrow's myth. And unless societies can change more rapidly than they have in the past, inaccurate perceptions of reality will continue to hinder social advancement and obscure great truths which humanity as a whole, and certainly the church, needs to discover.

The acknowledgment of myth within scripture is not to reject scripture as divinely inspired, but to gain a better understanding of inspiration and to make a more sensible application of scripture to the human life and to changing human societies. Yet it does require an abandonment of definitions and prescriptions that are self-contradictory and lead to absurd and ignoble conclusions. The concepts of plenary verbal inspiration and the inerrancy of scripture have done precisely this with regard to the church's position on the status of women. Therefore, resolution of the immediate dilemma requires giving up the fallacious foundation upon which patriarchy has rested in the Christian tradition.

Further, all this suggests that conservatives must give more careful attention to the common use made of the Old Testament by Jesus and by New Testament writers such as Paul.[27] And in the process consideration must be given to the possibility that Paul believed the Adam and

Eve story to be literally true, though it was not, and that neither inspiration nor apostleship made him infallible as a writer or evangelist. Attention also must be given to the historical process by which the New Testament came into being. Works such as I Timothy appear to form only a part of a much larger base of Christian literature from which the church selected documents it deemed suitable.[28] This process eliminated works that promoted female elevation,[29] and in turn canonized those that promoted traditional androcentricity. Therefore, neither the writing of New Testament works nor their collection and canonization bears the earmarks of total divine guidance, but often reflects the prejudice and bias of human social institutions and traditions. Unfortunately, this specific traditional bias robbed the church of a vital element of the Gospel and until the twentieth century hindered its full expression in socially meaningful terms.

III. Rethinking the Authority of Scripture

There arises also the need to rethink the traditional view of the authority of scripture for matters of church doctrine and practical Christian living.[30] The dilemma surrounding the status of women rests largely in the conservative view of the Bible, which tends to predetermine the outcome of biblical exegesis regardless of other relevant factors.[31] The question of the status of women is perhaps the clearest illustration of the theological cul de sac created by biblical literalism, which has been rejected by major theologians and scholars, some even calling it heresy.[32] Religious authority has been a point of contention for quite some time. Calvin and Luther both reacted strongly to the authority assumed by the Catholic Church in the form of tradition. But they were uncomfortable without some form of authoritative revelation of divine will. Calvin, in fact, saw authority as part of God's consideration of human need.[33] Wolfhart Pannenberg, noted theologian of the nineteenth century, concentrated much scholastic attention on several concepts of authority he deemed unacceptable, particularly that of Holy Scripture. Pannenberg was disturbed by the dangers of faith rooted in authority, and he faulted the Reformers for identifying human proclamation with the word of God.[34]

Thomas and Alexander Campbell saw the authority of scripture as the only means of uniting believers, and their movement resulted in numerous splits and divisions, compounding the problem they hoped to solve. Then in the early and middle twentieth century fear of modernism led to a revival of the apologetics of fundamentalism, led by Presbyterians of the caliber of John Machen, Cornelius Van Til and E.J. Young.[35]

The protective wall of authority erected in the last two centuries against attack by modern science brought about a crisis for modern evangelical theology. This is significant because conservative Christians, particularly fundamentalists, declare their allegiance to an inerrant Bible, including the Garden of Eden story upon which rabbinic views of women clearly rest. This forces a conclusion that has become in our time socially and theologically untenable.

For these reasons it is becoming increasingly difficult for Christians to refer to scripture for a detailed blueprint for social behavior and religious doctrine. It has been impossible for Protestants, as it has been also for Roman Catholics, to find in scripture a clear theology of womanhood. We have demanded of the Bible as a whole what it cannot produce. As the French theologian Francoise Florentin-Smith has stated:

> ...the Bible, which provides us with recipes for nothing, will not give us, with a theology of woman, the excuse for a laziness which runs the danger of being satisfied with compelling myths and sacred or magic meanings, instead of a passionate and always approximate investigation. Instead of a metaphysical order to which we should conform, and of consolations that may be found in the sublimation of intolerable or false situations into parables, the Bible frees us from all archetypal forms to throw us forward into the ways of love, where one gropes for an acknowledgement of the contradictions and diversities which love assumes and reconciles.... We are therefore reduced, be it with joy, to share the uncertainties and the impatient reflection of our contemporaries on woman's becoming.[36]

Bruce Waltke is representative of the entire conservative tradition in his defense of hierarchism, which he states is based on "three truths self-evident in scripture." These three are: first, that man and woman are equal in bearing the image of God and in their standing before God; second, that God prescribed that the husband is the head of the wife; third, that church administration must be consistent with the home, and therefore all church leadership must be male.[37] To him the issue is quite simple: "The Bible says it, and that is that." In this way Christians have come to employ the Bible as the ultimate authority in defense of traditional views.

The discovery of certain myths within orthodox tradition does indeed affect the authoritative station of the Bible, and the resolution of the present dilemma requires the acknowledgement of this fact by churches where the problem is most acute. It has become clear to many Christians that other self-evident truths, both within scripture and without, force a reconsideration of Waltke's assessment of truth. James Barr observes this very problem in fundamentalism, stating:

> Against these uses (or abuses) of scripture, the majority judgment has insisted upon the balance of scripture as a whole: for instance, though there are individual passages of scripture that seem to emphasize the subservience of women, the total impact of scripture and the final implication of its entire message must be such as to counter that subservience and to work for the full equality and honour of women in the eyes of God.[38]

Therefore, a balanced view of scripture is to accept that certain doctrines taught by biblical writers, more specifically New Testament writers, might not be ideal, good, universally appropriate, or even true. The Pauline doctrine on women, for example, stands in direct conflict with the tone and spirit of the Gospel. Conversely, gender equality and female leadership in the church might be technically in conflict with the teachings of Paul but in harmony with the overall spirit and tone of the Gospel. In examining the rituals and customs of a variety of cultures, sociologists Nancy Hardesty and Letha Scanzoni found four ways religious systems have attempted to deal with the very obvious distinction between the sexes.[39] One approach stresses the antithesis, or polarity of the sexes, with a concomitant exclusion of one from the rights, privileges and status of the other. A second approach stresses the complementary nature of the sexes, each being equal to the other, a counterpart to the other, but one being active and the other passive. A third approach stresses the blending or synthesis formed when the two become one, specifically in marriage. And the fourth is a transcendent approach, overlooking or denying sexual distinction, at least as far as religion is concerned. A major source of confusion about the Judaeo-Christian tradition is that all four of these approaches can be found in the Bible, and it is the Bible which Christians claim as the basis for their faith. It is this awareness that has led many scholars to conclude that the Bible is in fact ambivalent on the subject of women, and as a whole cannot be viewed as an authoritative pattern for doctrine and practice because it does not present a clear or consistent picture.

The great number of works published recently by conservatives on the subject of women reflects a desperation to resolve this very significant issue. There are two approaches to the status of women which are finding a large degree of acceptance. One is simply to reinterpret each relevant passage so as to extrapolate a less discriminatory doctrine, thereby preserving a conservative view of biblical authority and at the same time granting to women a measure of freedom and equality which will ease the present tension.[40] This is what Verdesi calls "co-optation," which amounts to a token gesture with no practical substance.[41]

The other approach is to view Pauline doctrines as inspired and authoritative, but often directed to transient cultural problems irrelevant today. This would allow Paul to instruct wives to be subordinate simply because it was the expected demeanor of the first century, but not require that Christians of another time and place follow his instructions explicitly. We must even consider the possibility that a writer such as Paul might encourage believers to endure and submit to social evils such as imperialism, slavery and patriarchy, without intentionally endorsing them or imposing them as a divine rule.

Both of these approaches represent a search for a solution without yielding ground on invalid presuppositions, and consequently they depend on speculations, dubious theories, and conjectures, rather than following logically upon the weight of historical evidence. They are merely apparent and temporary solutions. Furthermore, both approaches create a tension equal to that caused by traditional patriarchy by advocating a hermeneutical method which is inconsistent and self-contradictory.[42] It is more sensible to conclude that inspired scripture has room for certain concessions and there is no need to frantically reinterpret problem passages to make them harmonize with a newly discovered truth. Madeleine Boucher assesses the obvious failure of such methods, asserting that the real cause of the dilemma lies in traditional views of biblical authority:

> Theologians are often led to fresh insights by the new factors operating in their own time, especially intellectual and social factors. Then, because they stand in the Judaeo-Christian tradition, they turn to the Bible in search of texts with which to undergird these new insights. Yet, because they are seeking to answer contemporary questions, questions unknown to the biblical writers, they sometimes interpret the biblical texts in a way which is more true to contemporary thought than to the thought of the biblical writers. The recent discussion of the place of women in the church is an example. As said above, modern man, as a result of numerous and complex factors operating in the last three centuries, is no longer able to hold an abstract ideology of equality while refusing to translate it into practical terms.... Thus, a study of the New Testament teaching on the role of women leads finally to one of the important questions of theology today, that of the relationship between contemporary theology, on the one hand, and an authoritative Bible on the other hand.[43]

Many evangelical leaders and theologians realize that this is a fundamental issue, and are fearful of a trend leading their fellows to "jump on the bandwagon" without resolving more significant underlying questions.

Carl Henry, for example, acknowledges that stifling women's creative gifts is desperately wrong. But he adds:

> If you're willing to move with the tide of culture without having resolved how this bears on the authority of Scripture, which the church claims to salute, it has all sorts of implications on other issues.[44]

In this regard Landman expresses her rejection of "anxious exegetical methods" of evangelical feminists who attempt to plead their case, and at the same time defend a "once for all time" concept of revealed divine truth. We must accept, she says, that God is in a continual interaction with the world, unfolding truths at the right time and in the right way. On the issue of women, the authority of the letter gives way to the ongoing work of the Spirit.[45] Theology today may not be that concerned with the factuality of the literary devices employed by biblical writers, but it is concerned with the validity of the principles, lessons, or ideologies those devices communicate and their application in a modern circumstance. When biblical customs are enlisted as authoritative examples of "how things should be," the essential message of the New Testament becomes "time bound" and loses its universal and timeless thrust. Human conventions typically prove like old wineskins bursting at the seams, as the new wine of an ever unfolding Gospel strains for realization against the rigidity of human tradition. As Oliver expresses it, "If there is one truth at the heart of both Judaism and Christianity, it is that no representation of the divine—either visual or verbal—is finally adequate."[46] The Christian tradition must be seen as living and progressive, and constantly requiring self-examination. It is never threatened by any sincere critique.[47] This of necessity requires continual course adjustment. Therefore, as the church's social environment changes, so will her understanding of the Word change; and in turn, so will her response to it.

IV. Developing Appropriate Hermeneutics

The fundamentalist generally seeks to define, codify and delineate rather than allowing subjective issues to remain moot, since compromises weaken the concept of authority upon which such a hermeneutic rests. A major problem with this hermeneutic its common inconsistency of application. Many advocates of feminine equality have noticed that the rules are set aside on occasion by almost all exegetes when in their own minds there is a sensible and logical reason to do so.[48] In spite of slavish devotion to the letter in some instances, on other issues a scriptural teaching might be explained as purely cultural in nature, in which case it becomes benign and virtually irrelevant as a twentieth century doctrine. For example, not many fundamentalist churches have made a ritual of footwashing, despite Jesus' instructions to his disciples to follow his example.[49] The reason is that most can see the symbolism in his action, and realize that its application is in daily service rather than liturgical ritual. The same is true of "lifting holy hands" in prayer (I Timothy 2:8) and the "holy kiss" (I Corinthians 16:20), although some churches have applied even these fundamentally. A few also appeal to I Corinthians 11 against men having long hair, although generally the same passage is not enforced against women cutting their hair short. But the same passage is the classic proof text for females wearing veils in church. Conversely, very few churches prohibit women from wearing jewelry, plaited hair or expensive garments in spite of New Testament teachings against it.[50] Virginia Hearn summarizes the problem: "The hermeneutical question for evangelicals arises over how to distinguish between what is universal and timeless and what was local and particular in Paul's statements."[51] However, it seems that the real problem lies within the presumptions implied in her statement.

This sort of inconsistency in hermeneutics is not unnoticed among lay church members, and has contributed to confusion, mistrust and disillusionment, even loss of faith. If the letter of the word can be overlooked in some instances because it was addressed to a transient cultural issue, why can this not be so with regard to the status of women? To recognize this possibility with regard to all New Testament restrictions on the status of women is perhaps the simplest solution to the conservative dilemma. But the change creates enormous embarrassment, even guilt, since denominational doctrines based on a conservative hermeneutic are generally presented as sacrosanct, timeless, and immutable. To change, to embrace a doctrine, after having disfellowshipped people for teaching it in the past, places us in the camp of those in history whose hands remain forever stained with the blood of martyrs. Jesus castigated the religious leaders of his day for imposing laws in the name of God that were in fact of their own making. The Apostle Paul dragged about the corpse of guilt for persecution and murder prompted by his misguided zeal. So now, to reverse a position held so staunchly and argued so vigorously leaves a sickening taste in the mouth. In the words of an interlocutor, Bill Love expresses the frustration that is no doubt common among members of the Church of Christ at the thought of all that is implied by a change in their traditional hermeneutic:

> We have, as a movement, been studying the Bible for over 150 years.
> Are you telling me that now, all of a sudden, this generation of schol-
> ars is the first one smart enough to understand what the Bible is really
> saying?[52]

The answer, of course, is no. But previous generations felt no pressure to
reexamine their position. Their hermeneutical approach and their traditional interpretations seemed solid, at least while the majority agreed. But
the presumed universality of their conclusions became a stumbling block.
Different times and circumstances demanded a different approach.
Thomas Olbricht, Professor of Religion at Pepperdine University, vividly
demonstrates that among Churches of Christ the hermeneutic applied by
previous generations, the tripartite formula of command, example, and
necessary inference, no longer seems appropriate for resolving major issues
like the status of women.[53]

This leads to the conclusion that the most consistent and sensible
hermeneutic is one which remains flexible, allowing the principles within
scripture to speak to each human circumstance and allowing for many vari-
ations in human response and application. With particular reference to
the status of females, at least three principles must govern the interpretation and application of the Bible to a modern context: (1) Recognition
that traditional subordination of women is contrary to certain truths
undergirding the Christian message, and therefore any hermeneutic which
forces an interpretation or practice in opposition to those basic truths is
to be rejected. (2) Any hermeneutic that makes absolute a given historical social order or hierarchy is to be rejected. (3) Any hermeneutic which
fails to allow equal response to divine calling and limits roles of Christian service on the basis of nationality, class or sex is to be rejected.[54]

V. Abandoning Traditionalism

A major hurdle many churches face is the sacrosanct aura around religious tradition. Each group, and indeed the membership as a body, must
learn to feel comfortable with changes in doctrine and policy to suit human
needs in an ever changing world. The Roman Catholic Church for centuries has claimed divine authority for its tradition. Judaism also has survived over the centuries largely because of an ardent devotion to tradition.
But today we are discovering that changes in world view and styles of life
render many customs and traditions meaningless and out of touch. Jesus
himself was critical of human traditions simply because of their tendency

to supplant concern for human welfare and to be elevated to a status of eternal truth.[55]

Traditions in themselves are valuable. There is nothing wrong with traditions. Family and cultural traditions can be very positive, having the effect of bonding people together and providing a sense of worth and dignity even in difficult times. The problem lies in what might be called "traditionalism," which is the undesirable result of tradition becoming a constricting force, a ruling mandate that binds or discriminates without latitude for personal choice or social change. For this reason marriage customs have changed in most of the free world. Modern society can no longer abide traditions in which couples are assigned to each other by familial contract without personal consent. Love and courtship have taken the place of patriarchal selection and blessing, matchmaking and political alliances through token marriages. Therefore, the dilemma faced by churches over the status of women points to a dilemma concerning religious tradition. It demands the reexamination of the religious impetus for traditions and a willingness to look beyond them for the spiritual meaning of man's existence. Susanne Langer writes:

> We are faced with an unintended, unguided, but irresistible revolution in all human relations, from the marriage bonds and family controls whereby personal life has traditionally been ordered, to the religious and patriotic loyalties that were wont to rule people's wider activities. Such a change in the human scene requires and effects a change in the concepts with which we operate practically and intellectually, but few people realize that their basic social conceptions have changed.... Our profoundest metaphors have lost their moral import.[56]

If she is correct, and evidence is abundant that she is, the interest of the church can no longer lie in what was believed or how things were done in the past. Instead, we must simply determine what is good, right, noble, and just—today, and moving into tomorrow—and have the courage to act on our decision.

Chapter Nine Notes

1. Roberta Green, "Cutting Across Convention," *United Evangelical Action* (January–February, 1984), p. 7.

2. Beth Spring and Kelsey Menehan, "Women in Seminary: Preparing for What? *Christianity Today* (November 5, 1986), pp. 18–23.

3. Elsie Gibson, *When the Minister is a Woman*, pp. 34–59; Kenneth S. Kantzer, "Proceed With Care," *Christianity Today*, Vol. 30, No. 14 (October 3, 1986), p. 14–I.

4. John C. Brunt, "Ordination of Women: A Hermeneutical Question," *Ministry* (September, 1988), p. 14.

5. Dean Pederson, Gordon-Conwell Theological Seminary; Spring and Menehan, p. 19.

6. Roberta Hestenes, "Women in Leadership: Finding Ways to Serve the Church," *Christianity Today*, Insert (September 3, 1986), p. 10. Cf. Hestenes, *The Next Step: Women in a Divided Church* (Waco: Word, 1987).

7. Harold H. Oliver, "Beyond the Feminist Critique: A Shaking of Foundations," *The Christian Century* (May 1, 1985), p. 446.

8. George Tavard, *Women in Christian Tradition* (Notre Dame, Indiana: Notre Dame Press, 1973), p. 218.

9. Roger Haight, "Women in the Church: a Theological Reflection," *Toronto Journal of Theology*, Vol. II, No. 1 (1986), pp. 108.

10. F. Edwards, "God from a feminist perspective," *Sexism and Feminism in Theological Perspective*, W.S. Vorster, ed. (Pretoria, University of South Africa, 1984), pp. 36–7.

11. Denise Ackerman, "Women Barred in Christian Church," *Seek* (June–July, 1989), pp. 8–9.

12. Robert H. King, "The Task of Systematic Theology," *Christian Theology: An Introduction to Its Traditions and Tasks* (London: SPCK, 1983), pp. 21–27.

13. Mark Chavez, *Ordaining Women: Culture and Conflict in Religious Organizations* (Cambridge: Harvard, 1997), p. 192.

14. *Ibid*, p. 2.

15. Haight, p. 109.

16. Pivotal verse is II Timothy 3:16–17.

17. James Barr, *Escaping From Fundamentalism* (London: SCM, 1984), pp. 1–7.

18. The implications of this rationale are explored by E.E. Ellis, *Paul's Use of the Old Testament*. See also D.M. Beegle, *Scripture, Tradition and Infallibility* (Grand Rapids: Eerdmans, 1973).

19. Elisabeth Schussler Fiorenza, *In Memory of Her* (London: SCM, 1983), p. xv.

20. Fiorenza, p. 33.

21. Perhaps the finest recent analysis of the problem of fundamentalism is by James Barr, *Fundamentalism* (London: SCM Press, 1973); and *Escaping from Fundamentalism* (London: SCM Press, 1984). Of course, the status of women is only one of many issues which leads to this conclusion.

22. Elisabeth Schussler Fiorenza, "Women in the Early Christian Movement," *Womanspirit Rising*, Carol P. Christ and Judith Plaskow, eds. (San Francisco, Harper and Row, 1979), p. 85.

23. Any belief or ideology which has no basis in fact.

24. Elizabeth Janeway, *Man's World, Woman's Place* (New York: William Morrow and Company, Inc., 1971), pp. 136–7.

25. Bronislaw Malinowski, *Myth in Primitive Society*, 1926. Quoted by Janeway, p. 42.

26. Janeway, pp. 133.

27. James Barr, *Escaping Fundamentalism*, pp. 8–19.

28. James Barr, *Holy Scripture: Canon, Authority, Criticism* (London: Oxford University Press, 1983).

29. For example, *Acts of Paul and Thecla* discussed earlier.

30. This trend in modern times began with historical-critical approach to scripture, applied theologically by Rudolf Bultmann, Karl Barth, Emil Brunner, Reinhold Niebuhr, Paul Tillich, Ernst Kasemann, and others, spanning the nineteenth and twentieth centuries. In this century conservatism has been defended by Abraham Kuyper, Herman Bavinck, and Presbyterian theologian Gresham Machen. See Louis Praamsma, *The Church in the Twentieth Century*, Vol. VII (St. Catherines, Ontario: Paideia, 1981), pp. 226–234. Also in general by a broad range of conservative and fundamentalist churches, such as the Baptists, Seventh Day Adventists, Churches of Christ, Pentecostals, and others.

31. This is far more demanding than the plea of *sola scriptura* of the Reformation, which simply rejected tradition holding to the Bible only as the source and authority for church teaching.

32. James D. Smart, *The Past, Present and Future of Biblical Theology* (Philadelphia: Westminster, 1979), p. 147–52.

33. G.C. Berkouwer, *A Half Century of Theology* (Grand Rapids: Eerdmans, 1977), Lewis B. Smedes, ed. and trans., p. 161.

34. *Ibid.* p. 160.

35. Louis Praamsma, *The Church in the Twentieth Century*, Vol. VII (St. Catharines, Ontario: Paideia, 1981), pp. 226–233.

36. Francoise Florentin-Smith, "La femme en milieu protestant," Tatiana Struve, Agnes Cunningham, Francoise Florentin-Smith, *La Femme* (Paris, 1968), p. 150.

37. Bruce Waltke, "Male Headship," *Christianity Today*, Vol. 30, No. 16 (October 3, 1986), p. 13–I.

38. James Barr, *Escaping From Fundamentalism*, pp. 111–12.

39. Letha Scanzoni and Nancy Hardesty, *All We're Meant to Be* (Waco: Word Books, 1974), p. 14.

40. This has been the case on almost every related passage; i.e. the meaning of "head" in I Corinthians 11 and Ephesians 5, the meaning of "authority" in I Corinthians 11, the meaning of "silence" in I Corinthians 14 and I Timothy 2, etc.

41. E.H. Verdesi, *In But Still Out: Women in the Church* (Philadelphia: Westminster, 1976), p. 22. Co-optation occurs when an organization responds to wants or demands by appointing a special interest group and assigning them informal service roles to placate them, but granting no true authority or decision making powers. D.M. Ackermann, "The role of women in the church—certain practical theological perspectives," *Sexism and Feminism*, W.S. Vorster, ed. (Pretoria: University of South Africa, 1984), p. 77.

42. Papers published in *The Role of Women*, edited by Shirley Lees (several writers have been quoted in this thesis) is a good example of the polarity of these positions among conservatives.

43. Madeleine Boucher, "Some Unexplored Parallels to I Cor. 11:11–12 and Gal. 3:28; The New Testament on the Role of Women," *Catholic Biblical Quarterly*, 31:50–8 (June, 1969).

44. Green, p. 7.

45. C. Landman, "A Profile of Feminist Theology," *Sexism and Feminism in Theological Perspective*, W.S. Vorster, ed. (Pretoria: University of South Africa, 1984), p. 11.

46. Oliver, p. 446.

47. Edward Farley and Peter C. Hodgson, "Scripture and Tradition," *Christian Theology: An Introduction to Its Traditions and Tasks*, pp. 35–61.

48. Scanzoni and Hardesty, pp. 17–19.

49. John 13:14–15.

50. I Timothy 2:9; I Peter 3:3. Such strict applications can be found among certain Pentecostal and Holiness groups, the Amish in the Northeast United States, the Church of the Latter Rain, and others.

51. Hearn, p. 62.

52. Bill Love, "Practical Implications of a Change in the Role of Women," *Essays on Women in Earliest Christianity*, Vol. 2, p. 575.

53. Thomas H. Olbricht, "Women in the Church: The Hermeneutical Problem," *Essays on Women in Earliest Christianity*, Vol. 2, pp. 556, 568.

54. James Bodensieck, "Theological Principles Determining the Role of Christian Women in Church and Society," Lutheran Social Ethics Seminar, Valparaiso University (December, 1955), p. 1; see also Russell Prohl, pp. 18–19; Scanzoni and Hardesty, p. 20.

55. Mark 7:1ff.

56. Susanne K. Langer, "The Growing Center of Knowledge," *Philosophical Sketches* (Baltimore: Johns Hopkins Press, 1962), p. 147.

Chapter Ten

STRATEGY FOR CHANGE

Where do we go from here? Complex theological assertions are meaningless unless they are translated into practical application, and that must be genuine, not empty ritualization or patronization. In order to face the issue of the status of women constructively, conservative Christians must accept that both the church and New Testament theology must remain flexible. Both must experience continual reassessment, and both must keep pace with the advancing human situation. In the words of George Tavard:

> One cannot build a theology in historical isolation anymore than in the abstract. Consideration of woman today will avoid abstraction. Insertion of our thought in the continuity of Christian tradition will avoid isolation. What we see and think of woman today is necessarily tied to what was seen and thought formerly. The difficulty comes when we try to assess what in this tradition remains normative and what was too influenced by local or temporary conditions, by contingent cultural patterns, by human prejudice and by philosophical bias to be valid today.[1]

The Gospel message is not static, but experiences a continuous flow of unfolding and finding new applications within the flux of history becoming.[2] G.C. Berkouwer expresses it in this fashion:

> The Word has to be free to remake and reform the Church over and over again. The moment the Church loses interest in working the mines of the Word because it thinks it has seen all there is to see, that moment the Church also loses its power and its credibility in the world. When the Church thinks it knows all there is to know, the opportunity for surprising discovery is closed. The Church then becomes old, without perspective, and without light and labor and fruitfulness.[3]

Of course, the motive for remining the Word should not be to find supportive evidence for preconceptions, nor should it be to reinterpret critical passages so as to bury a problem and pretend it never existed. Instead, it must be to listen for the voice of God speaking to our time and act accordingly.

Having arrived at certain definitive conclusions, a resolution of the church's dilemma concerning the status of women will require a concerted collective effort at a practical and grass roots level. Nesbitt appropriately stresses that the flaw in deconstructive analysis is often the failure to offer reconstructive alternatives.[4] Therefore, corrective steps must include due consideration to such issues as socio-economic and political shifts, generational critique, mutilayered personal and interpersonal stresses, as well as the most obvious areas of female roles and status. Where change does not occur naturally and spontaneously it must be initiated and then nurtured with careful planning and great care. Numerous problems will be encountered in the reconstruction and reconciliation process.

I. Facing the Trauma of Change

Change is often painful and costly, especially where it involves established religious traditions. In fact, iconoclasts generally face ostracization by the establishment and by their peers, possibly perceived by some as the enemies of God. Despite efforts to maintain harmonious relationships while change is brought about slowly, often confrontation is forced by the incompatibility of enlightenment and tradition. That is to be expected. The process of change is unavoidably traumatic. Unfortunately, staunch traditionalism tends to resist to the point of revolution, which intensifies the trauma.

What has occurred in the past century is a combination of scholastic reexamination and collective protest, and there is a difference between protest and social change. Protest is a verbal and physical expression of disapproval, arising from inequity and injustice when the level of tolerance is exceeded. Positive change is the desired result of protest. Yet, such results are not typically realized by correcting documentation or even by modifying methodology. It usually begins there, but it must eventually extend deep into human attitudes and social views by replacing old ideologies through affirmative action. It is one thing for slaves to be declared free, but quite another to overcome the spirit of racism and discrimination within a society. It is one thing for a country to declare its independence from colonial rule. It is another thing to shoulder the responsibility for independence, to develop a government and economic structure whereby individuals may personally experience the privileges of free enterprise. Likewise, it is one thing to declare women legally, socially or spiritually equal, but another to break down time hardened traditions, enabling them to enjoy relationships and roles which truly reflect theoretical equality. However, the process of change must begin somewhere.

We have ample reason to believe that change is more difficult in more advanced societies, America being right at the top. A survey among Reformed churches by Henny Dirks-Blatt offers evidence that changes in the status of women in the church have been more difficult in the Western world than among churches in Africa, Asia, South America and Australasia.[5] For several centuries missionaries have managed to infuse into other societies a mixture of Christian doctrine and Western culture, all in the name of world evangelism. Their success is attributable, in part, to the link between the two in the minds of the recipients. Since Western culture is advanced and its collective knowledge greater, so the recipients conclude, its religious beliefs must be superior also. Therefore, Christian doctrine has been supported subliminally by the technological and socioeconomic superiority of its immediate point of origin. Since the Protestant Work Ethic interprets economic success and prosperity as a sign of spiritual rectitude, forcing self-examination and change at the headwaters of that belief is difficult.

Another hindrance to change among conservative churches in America has been that the United States Constitution protects the right of discrimination against women in religion, since this is an essential corollary to the freedom of worship based on each church's understanding of Holy Scripture.[6] In the same way, churches have the right to debar from membership practicing homosexuals, divorced persons, or any others whom they consider impenitent or morally unsuitable. This element of religious freedom is certain to be challenged in the future, because it flaunts class discrimination and social inequity. Religion cannot be exempt from, or a sanctuary from, essential human rights.

There are certain socio-economic difficulties to be faced. Chafetz points out the simple law of supply and demand, and the fact that if all the female seminarians were ordained today the result would reduce the number of available jobs for men by half.[7] A sudden radical change might be devastating. But that is no excuse for bad theology.

Excuses for resisting change are numerous. Some traditionalists fear disastrous moral consequences, viewing feminism as a herald of Armageddon, a virulent heresy that threatens to destroy the home and corrupt the values of future generations.[8] Then there are several hackneyed excuses like: "Some people won't like it," or "Introducing controversy is wrong," or "This is going to split the church."

Some churchmen argue that women are unsuitable for church leadership because they are sexually appealing to men and therefore become a distraction. If this is true, one must ask whether such has been prohibitive in the secular world, where women are capably filling responsible positions and overcoming the barriers created by "sex appeal." Surely the same could be said of female psychologists, business executives, politicians, university professors, attorneys, and physicians. Yet mature people recognize the individual responsibility to control his or her sexual urges, regardless of an attraction to an individual in a leadership position. Furthermore, it cannot be overlooked that in the past the subordination of women has no doubt contributed to common syndrome wherein women become sexually attracted to men in power positions. Clergymen are continually in this precarious situation and must guard against unwholesome relationships and the abuse of their position. Professional ethics demands this in virtually every field. If the desirability of women categorically eliminates them as candidates for the ministry, then males, especially young attractive ones, should be categorically prohibited from pastoring churches with female members. But this offers no logical rationale for generalizations or prohibitions. On the contrary, such are common obstacles to be overcome in the performance of noble and necessary tasks.

People are naturally prone to static conditions and are conservative with regard to collective patterns. Change does not occur without a disruption of the norm and a concerted effort to dispel mythical beliefs, which of necessity creates discomfort.[9] Such discomfort is evident among conservative Christians on the issue of women. A church elder summarized the dilemma in these words: "We have to change our beliefs about the role of women, but our people are too set in their ways to accept it gracefully. I just hope we can stall it long enough so that we can pass the problem on to the next generation to deal with."

In contrast, it seems abundantly clear that believers are compelled to shoulder responsibility for practicing and promoting the principles of the Gospel. Church leaders should play a key role in assisting their members to adjust, rather than complicating modern living by demanding allegiance to antiquated and inferior ideologies, or by balking at responsibility and stalling essential progress under the banner of "preserving peace."

II. Restructuring Male and Female Roles in Marriage

Many churches also have upheld mutually conflicting ideals concerning roles and relationships in the home. There is a general trend today to encourage attitudes of sharing, mutual support and understanding between husbands and wives, while at same time holding to a biblical pattern of the wife's subordinate role and husband's headship. In the attempt to build more stable homes, fathers have been urged to spend more time with their children, share in domestic chores and interests, and such like, yet at the same time they are instructed to shoulder their responsibility as familial head. Wives, in turn, may be encouraged obtain education and develop skills which might place them above certain men, even their own husbands, yet they are taught that happiness and fulfillment is to obtained by submission. Some husbands have welcomed the supplementary income from working wives, but are unwilling to share in domestic chores and child supervision and deny their wives the dignity of partnership. These positions are incompatible and contradictory.[10]

For some time it has been apparent that the rising divorce rate is directly related to the stress of conflicting ideologies. While conservatives advocate a return to the "husband as head of the wife" paradigm, there is a growing body of evidence that such marriages in our day are not as healthy as has been supposed. It is likely that this kind of structure, especially in "religious addictive" families, leads to dysfunctional relationships and has pathological effects on children and wives.[11] There is a growing emphasis on marriage in which each partner sees the other as an equal, in a mutually dependent and mutually submissive relationship void of power, headship, and authority overtones characteristic of traditional patriarchal marriages. Such relationships are proving superior because they are void of competition, feelings of threat, neurotic dependency, and low self-esteem, and are not based on ego gratification or the pathological domination of one individual by another.

To assist such changes at the individual and family level, churches should engage in an active effort to promote concepts of love, cooperation, and partnership in marriage, without attempting to defend female submission and male headship. Opportunities for such guidance are especially plentiful in the context of marital and premarital counseling, but this requires the attention of ministers or psychotherapists who are fully informed of recent developments in both psychology and theology. With time, the superior ideologies will supplant antiquated tradition and the unpleasantness of transition will pass.

The future of equality may depend as much on personal relationships as on legislation, social approval and church doctrine. As Chafe points out, it is a reciprocal process taking place between cultural values, social institutions, individual life choices and interpersonal relationships. The personal becomes both social and political.[12] Therefore, it seems that the church, by assisting its members to learn equity in heterosexual relationships, can and will have a marked effect on the attainment of justice and equity on a social level, and the development of healthier personal and interpersonal relationships in future generations.

It is likely that divorce trends will reverse as the present stress of conflicting ideologies gives way to a new norm. Studies of marital stability since the 1930s suggest that where both partners in a marriage work or remain intellectually active, with neither significantly more successful than the other, the relationship is likely to have balance and stability.[13] A significant factor in attaining equality is a willingness on the part of both to sacrifice some of society's present obsession with individualism in order to be mutually supportive. The future is likely to see a revival of the concept of shared vision in marriage, a characteristic of many marriages in pioneer, colonial, medieval, and various ancient cultures, allowing the husband and wife to work together in the same career and provide mutual support in individual pursuits without overt male domination.

III. Taking Definitive Steps in Church Polity and Liturgy

Mary Van Leeuwen states that throughout the modern feminist movement good churches have cushioned the negative effects of social change by operating as extended families, and by encouraging women to minister and to improve themselves to whatever degree they find acceptance.[14] But the most difficult aspects of this change have been pushed back, awaiting some definitive action that never comes. Clearly, at some point a visible change has to be made. Patronization and token gestures will only intensify general dissatisfaction and will lead to more aggressive forms of revolt.

The best approach is simply to outline a program for genuine change, with clear objectives, goals and a definitive structure void of discriminatory mechanisms and regulations. This must include placing women into positions that represent genuine expressions of equality. Maitland describes such an approach as "process theology," which is best defined in terms borrowed from popular psychology: "We do not think ourselves into better ways of acting; we act ourselves into better ways of thinking."[15] Genuine change can only occur through genuine action. As Dirks-Blatt points out, "learning by doing" is essential in this kind of change, and churches, as well as the men and women who constitute them, will only be able to adjust to participation by women once those changes are enacted.[16]

Schmidt lists seven crucial and immediate tasks, even for churches that have already taken the first step by granting women the right to ordination:

1. Develop strong denominational leadership to promote values, direction and role modeling toward the inclusion of women at every level.
2. Include women in larger numbers at higher echelons.
3. Set quotas and extend to every level of church role so as to distribute power.
4. Assure that male leaders remain visibly active and supportive of change.
5. Issue a clear and unambiguous directive to ordain women.
6. Help the church move beyond the debate over sameness by practicing equality.
7. Teach males to adopt some of the characteristics, values and commitments generally attributed to women.[17]

Here is the crux of the matter. Someone must take the first step. Even among fundamentalist churches like the Church of Christ, with all the unpleasantness and fear of change, someone eventually must initiate it and accept the consequences. Playing on a scenario from a paper by Nancy Sehested,[18] one Sunday morning somewhere a congregation will assemble, and all the signs of change will be visible. The marquee might still read "Church of Christ," or "Baptist Church" but certain aspects of structure and assembly format will be different. A woman will conduct the adult Bible class, another will lead the opening prayer, and perhaps three others along with three men will serve the Lord's Supper. The pulpit minister of this particular congregation might even be a woman. If not, on this Sunday there is a guest speaker, a minister from another church across town. She holds the same degrees and the same recognized paid position. Further differences appear on the church bulletin where the names of elders and deacons are given. Perhaps the term "shepherd" is used instead of "elder," and the list includes both men and women. Perhaps instead of deacons and deaconesses, the bulletin lists twenty-five "ministry leaders," both men and women. But the change is evident, nonetheless. This is how it must be. This is the new wine that cannot be put into old skins.

IV. Taking a Lead in Social Advances

The World Council of Churches' Decade for Women followed upon the United Nations Decade for Women, seeking to advance the status of

women in the church and world by addressing the obstacles still standing in the way of total equity, wholeness and mutuality among the people of God. The issues faced by women in society in the '90s continue
into the twenty-first century. Among them are the feminization of
poverty, teenage pregnancy, abortion and surrogacy, alcohol and drug
abuse, wife beating, and racism among women. In spite of advances there
is still a great deal to be overcome before women enjoy equal pay for equal
work, and before discrimination and sexism are overcome with regard to
positions of responsible leadership.

Tavard suggests that there has always been a tendency for the church
to hold back rather than taking the lead in any form of social advancement. Many progressive churches have attempted to do so in this century, but conservative churches avoid being associated with the
avant-garde in a movement away from tradition. The rationale for this,
it seems, is to maintain a quiet and orderly profile within the cultural status quo. While this is quite sensible with reference to matters of propriety, such as modest dress and general social conduct, the principle cannot
apply to issues of ethics and justice.

For this reason Biblical Feminist Theology arises in response to desperate human need at a time when world consciousness is turned to issues
such as international peace, social injustice and world hunger.[19] Women
are especially sensitive to these great social needs largely because they as
a class, and in various ways each one as an individual, have suffered what
Schillebeeckx has called a "contrast experience."[20] This is an experience
of events or circumstances which are essentially negative, perhaps even
shocking and scandalous, the result of which one intuitively knows it to
be morally unjust or evil … that it should not exist. Slavery, Apartheid,
genocide, tyranny, and terrorism are extreme examples. The church cannot close its eyes to great social evils. But action is typically taken only
when sufficient numbers of its members experience a certain form of evil
to recognize it, or come to feel strongly enough to take action. Such action
inevitably brings with it a perspective and community structure quite
different from that of the previous era simply because it is born of revolution, which is in fact a collective reaction against perceived evil. Sexism is one of the great historical evils opposed by the spirit of the Gospel,
and against which the church must take a stand.

Sehested suggests that the liberation of women in churches calls for
a new vision of power and authority in terms of servant leadership.[21]
Women are stepping into roles of authority without sufficient personal
and historical experience to deal with it well. Yet it may be that because
of their experience as women they will be able to bring with them a clearer

perception of servanthood than men have been able to learn, and therefore offer a dimension to leadership that has been lacking. Of particular concern to Sehested is the role women need to play in determining the direction of the world, considering the vital issues going into the twenty-first century. The quest for liberation by financially secure women in the Western world hardly compares to massive starvation, civil war, ethnic cleansing and brutality against women in certain Islamic cultures, and the "churches' complicity with a nuclear arms race that sucks the life out of our economy and threatens Armageddon for the whole creation." She concludes:

> I have only an indirect interest in promoting equal opportunity for women. My major concern is that women be allowed to take up equal responsibility, equal "ability to respond" to the crises of our world.[22]

V. Changing Self-Perception in Women

In a letter to the women of the Anglican Community, Pamela Chinnis outlines what she sees as needs still to be addressed:

> It may be that the most blatant forms of bias are behind us, but they were the easier ones to fight. Now the most significant obstacles may be the inner barriers—inner barriers for men and women both that have been bred into us by generations and acculturization.[23]

Clearly female liberation is not merely a battle against male chauvinism. It is also a battle against a traditional orientation in women themselves. Letha Scanzoni states that liberation should be defined as a "state of mind" in which woman comes to see herself as Jesus sees her.[24] This means that each woman who has been locked into the traditional model of subjection faces a personal struggle to view herself and other women differently.

In many churches opposition to change has come from women as strongly as from men and from church leadership. This is not surprising, for several reasons. Many women feel threatened by feminism. The old view of women at least provides the traditional housewife with a certain degree of security, as long as she remains in submission. Her glory has been in whatever role her husband has found success and acceptance. She has basked in his limelight and has been afforded at least some share in the credit, if only in patronizing accolades such as: "Behind every great man is a great woman." To such women liberation appears to demand independence and competition in a world where they do not feel comfortable ... where in fact they feel incompetent. Some women will resist change because of timidity and fear of accepting new areas of responsibility. But facing these challenges will have to become as critical in the preaching and teaching of the church as, for example, teaching ethics, morality, family and home, parenthood, or church doctrine has been in the past.

Some women also will experience jealousy, perhaps feeling threatened by those women who are ready to take the quantum leap to equality. Church membership under the pastoral care of another woman might bring personal feelings of inferiority. This is no cause for retreat, since in the secular world women have adjusted quite well to employment under female executives, treatment by female physicians, education under female professors, or advisement by female counselors and attorneys. Nonetheless, religious tradition is resilient and the male clerical mystique will die hard in the minds of many women. Some scholars are convinced that should women be invited immediately to join the sacramental ministry, the work of changing women's conception of themselves as silent, passive receptacles of grace will take generations.[25]

Naturally, women who step into positions of leadership initially will suffer because of the absence of role models.[26] But this also will be overcome only though positive and visionary participation in change. The brave new generation will follow a trail blazed by brave pioneers. Someone has to face new challenges without the benefit of role models. Therefore, one of the essentials in this challenging era is that capable women must be placed in positions of responsibility, and within a decade role models will be established for successive generations. Then women will no longer perceive themselves as timid creatures of the house, inferior and subordinate. They will no longer identify with shy women of ancient Greece, venturing into the streets for the first time, defying the authority of their husbands and embarrassing the angels of heaven by asking questions or speaking out in church. Instead, they will see themselves as mature women, the equals and partners of men, filling responsible roles in the service of God in a world where their abilities and opinions are welcome.

VI. Regaining Purpose and Credibility

Some churches are in danger of choosing a destructive course, refusing to acknowledge the need for change and excommunicating all feminist sympathizers. As has been the case over past issues, in many churches there is the possibility of large scale splits resulting in liberal and conservative branches. Both Protestant and Catholic Christianity are already riddled with doctrinal confusion and conflict, and an issue such as this could bring disastrous consequences where leaders do not exercise caution and patience. Therefore, great care should be taken to maintain dialogue and openness, although in some churches either a split or a massive loss of membership seems inevitable.

Over the centuries the church as an institution has found itself fighting senseless battles while significant human needs were left unattended, largely because churchmen have taken a dogmatic stand on mistaken beliefs. In the nineteenth and twentieth centuries an unnecessary warfare between science and scripture has continued. Among university students and academics in general, the Bible and Christianity have lost credibility, and many lay persons have left their traditional churches and lost faith in God altogether over relatively insignificant issues. Some denominations have lost credibility with their members because of a lack of vision and purpose, devoting themselves to the task of defending and promoting a sectarian identity without a truly meaningful reason for existing. Obsession with doctrines that have little contemporary significance renders the church ineffective and worthless.

Clearly the failure of the church to acknowledge the rightful place of women in society, in the home and in church leadership has seriously damaged the credibility of the Bible and Christianity as a whole. Churches are not only challenged to make essential changes on this vital issue, but also to overcome the damage inflicted upon their people in the process. In the twenty-first century and beyond church leaders and theologians must engage in a careful reexamination of the *raison d'être* of all organizational forms of Christianity, both historically and spiritually, as well as determining immediate and long range goals. The church must rediscover its purpose, its relevance to human existence, and its objectives in human history, or it has no reason to continue. Robert King suggests that such a task is the major concern of theology today:

> If there can be said to be a single overriding task for theology at the present time, it is to recover a sense of the wholeness, the unity and integrity, of the Christian witness.[27]

His words express a hope for a greater awareness and understanding of theological trends by tradition-bound churchmen, allowing a healthy assimilation of wisdom from nontraditional sources. In this process, each Christian denomination should reassess the Gospel message with respect to spiritual, political and sociological needs of humanity, and all church doctrines should be examined in terms of legitimate value. If this occurs the result will certainly be an enhancement of the influence of Christianity in a world of religious pluralism, as well as a degree of unification and revitalization among Christians.

In Ephesians 4:11–16 Paul writes about the church growing to maturity. His vision of the church building itself in love was merely an internalized expression of the Great Commission, in which apostles were sent by Christ into all the world with a message of hope, peace, freedom and salvation. The church has a two-fold purpose of ministering to the needs of its people while at the same time ministering to the needs of the world. Such a mission is attainable only for a church with responsible spiritual perception, which demands facing change and dealing with the needs of a rapidly changing and increasingly complex world. Dietrich Bonhoeffer asked: "How can we reclaim for Christ a world which has come of age?"[28] Paul's visionary answer is, "By means of a church come of age."

Such a church will acknowledge the great historical evil of patriarchy which has held women in subjection to the present time and will set them free. Further, such a church will recognize the vast resources and potential for good in its women, encouraging in them full participation in roles of service and leadership of which they are fully capable, for which they are equally suitable and have been equally trained, and to which they have been called by the Spirit of God.

Chapter Ten Notes

1. Tavard, pp. 187–8.

2. The concept of "word event" in an unfolding flow of history was pioneered by Martin Heidegger and developed by Gerhard Ebeling, Ernst Fuchs, and others. See Robert King, "The Task of Systematic Theology," *Christian Theology: An Introduction to Its Traditions and Tasks*, Peter C. Hodgson and Robert H. King, eds. (London: SPCK, 1983), p. 23.

3. G.C. Berkouwer, "Understanding Scripture," *Christianity Today* 14 (May 22, 1970), p. 40.

4. Nesbitt, p. 175.

5. Henny Dirks-Blatt, "Women Ministers of WARC Member Churches on the Ordination of Women," *Reformed World*, Vol. 39, No. 1 (1986), pp. 490–1.

6. Elmer T. Clark, *The Small Sects in America* (New York: Abingdon Press, 1949), pp. 13–20.

7. Janet Saltzman Chafetz, *Gender Equality: An Integrated Theory of Stability and Change* (Newbury Park: Sage, 1990), p. 122.

8. Kenneth S. Kantzer, "Proceed With Care," *Christianity Today*, Vol. 30, No. 16 (October 3, 1986), p. 15–I.

9. Jo Freeman, *The Politics of Women's Liberation* (New York: David McKay Co., 1975), pp. 13, 16.

10. D.M. Ackermann, "The Role of Women in the Church, Certain Practical Theological Perspectives," *Sexism and Feminism in Theological Perspective*, W.S. Vorster, ed. (Pretoria: University of South Africa, 1984), p. 79.

11. Jack O. and Judith Balswick, *The Family: A Christian Perspective on the Contemporary Home* (Grand Rapids: Baker, 1989), pp. 91ff., p. 281.

12. Chafe, p. 155.

13. Chafe, p. 163.

14. Van Leeuwen, p. 12.

15. Sara Maitland, *A Map of the New Country: Women and Christianity* (London: Routledge and Kegal Paul, 1975), p. 191.

16. Henny Dirks-Blatt, Part I, p. 443.

17. Frederick W. Schmidt, *A Still Small Voice: Women, Ordination and the Church* (New York: Syracuse University Press, 1996), p. 173.

18. Nancy Hastings Sehested, "Women and Ministry in the Local Congregations," *Review and Expositor*, Vol. 83, No. 1 (1986), p. 71–9.

19. Virginia Hearn, "Christian Feminists in North America: The Experience of Evangelical Women," *Dialogue & Alliance*, Vol. II, No. 3 (Fall, 1988), p. 70.

20. Haight, p. 110; Edward Schillebeeckx, *God the Future of Man*, N.D. Smith, trans. (New York: Sheed and Ward, 1968), pp. 136–64.

21. Sehested, pp. 71–9.

22. *Ibid.*, p. 78.

23. Pamela P. Chinnis, The Episcopal Church Center, 815 Second Avenue, New York, N.Y. 10017 (September 15, 1987).

24. Scanzoni, p. 12.

25. "Ordination of women: more debate on topic is imperative," *Seek* (June–July, 1989), p. 8. This article pertains to the 1989 diocesan conference on the ministry in the Anglican Church, held in Pietermaritzburg.

26. Kelsey Menehan, "Women in Seminary: Preparing for What?" *Christianity Today* (September 5, 1986), p. 20.

27. Robert H. King, "The Task of Systematic Theology," *Christian Theology: An Introduction to its Traditions and Tasks*, Peter Hodgson and Robert King, eds. (London: SPCK, 1983), p. 26.

28. Dietrich Bonhoeffer, *Letters and Papers from Prison* (Edinburgh: Macmillan, 1953).

BIBLIOGRAPHY

Scholarly Journal Articles

Ackermann, Denise. "Feminist Liberation Theology: a Contextual Option," *Journal of Theology for Southern Africa*, No. 62 (March, 1988), pp. 14–28.

Allison, Robert W. "Let Women Be Silent in the Church (I Cor. 14:33b–36): What Did Paul Really Say, and What Did It Mean?" *Journal for the Study of the New Testament*, 10 (1988): 27–60.

Bartchy, S. Scott. "Issues of Power and a Theology of the Family," Parts I and II, *Mission* (July-August, 1987), pp. 3–15; (September, 1987), pp. 3–11.

Blood, Robert O. "Long-Range Causes and Consequences of the Employment of Married Women," *Journal of Marriage and the Family*, 27:43–47 (February, 1965).

Boucher, M. "Some Unexplored Parallels to I Corinthians 11:11–12 and Galatians 3:28; The New Testament on the Role of Women," *Catholic Biblical Quarterly*, 31:50–8 (June, 1969).

Brown, Raymond E. "Roles of Women in the Fourth Gospel," *Theological Studies* (December, 1975), 36:688–99.

Bunkle, Phillida. "Sentimental Womanhood and Domestic Education, 1830–1870," *History of Education Quarterly* (Spring, 1974).

Busenitz, Irvin A. "Woman's Desire for Man, Gen. 3:16," *Grace Theological Journal*, 7, No. 2 (Fall, 1986), pp. 203–212.

Carnelley, Elizabeth. "Tertullian and Feminism," *Theology* (January, 1989), pp. 31–35.

Davis, John. "Some Reflections on Galatians 3:28, Sexual Roles, and Biblical Hermeneutics," *Journal of Evangelical Theological Society*, 19 (1976).

de Vaux, Roland. "Sur le Voile des Femmes dans l'Orient Ancien," *Review Biblique*, 44 (1935), p. 400.

Dieter, Melvin E. "Women and Ministry in the Methodist Tradition," *Asbury Seminary*, 39, No. 4 (Spring, 1985), pp. 3–7.

Dirks-Blatt, Henny G. "Ordination of Women to Ministry in Member Churches of the World Alliance of Reformed Churches," pt. 2. *Reformed World*, 39, No. 1 (1986), pp. 484–489.

Feuillet, A. "La dignité et le role de la femme d'apies quelques textes pauliniens," *New Testament Studies*, 21:2 (January, 1965).

Fiddes, Paul S. "Woman's Head is the Man," *Baptist Quarterly*, 31, No. 8 (October, 1986), pp. 370–383.

Fitzmeyer, J.A. "A Feature of Qumran Angelology and the Angels of I Corinthians 11:10," *New Testament Studies*, 4:48–58 (1957).

Ford, J. Massyngberde. "Biblical Material Relevant to the Ordination of Women," *Journal of Ecumenical Studies*, X, 4:669–94 (Fall, 1973).

_____. "Levirate Marriage in St. Paul (I Cor. 7)," *New Testament Studies*, 10:3 (April, 1964).

_____. "The Meaning of Virgin," *New Testament Studies*, 12:3 (April, 1966).

_____. "St. Paul the Philogamist (I Cor. 7 in Early Patristic Exegesis)," *New Testament Studies*, 11:4 (July, 1965).

Franklin, Doris. "Impact of Christianity on the Status of Women," *Religion and Society*, 32, No. 2 (June, 1985), pp. 43–55.

Gundersen, Joan R. "The Local Parish as a Female Institution: the Experience of All Saints Episcopal Church in Frontier Minnesota." *Church History*, 55, No. 3 (Spring, 1986) pp. 307–322.

Haight, Roger. "Women in the Church: a Theological Reflection," *Toronto Journal of Theology*, 2, No. 1 (Spring, 1986), pp. 105–117.

Hall, Barbara. "Church in the World: Paul and Women," *Theology Today*, 31:50–55 (April, 1974).

Hastings, Nancy. "Women and Ministry in Local Congregations," *Review and Expositor* 83, No. 1 (Winter, 1986), pp. 71–9.

Hearn, Virginia. "Christian Feminists in North America: The Experience of Evangelical Women," *Dialogue & Alliance*, 2, No. 3 (Fall, 1988), pp. 57–75.

Holley, Bobbey Lee. "God's Design: Women's Dignity," Part Two, *Mission*, VIII, 10:291–5 (April, 1975).

Hommes, N.J. "Let Women Be Silent in the Church: a Message Concerning the Worship Service and the Decorum to be Observed by Women," *Calvin Theological Journal*, 4:5–22 (April, 1969).

Hooker, Morna D. "Authority On Her Head; an Examination of I Corinthians 11:10," *New Testament Studies*, 10:410–16 (April, 1969).

Hurley, James B. "Did Paul Require Veils or the Silence of Women? A Consideration of I Corinthians 11:2–16 and I Corinthians 14:33b–36," *The Westminster Theological Journal*, XL, 2:190–220 (Winter, 1973).

Keane, Marie-Henry. "Woman in the Theological Anthropology of the Early Fathers," *Journal of Theology for Southern Africa*, No. 62 (March, 1988), pp. 3–13.

Lagerwerf, Leny. "South Africa—Women's Struggle in Theology, Church and Society," *Exchange*, 48:33–61 (December, 1987).

Ledbetter, Hoy. "The Prophetess," *Integrity*, January, 1973.

Leonard, E.A. "Paul's View of Women," *Catholic Biblical Quarterly*, 12:311–20 (July, 1950).

Maahs, Kenneth H. "Male & Female in Pauline Perspective: A Study in Biblical Ambivalence," *Dialogue & Alliance*, 2, No. 3 (Fall, 1988), pp. 17–34.

Martin, V.M. and G.M. Rogerson. "Women and Industrial Change: The South African Experience," *South African Geographical Journal*, 66:32–46 (April, 1984).

Nauta, Rommie. "Latin American Women Theology," *Exchange*, 48:7–31 (December, 1987).

Olbricht, Thomas. "Hermeneutics in the Churches of Christ," *Restoration Quarterly* (37, 1995).

_____. "Hermeneutics: The Beginning Point," *Image* (September-October, 1989).

Orden, Susan and Norman Bradburn. "Working Wives and Marriage Happiness," *The American Journal of Sociology* (January, 1969), p. 395.

Parks, Normon L. "Set Our Women Free," *Integrity* (January, 1973).

Paterson, Torquil. "The Ordination of Women: A Contribution to the Debate within the CPSA," *Journal of Theology for Southern Africa*, No. 66 (March, 1989), pp. 21–33.

Pelser, G.M.M. "Women and Ecclesiastical Ministries in Paul," *Neutestamentica*, 10 (1976).

Peterson, David. "The Ordination of Women: Balancing the Scriptural Evidence," *St. Mark's Review*, No. 125 (March, 1986), pp. 13–21.

Sehested, Nancy Hastings. "Women and Ministry in the Local Congregations." *Review and Expositor*, 83:1 (Winter, 1986), pp. 71–9.

Shapiro, J. "Political Organization of Women in South Africa," *African Perspective* 15:1–15 (1980).

Shideler, Mary McDermott. "Male and Female Created He Them," *Religion in Life*, 43:60–7 (Spring, 1974).

Steele, Elizabeth. "The Role of Women in the Church," *Currents in Theology and Mission*, 13, No. 1 (February, 1986), pp. 13–21.

Stockton, Eugene D. "The Woman: A Biblical Theme," *Australian Journal of Biblical Archaeology*, I:6, 106 (November, 1973).

Swart-Russel, Phoebe. "Towards Our Liberation: A New Vision of Church and Ministry," *Journal of Theology for Southern Africa*, No. 66 (March, 1989), pp. 34–47.

Swidler, Leonard. "Jesus Was a Feminist," *South East Asia Journal of Theology*, XII:1, 102 (October, 1971).

Tanner, Mary. "The Ministry of Women; an Anglican Reflection," *One In Christ*, 21, No. 4 (1985) pp. 284–292.

Tisani, Nomathamsanqua. "Christ the Liberator; The Attitude of the Church to the Oppression of Women," *Journal of Theology for Southern Africa*, No. 66 (March, 1989), pp. 79–83.

Tobin, Mary Luke. "Women in the Church Since Vatican II," *America*, 155:243–46 (November 1, 1986).

Wagner, Walter. "The Demonization of Women," *Religion in Life*, XLII (Spring, 1973).

Other Periodical Articles

Ackermann, Denise. "Women Barred in Christian Church," *Seek* (June-July, 1989), p. 8.

Barr, Browne. "The Ordination of Women and the Refreshment of the Sacraments," *The Christian Century* (September 25, 1985), pp. 823–24.

Benton, Catherine. "Does the Church Discriminate Against Women on the Basis of Their Sex?" *Critic*, 24:22 (June-July, 1966).

Berkouwer, G.C. "Understanding Scripture," *Christianity Today*, 14 (May 22, 1970).

Brunt, John C. "Ordination: A Hermeneutical Question," *Ministry* (September, 1988).

"Ecumenical Decade 1988–1998," *South African Outlook* (April, 1988), pp. 57–8.

Eenigenburg, E.M. "The Ordination of Women," *Christianity Today*, 3:15–16 (April 27, 1959).

Florentin-Smith, Francoise. "La femme en milieu protestant," Tatiana Struve, Agnes Cunningham, Francoise Florentin-Smith, *La Femme* (Paris, 1968).

Gaden, J.R. "For the Ordination of Women," *MOW* (Melbourne, 1985).

Green, Roberta. "Cutting Across Convention," *United Evangelical Action* (January-February, 1984).

Hestenes, Roberta. "Women in Leadership: Finding Ways to Serve the Church," *Christianity Today*, Insert (September 3, 1986), p. 10.

Jung, Anees. "Modern Woman, Ancient Religions," *Vogue* (April, 1986).

Kaiser, Walter C., Jr. "Shared Leadership or Male Leadership," *Christianity Today*, 30, No. 14 (October, 1986), pp. 121–131.

Mailer, Norman. "The Prisoner of Sex," *Harper's Magazine* (March, 1971), p. 66.

Neff, David. "The Battle of the Lexicons: Scholars Debate Biblical Roles of Men and Women," *Christianity Today*, 31:44 (January 16, 1987).

Oliver, Harold H. "Beyond the Feminist Critique: A Shaking of the Foundations," *The Christian Century* (May 1, 1985), pp. 446–447.

Riley, Janet. "The Ordination of Disciples Women: A Matter of Economy or Theology?" *Encounter*, 50:3 (Summer, 1989).

Ryrie, C.C. "Women in the Church," *Christianity Today*, 3:13–14 (April 27, 1959).

Slack, Kenneth. "Women's Ordination: The Fight is On," *The Christian Century* (December 4, 1985), pp. 1108–9.

Thompson, Betty. "UM Women: On a Journey to Peace," *The Christian Century* (July 7–14, 1982), pp. 758–9.

Van Leeuwen, Mary Stewart. "The End of Female Passivity," *Christianity Today* (January, 1986, insert), pp. 12–13.

Waltke, Bruce. "Male Headship," *Christianity Today*, Vol. 30, No. 16 (October 3, 1986).

Wright, Susan Lockwood. "SBC Women Ministers Break Their Silence," *The Christian Century* (November 12, 1986).

Yust, Karen-Marie. "Women: Remaking Ministry," *The Disciple* (June, 1998).

Commentaries

Abbot, T.K. "Ephesians and Colossians," *International Critical Commentary*. Edinburgh: T & T Clark, rep. 1968.

Allen, W.C. "The Gospel According to St. Matthew," *International Critical Commentary*. Third Edition. Edinburgh: T & T Clark, rep. 1965.

Barclay, William. *The Gospel of Luke*. Philadelphia: Westminster Press, 1955.

_____. *The Gospel of Mark*. Second Edition. Edinburgh: St. Andrews Press, rep. 1973.

_____. *The Letter to the Romans*. Edinburgh: The St. Andrews Press, 1969.

_____. *The Letters to the Corinthians*. Philadelphia: Westminster Press, 1956.

Barrett, C.K. *A Commentary on the Epistle to the Romans*. New York: Harper and Row, 1957.

_____. *A Commentary on the First Epistle to the Corinthians*. New York: Harper and Row, 1968.

_____. *The Gospel According to St. John*. London: SPCK, rep. 1962.

Barth, Karl. *The Epistle to the Romans*. Sixth edition. E.C. Hoskyns (trans.). Oxford: University Press, rep. 1968.

Bernard, J.H. "Gospel According to John," *International Critical Commentary*. 2 Vols. Edinburgh: T & T Clark, rep. 1969.

_____. "The Second Epistle to the Corinthians," *The Expositor's Greek Testament*, Vol. II. Grand Rapids: Eerdmans, rep. 1970.

Bigg, Charles. "Epistle of St. Peter and St. Jude," *International Critical Commentary*. Edinburgh: T & T Clark, rep. 1969.

Bornkamm, Gunther, G. Barth and H.J. Held. *Tradition and Interpretation in Matthew*. London: SCM, 1963.

Bruce, F.F. *The Acts of the Apostles*. Grand Rapids: Eerdmans, rep. 1970.

Bultmann, Rudolf. *The Gospel of John: A Commentary*. G.R. Beasley-Murray (trans.). Oxford: Basil Blackwell, 1971 edition.

Burton, Ernest de Witt. "The Epistle to the Galatians," *International Critical Commentary*. Edinburgh: T & T Clark, rep. 1968.

Caird, G.B. *Commentary on the Revelation of St. John the Divine*. New York: Harper and Row, 1966.

Calvin, John. *Commentary on the Epistles of Paul the Apostle to the Corinthians*. John Pringle (trans.). 2 vols. Edinburgh: Calvin Translation Society, 1848.

Charles, R.H. "A Critical and Exegetical Commentary on the Revelation of St. John," Vol. I. *International Critical Commentary*, rep. 1963.

Conzelmann, Hans. *Der Erste Brief an die Corinther*. Gottengen: Vanderhoeck and Ruprecht, 1969.

Davidson, F., ed. *The New Bible Commentary*. London: Inter-Varsity Fellowship, rep. 1967.

Dodd, C.H. "The Epistle of Paul to the Romans," *The Moffatt New Testament Commentary*. James Moffatt (ed.). New York: Harper and Brothers, 1932.

_____. *The Interpretation of the Fourth Gospel*. Cambridge: University Press, 1953, rep. 1972.

Dods, Marcus. *The First Epistle to the Corinthians*. London: Hodder and Stoughton, 1900.

Edwards, T.C. *A Commentary on the First Epistle to the Corinthians*. London: Hodder and Stoughton, 1885.

Ellicott, Charles J. *The Pastoral Epistles of St. Paul*. Third edition. London: Longman, Roberts and Green, 1864.

Ferneaux, William Mordaunt. *The Acts of the Apostles*. Oxford: Clarendon Press, 1912.

Filson, Floyd V. *A Commentary on the Gospel According to St. Matthew*. Second edition. London: Adam and Charles Black, 1971.

Gealy, F.D. "I Timothy," *The Interpreter's Bible*, G.A. Butterick, ed. Vol. XI. New York: Abingdon, 1955.

Glen, John Stanley. *Pastoral Problems in First Corinthians*. Philadelphia: Westminster Press, 1964.

Godet, Frederick Louis. *Commentary on the Epistle to the Romans*. Grand Rapids: Zondervan, 1969.

Goudge, Henry Leighton. *The First Epistle to the Corinthians*. Third edition. London: Methuen, 1911.

Grosheide, F.W. *Commentary on the First Epistle to the Corinthians*. Grand Rapids: Eerdmans, 1953.

Hendriksen, William. *A Commentary on I and II Timothy and Titus*. London: Banner of Truth, 1964.

Hertz, J.H., ed. *The Pentateuch and Haftorahs*. Second edition. London: Soncino Press, 1975.

Lenski, R.C.H. *The Interpretation of Acts of the Apostles*. Columbus, Ohio: Lutheran Book Concern, 1934.

_____. *The Interpretation of Galatians, Ephesians, Philippians*. Minneapolis: Augsburg, 1961.

_____. *The Interpretation of St. Paul's Epistle to the Romans*. Minneapolis: Augsburg, rep. 1961.

_____. *The Interpretation of St. Paul's Epistles to the Colossians, to the Thessalonians, to Timothy, to Titus and to Philemon*. Minneapolis: Augsburg, 1961.

_____. *The Interpretation of St. Paul's First and Second Epistles to the Corinthians*. Columbus, Ohio: Lutheran Book Concern, 1946.

_____. *Interpretation of the Epistles of St. Peter, St. John and St. Jude*. Minneapolis: Augsburg, rep. 1961.

Lightfoot, J.B. *The Epistle of St. Paul to the Galatians*. Grand Rapids: Zondervan, rep. 1972.

_____. *St. Paul's Epistle to the Philippians*. Twelfth edition. London: Macmillan and Co. Ltd., 1898.

_____. *St. Paul's Epistles to the Colossians and Philemon*. Grand Rapids: Zondervan, rep. 1971.

Lock, Walter. "A Critical and Exegetical Commentary on the Pastoral Epistles," *International Critical Commentary*. Edinburgh: T & T Clark, 1966.

Luther, Martin. *Commentary on Genesis*, J. Theodore Mueller (trans.). Grand Rapids: Zondervan, 1958.

MacGregor, G.H.C. "The Acts of the Apostles," *The Interpreter's Bible*. Vol. IX. New York: Abingdon, 1954.

Metzger, Bruce M. *A Textual Commentary on the Greek New Testament*. London: United Bible Society, 1971.

Meyer, Heirich August Wilhelm. *Critical and Exegetical Handbook to the Epistles to the Corinthians*. New York: Funk and Wagnalls, 1884.

Micklem, Nathaniel. "II Corinthians," *The Interpreter's Bible*, G.A. Buttrick (ed.). Vol. II. New York: Abingdon, 1953.

Moffatt, James. *The First Epistle of Paul to the Corinthians*. New York: Harper, (n.d.).

_____. "Hebrews," *International Critical Commentary*. Edinburgh: T & T Clark, 1952.

Morgan, G.C. *The Corinthian Letters of Paul*. New York: Fleming H. Revell Co., 1946.

Morris, Leon. *The First Epistle of Paul to the Corinthians; an Introduction and Commentary*. Grand Rapids: Eerdmans, 1958.

_____. *The Gospel According to John*. Grand Rapids: Eerdmans, 1971.

Murray, John. *The Epistle to the Romans*, Vol. II. Grand Rapids: Eerdmans, 1965.

Plummer, Alfred. "The Gospel According to Luke," *International Critical Commentary*. Fifth edition. Edinburgh: T & T Clark, rep. 1964.

_____. "Second Epistle of St. Paul to the Corinthians," *International Critical Commentary*. Edinburgh: T & T Clark, rep. 1966.

Rackham, A.B. *The Acts of the Apostles*. Grand Rapids: Baker, 1964.

Ridderbos, H.N. *The Epistle of Paul to the Churches of Galatia.* Grand Rapids: Eerdmans, 1970.

Rist, Martin. "The Revelation of St. John the Divine," *The Interpreter's Bible*, Vol. XII. New York: Abingdon, 1957.

Robertson, A. "I Corinthians," *International Critical Commentary.* New York: Charles Scribner's Sons, 1925.

Robertson, A. and A. Plummer. "First Epistle of St. Paul to the Corinthians," *International Critical Commentary.* Edinburgh: T & T Clark, reprint 1967.

Sanday, W. and A.C. Headlam. "The Epistle to the Romans," *International Critical Commentary.* Edinburgh: T & T Clark, rep. 1968.

Schnackenburg, Rudolf. *The Gospel According to St. John*, Volume I, K. Smith (trans.). New York: Herder and Herder, 1968.

Shedd, W.G.T. *A Critical and Doctrinal Commentary on the Epistle of St. Paul to the Romans.* Grand Rapids: Zondervan, 1879, rep. 1967.

Stanley, A.D. *The Epistles of Paul to the Corinthians.* London: John Murray, 1882.

Vincent, Marvin R. "The Epistles to the Philippians and to Philemon," *International Critical Commentary.* Edinburgh: T & T Clark, rep. 1968.

Vine, W.E. *I Corinthians.* London: Oliphants, rep. 1965.

Wedel, T.O. and F.W. Beare. "Ephesians," *The Interpreter's Bible*, G.A. Buttrick (ed.). Vol. X. New York: Abingdon, rep. 1953.

History

Bruce, F.F. *The Spreading Flame.* London: Paternoster, 1970.

Campbell, Alexander, ed. *The Christian System, in Reference to the Union of Christians and a Restoration of Primitive Christianity as Plead in the Current Reformation.* Salem: Ayer, Reprint Edition, 1988.

_____. *The Millennial Harbinger.* 1830–1870. Joplin: College Press, Reprinted Edition, 1987.

Carrington, Philip. *The Early Christian Church.* 2 Vols. Cambridge: University Press, 1957.

Chadwick, Henry. *The Early Church.* Grand Rapids: Eerdmans, 1967.

Cullmann, Oscar. *The Early Church.* A.J.B. Higgens (ed.). London: SCM Press, 1956.

Deissmann, Adolf. *Paul: A Study in Social and Religious History.* William E. Wilson (trans.). Second edition. London: Hodder and Stoughton, 1926.

Dods, Marcus. *Introduction to the New Testament.* London: Hodder and Stoughton, 1891.

Donaldson, James. *Woman: Her Position and Influence in Ancient Greece and Rome, and Among the Early Christians.* London: Longmans, Green and Co., 1907.

Ember, Carol R. and Melvin Ember. *Cultural Anthropology.* New York: Appleton-Century-Crafts, 1973.

Enslin, M.S. *Christian Beginnings.* New York: Harper, 1956.

Ferguson, Everett. *Early Christians Speak.* Austin: Sweet, 1971.

Ferguson, John. *The Heritage of Hellenism.* New York: Science History Publications, 1973.

Foakes-Jackson, F.J., and Kirsopp Lake, eds. *The Beginnings of Christianity.* 5 vols. London: Macmillan, 1926–42.

_____. *Studies in the Life of the Early Church*. New York: George H. Doran Company, 1924.

Gasque, Ward and R.P. Martin, eds. *Apostolic History and the Gospel*. Grand Rapids: Eerdmans, 1970.

Halliday, W.R. *The Pagan Background of Early Christianity*. London: Hodder and Stoughton, 1925.

Harnack, Adolf. *The Mission and Expansion of Christianity in the First Three Centuries*. James Moffat (trans.). Second edition, 2 vols. London: Williams and Norgate, 1908.

Hedlund, Mary F., and H.H. Rowley, trans. and eds. *Atlas of the Early Christian World*. London: Thomas Nelson, 1958.

Hophan, Otto. *Maria*. Turin: Marietti, 1953.

Humbert, Royal, ed. *A Compend of Alexander Campbell's Theology, with Commentary in the Form of Critical & Historical Footnotes*. St. Louis: Bethany, 1961.

Lightfoot, J.B. *The Apostolic Fathers*, Parts I and II. London: Macmillan, 1890.

Lowenberg, James and Ruth Bogen, eds. *Black Women in Nineteenth-Century American Life*. University Park: Pensylvannia State University Press, 1976.

McAllister, Lester G., ed. *An Alexander Campbell Reader*. St. Louis: CBP, 1988.

Nock, A.D. *Early Gentile Christianity and Its Hellenistic Background*. New York: Harper and Row, 1964.

Osburn, Carroll D., ed. *Essays on Women in Earliest Christianity*, Volumes 1 and 2. Joplin: College Press, 1993.

Ramsay, W.M. *The Church in the Roman Empire*. Eighth edition. London: Hodder and Stoughton, 1914.

_____. *St. Paul the Traveller and Roman Citizen*. London: Hodder and Stoughton, 1897.

Randall, Max Ward. *The Great Awakenings and the Restoration Movement: A Study of the 1790–1860 History of the Awakenings and Their Impact Upon the Formation and Early Development and Growth of the Christian Churches—Churches of Christ*. Joplin: College Press, 1983.

Richardson, Robert. *Memoirs of Alexander Campbell*. Philadelphia: Lippincott, 1871.

Schaff, Philip. *History of the Christian Church*. Vols. I–II. Grand Rapids: Eerdmans, rep. 1968.

Stendahl, Krister. *The Bible and the Role of Women: A Case Study in Hermeneutics*, Emile T. Sanders (trans.). Philadelphia: Fortress, 1966.

Unger, Merrill F. *Archaeology and the New Testament*. Grand Rapids: Zondervan, 1962.

Vigeveno, H.S. *Jesus Was a Revolutionary*. Glendale: G/L Publications, reprint 1972.

Weiss, Johannes. *Earliest Christianity, A History of the Period A.D. 30–150*. F.C. Grant (ed. and trans.). Vols. I and II. New York: Harper and Brothers, 1959.

_____. *The History of Primitive Christianity*. F.C. Grant (ed.). 2 vols. New York: Wilson-Erickson, 1937.

Williams, D. Newell, ed. *A Case Study of Mainstream Protestantism: The Disciples' Relation to American Culture, 1880–1989*. Grand Rapids: Eerdmans, 1991.

General Works

Allen, C. Leonard and Richard T. Hughes. *Discovering Our Roots: the Ancestry of Churches of Christ*. Abilene: ACU Press, 1988.

Backman, Milton V., Jr. *Christian Churches of America*. New York: Charles Scribner's Sons, 1976.

Barnhouse, Ruth Tiffany and Urban T. Holmes III, eds. *Male and Female*. New York: The Seabury Press, 1976.

Barr, James. *The Bible in the Modern World*. London: SCM Press, 1973.

_____. *Escaping from Fundamentalism*. London: SCM Press, 1984.

_____. *Fundamentalism*. Philadelphia: Westminster Press, 1978.

Becker, Ernest. *Escape from Evil*. New York: The Free Press, 1975.

Bedell, George C., Leo Sandon and Charles T. Wellborn. *Religion in America*. Second edition. New York: Macmillan, 1982.

Bennison, Charles E. *In Praise of Congregations: Leadership in Local Churches Today*. Cambridge: Cowley, 1999.

Bilezikian, Gilbert. *Beyond Sex Roles*. Grand Rapids: Baker, 1985.

Bonhoeffer, Dietrich. *Letters and Papers from Prison*. Edinburgh: Macmillan, 1953.

Brooke, G.J., ed. *Women in Biblical Tradition*. Lewiston: Edwin Miller, 1992.

Brun, Henry J. *Women of the Ancient World*. New York: Richards Rosen Press, Inc., 1976.

Caird, G.B. *Paul and Women's Liberty*. The Manson Memorial Lectures, University of Manchester, 1971.

Chafe, William H. *Women and Equality*. New York: Oxford University Press, 1977.

Chafetz, Janet Saltzman. *Gender Equality: An Integrated Theory of Stability and Change*. Newbury Park: Sage, 1990.

Chavez, Mark. *Ordaining Women: Culture and Conflict in Religious Organizations*. Cambridge: Harvard, 1997.

Christ, Carol P. and Judith Plaskow, eds. *Womanspirit Rising: A Feminist Reader in Religion*. San Francisco: Harper and Row, 1979.

Christenson, Larry. *The Christian Family*. Minneapolis: Bethany Fellowship, 1970.

Cone, James H. *For My People; Black Theology and the Black Church*. Johannesburg: Skotaville, 1985.

Culver, Elsie Thomas. *Women in the World of Religion*. Garden City: Doubleday, 1967.

Culwell, Kitty Jones. *Sarah's Daughters*. Murfreesboro: Dehoff Publications, 1958.

Davenport, T.R.H. *South Africa: A Modern History*. Bergvlei: Southern Books, rep. 1987.

Deen, Edith. *All the Women of the Bible*. New York: Harper and Brothers, 1955.

de Gruchy, John W. *The Church Struggle in South Africa*. Grand Rapids: Eerdmans, 1986.

de Moubray, GA. de C. *Matriarchy in the Malay Peninsula*. London: George Routledge and Sons, 1931.

Doely, Sarah Bentley, ed. *Women's Liberation and the Church*. New York: Association Press, 1970.

Donne, John. "First Anniversary." *The Complete English Poems of John Donne*. C.A. Patrides, ed. London: Dent, 1985.

Erickson, Erik. *Identity, Youth and Crisis*. New York: W.W. Norton, 1968.

_____. *Childhood and Society*, second edition. New York: W.W. Norton, 1963.

Ferriss, Abbott L. *Indicators of Trends in the Status of American Women*. New York: Russell Sage Foundation, 1971.

Fiorenza, Elizabeth Schüssler. *In Memory of Her*. London: SCM, 1983.

Fiorenza, Elizabeth Schüssler and Mary Collins, eds. "Women: Invisible in Church and Theology," *Concilium: Religion in the Eighties*. Edinburgh: T & T Clark, 1985.

Fitzwater, Perry B. *Woman, Her Mission, Position and Ministry*. Grand Rapids: Eerdmans, 1949.

Flexner, Elenor. *Century of Struggle*. New York: Atheneum, 1959.

Foh, Susan. *Women and the Word of God: A Response to Biblical Feminism*. Phillipsburg: Presbyterian and Reformed Publishers, 1979.

Freeman, Jo. *The Politics of Women's Liberation*. New York: David McKay, 1975.

Friedan, Betty. *The Feminine Mystique*. New York: Dell, 1963.

Gibson, Elsie. *When the Minister is a Woman*. New York: Holt, Rinehart and Winston, 1970.

Gilman, Charlotte Perkins. *Women and Economics*. New York: Harper & Row, 1966. Original edition, 1898.

Glasgow, Maude. *The Subjection of Women and the Traditions of Men*. New York: Maude Glasgow, 1940.

Goode, William. *World Revolution and Family Patterns*. Glencoe, Illinois: Free Press, 1963.

Gouge, Henry Leighton. *The Place of Woman in the Church*. London: R. Scott, 1917.

Grant, Robert M. *A Short History of the Interpretation of the Bible*. Revised edition. New York: Macmillan, 1963.

Green, Marge. *Martha, Martha!* Abilene: Quality, 1964.

Grenz, Stanley J. *Women in the Church: A Biblical Theology of Women in the Ministry*. London: Inter-Varsity Press, 1995.

Hays, H.A. *The Dangerous Sex: The Myth of Feminine Evil*.

Hecker, Eugene A. *A Short History of Women's Rights*. New York: George Putnam's Sons, 1910.

Heine, Susanne. *Women and Early Christianity: Are Feminist Scholars Right?* London: SCM, 1987.

Hestenes, Roberta. *The Next Step: Women in a Divided Church* (Waco: Word, 1987).

Hobbs, Lottie Beth. *Daughters of Eve*. Ft. Worth: Harvest Publications, 1963.

Hodgson, Peter C. and Robert H. King, eds. *Christian Theology: An Introduction to its Traditions and Tasks*. London: SPCK, 1983.

Hopko, Thomas, ed. *Women and the Priesthood*. St. Vladimir's Seminary Press, 1999.

House, Wayne. *The Role of Women in Ministry Today*. Grand Rapids: Baker, 1995.

Hull, Debra B. *Christian Church Women: Shapers of a Movement*. St. Louis: Chalice, 1994.

Hunt, Susan. *Leadership for Women in the Church*. Grand Rapids: Zondervan, 1991.

Inkeles, Alex. *What Is Sociology?* Englewood Cliffs: Prentice-Hall, 1964.

Isaksson, Abel. *Marriage and Ministry in the New Temple; A Study with Special Reference to Matthew 19:3–12 and I Corinthians 11:3–16*. Lund: Gleerup, 1965.

Janeway, Elizabeth. *Man's World, Woman's Place*. New York: William Morrow, 1971.

Jewett, Paul K. *Man as Male and Female*. Grand Rapids: Eerdmans, 1975.

_____. *The Ordination of Women*. Grand Rapids: Eerdmans, 1980.

King, Robert H. "The Task of Systematic Theology," *Christian Theology: An Introduction to its Traditions and Tasks*, Peter Hodgson and Robert King (eds.). London: SPCK, 1983.

Knight, Charles H. *Christianity in Culture*. Maryknoll: Orbis, 1979.

Kroeger, Richard C. and Catherine C. *I Suffer Not a Woman: Rethinking I Timothy 2:11–15 in Light of Ancient Evidence*. Grand Rapids: Baker, 1992.

Kuyper, Abraham. *Women of the New Testament*. Henry Zylstru (trans.). Grand Rapids: Zondervan, 1973.

Langer, Susanne K. "The Growing Center of Knowledge," *Philosophical Sketches*. Baltimore: Johns Hopkins Press, 1962.

Lees, Shirley, ed. *The Role of Women*. Leicester: Inter-Varsity Press, 1984.

Lillie, William. *Studies in New Testament Ethics*. London: Olive and Boyd, 1961.

Lindley, D. Ray. *Apostle of Freedom*. St. Louis: Bethany, 1957.

Mace, David and Verna. *Marriage East and West*. New York: Doubleday, 1960.

Mack, Wayne. *The Role of Women in the Church*. Cherry Hill: Mack Publishing Co., 1972.

Maitland, Sara. *A Map of the New Country: Women and Christianity*.London: Routledge & Kegal Paul, 1975.

Massey, Lesly F. *Women and the New Testament*. Jefferson: McFarland, 1989.

Mathews, Shailer. "Jesus' Philosophy of Social Progress," *Great Lives Observed Jesus*, Hugh Anderson, ed. Englewood Cliffs, N.J.: Prentice Hall, 1967.

McAllister, Lester G. and William E. Tucker. *Journey in Faith. A History of the Christian Church (Disciples of Christ)*. St. Louis: Bethany, 1988.

McLaughlin, E.C. "Equality of Souls, Inequality of Sexes: Women in Medieval Theology" *Religion and Sexism*, R.R. Ruether (ed.). New York: Simon and Schuster, 1974.

Moody, J.B. *Women in the Churches*, Second edition, revised. Martin: Hall-Moody Institute, 1910.

Morris, Joan. *The Lady Was a Bishop*. New York: Macmillan, 1973.

Nesbitt, Paula D. *Feminization of the Clergy in America: Occupational and Organizational Perspectives*. New York: Oxford, 1997.

Pape, Dorothy. *God & Women*. London: Mowbrays, 1977.

Paterson, Gillian. *Still Flowing: Women, God and Church*. Geneva: WCC Publications, 1999.

Piper, John and Wayne Grudem, eds. *Recovering Biblical Manhood and Womanhood: A Response to Evangelical Feminism*. Wheaton: Crossway, 1991.

Praamsma, Louis. *The Church in the Twentieth Century*. Vol. VII. Ontario: Paideia, 1981.

Price, Eugenia. *The Unique World of Women*. Grand Rapids: Zondervan, 1969.

Prohl, Russell C. *Woman in the Church: a Restudy of Woman's Place in Building the Kingdom*. Grand Rapids: Eerdmans, 1957.

Roberts, B.T. *Ordaining Women*. Rochester: Earnest Christian Publishing House, 1891.

Rosaldo, Michelle Zimbalist and Louise Lampere, eds. *Women, Culture and Society*. Stanford: Stanford University Press, 1974.

Ruether, Rosemary Radford. *Liberation Theology*. New York: Paulist Press,1972.

_____. *Religion and Sexism*. New York: Simon and Schuster, 1974.

_____. *Sexism and God-Talk*. London: SCM, 1983.

Ryrie, Charles Caldwell. *The Place of Women in the Church*. New York: Macmillan, 1958.

Sandifer, J. Stephen. *Deacons: Male and Female?* Houston: Keystone, 1989.

Scanzoni, Letha and Nancy Hardesty. *All We're Meant to Be*. Waco: Word, 1975.

Schmidt, Frederick W. *A Still Small Voice: Women, Ordination and the Church*. New York: Syracuse University Press, 1996.

Smart, James D. *The Past, Present and Future of Biblical Theology*. Philadelphia: Westminster, 1979.

Stendahl, Krister. *The Bible and the Role of Women: a Case study in Hermeneutics*, Emile T. Sanders (trans.). Philadelphia: Fortress Press, 1966.

Stone, Merlin. *The Paradise Papers*. London: Virago, 1979.

Swidler, Leonard. *Biblical Affirmations of Women*. Philadelphia: Westminster, 1979.

Tavard, George H. *Woman in Christian Tradition*. Notre Dame, Indiana: Notre Dame Press, 1973.

Thomas, H.F. and R.S. Keller, eds. *Women in New Worlds*. Nashville: Abingdon, 1981.

Toulouse, Mark G. *Joined in Discipleship*. St. Louis: Chalice, 1992.

Vorster, W.S., ed. *Sexism and Feminism: In Theological Perspective*. Pretoria: UNISA, 1984.

Vos, Clarence J. *Women in Old Testament Worship*. Delft: N.V. Verenigde Drukkerijn Judels und Brinkman (n.d.).

Waddey, John, ed. *Introducing the Church of Christ*. Ft. Worth: Star, 1981.

Webster, Ellen Low and C.B. John, eds. *The Church and Women In the Third World*. Philadelphia: Westminster, 1985.

Welsh, William. *Women Helpers in the Church*. Philadelphia: J.B. Lippencott, 1872.

Where We Stand. Springfield: Missouri, Gospel Publishing House, 1994.

Willard, Frances E. *Women in the Pulpit*. Chicago: Woman's Temperance Publication Association, 1889.

Wilson-Kastner, Patricia. *Faith, Feminism and the Christ*. Philadelphia: Fortress, 1983.

Witherington, Ben. *Women in the Earliest Churches*. Cambridge: University Press, 1988.

_____. *Women in the Ministry of Jesus*. Cambridge: University Press, 1984.

Yee, Shirley J. *Black Women Abolutionists: a Study in Activities*. Knoxville: University of Tennessee Press, 1992.

Zerbst, Fritz. *The Office of Women in the Church; A Study in Practical Theology*. St. Louis: Concordia, 1955.

Zikmund, Barbara Brown. *Clergy Women: An Uphill Calling*. Louisville: Westminster, 1998.

Dictionaries and Encyclopedias

Musurillo, H. "Basil of Ancyra." *New Catholic Encyclopedia*, Vol. II. New York: McGraw-Hill, 1967.

Nash, H.S. "Prayer," *New Schaff-Hersog Encyclopedia of Religious Knowledge*, Vol. IX. Grand Rapids: Baker, 1964.

Oepke, Albrecht. "Gune," *Theological Dictionary of the New Testament*, Vol. I, G. Kittel (ed.). Grand Rapids: Eerdmans, Rep. 1969.

Pratt, Dwight M. "Women," *International Standard Bible Encyclopedia*, Vol. V. Grand Rapids: Eerdmans, rep. 1955.

Scroggs, Robin. "Women in the New Testament," *The Interpreter's Dictionary of the Bible*, suppl. Vol. Nashville: Abingdon Press, 1976.

Vermeersch, A. "Nuns," *Catholic Encyclopedia*, Vol. 11. New York: Encyclopedia Press, 1911.

Classical Works and Multi-Volume Collections

Bohn's Classical Library. London: George Bell and sons, 1900–1903.

Halton, Thomas P. (ed. dir.). *Fathers of the Church*. Washington D.C.: Catholic University of America Press, 1986.

Loeb Classical Library, London: William Heinemann, 1921–40.

Quasten, Johannes, Walter J. Burghardt, and Thomas C. Lawler (eds.) *Ancient Christian Writers*. New York: Newman Press, 1982.

Roberts, Alexander and James Donaldson (eds.). *The Ante-Nicene Fathers*. Grand Rapids: Eerdmans, 1953.

Robinson, J.M. and H.J. Klimkeit (eds.). *Nag Hammadi and Manichean Studies*. New York: Leiden, 1994.

Schaff, Phillip (ed.). *Nicene and Post–Nicene Fathers*. Grand Rapids: Eerdmans, rep. 1969.

Shore, Sally R. (trans.) John Chrysostom, *On Virginity* (*Studies in Women and Religion*), Vol. 9. New York: Edwin Mellen Press, 1983.

Summa Theologica. Fathers of the English Dominican Province, trans. *Great Books of the Western World*, Vols. 19–20. Revised by Daniel J. Sullivan. London: Burns, Oates & Washbourne, rev. 1952.

Tappert, Theodore G. (ed. and trans). *Luther's Works*. Philadelphia: Fortress Press, 1967.

Unpublished Sources

Chinnis, Pamela P. A General Letter. The Episcopal Church Center, New York, September 15, 1987.

Duggins, Davis. Personal Correspondence, December 28, 1987.

Hagee, Diana. "Submission and How I Conquered It." Televised Lecture. San Antonio, Texas, 2000.

Ruether, Rosemary Radford. "Prophetic Tradition and the Liberation of Women: A Story of Promise and Betrayal." A paper read at the University of Natal, Pietermaritzburg, South Africa, 1989.

INDEX